Once upon an open book
I dreamed I saw the sun—
It came down to my little house
And stayed 'til day was done.

Once upon an open book
I dreamed I saw the moon—
It spoke with me from up the sky
And left me all too soon.

Once upon an open book
I dreamed I saw the stars—
They wrapped me in their billion rays
And carried me afar.

—Nancy Bopp

Reading 3 A & B Worktext for Christian Schools®

Not so very long ago
(Or was it years before?)
I opened up a storybook
The way I open up a door.

Not so very long ago
(Just the turning of a page!)
I stepped into a storybook
The way I step onto a stage.

Not so very long ago
(It was just yesterday)
I lived inside a storybook
A hundred worlds away.

—Dawn L. Watkins

TEACHER'S EDITION
Second Edition

Bob Jones University Press, Greenville, South Carolina 29614

NOTE:
The fact that materials produced by other publishers may be referred to in this volume does not constitute an endorsement by Bob Jones University Press of the content or theological position of materials produced by such publishers. The position of Bob Jones University Press, and the University itself, is well known. Any references and ancillary materials are listed as an aid to the student or the teacher and in an attempt to maintain the accepted academic standards of the publishing industry.

READING 3 Worktext for Christian Schools® Teacher's Edition
Second Edition

Produced in cooperation with the Bob Jones University School of Education and Bob Jones Elementary School.

for Christian Schools is a registered trademark of Bob Jones University Press.

"My Dad's a Secret Agent," copyright © 1998, Kenn Nesbitt. All rights reserved. Used by permission. http://www.poetry4kids.com

Photograph Credits
The following agencies and individuals have furnished materials to meet the photographic needs of this textbook. We wish to express our gratitude to them for their important contribution.

Corel Corporation
PhotoDisc, Inc.
Telephone Pioneers of America
Unusual Films
www.arttoday.com

Telephone Pioneers of America, 41
Corel Corporation 210 (all), 229
PhotoDisc, Inc., 233
www.arttoday.com, 308, 309 (both)
Unusual Films, 338 (both), 339

The Knight Rides at Night

Name

> **Homonyms**
> Have the same sound.
> Have different meanings.
> Have different spellings.
> *often*

▸Choose One

Put an *X* on the word that does not fit the sentence.

1. The knight rode out to ___ the giant.   meet   meat

2. He stopped on the way to ___ a new lance.   bye   buy

3. The head was made of the finest ___.   steel   steal

4. It had a long ___ shaft.   red   read

5. Off he ___ with the lance at his side.   road   rode

▸Draw Both

Read each sentence and draw a picture to show the meaning of the underlined word.

The <u>sun</u> was so bright that the giant needed sunglasses.	The king has two daughters and one <u>son</u>.

Reading 3A: "The Singing Knight," pp. 2-6, Lesson 1
Vocabulary: choosing the correct homonym; interpreting homonyms in sentences

1

Old "Mask" Donald

▶Circle Them

Circle the consonant blend or blends in each word.

▶Choose and Write

From the truck choose a word to replace the colored words in each sentence and write it on the line.

Old Mask Donald had a farm, and on his farm . . .

1. He had some plants grown for food.

   crops

2. He had a four-wheeled something to take crops to market.

   truck

3. He had some narrow-leafed green plants for animals to eat.

   grass

4. He had a small, wild, partly tamed horse.

   bronco

5. He had a watery place for the animals to drink.

   pond

6. He had some animals that live in the pond and eat flies.

   frogs

Reading 3A: "The Singing Knight," pp. 2-6, Lesson 1
Phonics: using letter-sound association for consonant blends

A Little Knight Music

▶Choose One

Circle the note next to the answer that best completes each sentence.

1. The story of Sir Bryan takes place ___.
   - ♪ in America
   - ♪ in a faraway land
   - ♪ on another planet

2. Sir Bryan had a horse named ___.
   - ♪ Charger
   - ♪ Chester
   - ♪ Challenger

3. The other knights did not ___.
   - ♪ have horses
   - ♪ admire Sir Bryan
   - ♪ fight as bravely

4. The ladies laughed at Sir Bryan because ___.
   - ♪ he played the lute
   - ♪ he liked to ride his horse
   - ♪ he was not a brave knight

5. Sir Bryan was able to rescue the princess by ___.
   - ♪ fighting the giant
   - ♪ playing his lute
   - ♪ talking to the giant

6. Sir Bryan's reward was ___.
   - ♪ a new lute
   - ♪ a trip to America
   - ♪ half the kingdom

▶Think Big

Find and read Mark 6:17-28 in your Bible. It tells the story of a real person who was offered half a kingdom. Did she make the right choice? How did the king feel about her choice? What do you think would have happened if she had chosen half the kingdom? Write your answers on your own paper.

Reading 3A: "The Singing Knight," pp. 7-13, Lesson 2
Comprehension: recalling facts and details; thinking critically

3

A Short Note About Vowels

▶Listen and Color
Say the name of each picture. Color the note beside it to match the vowel sound on the larger note.

▶Choose One
Fill in the circle beside the correct word.

1. "I don't want to practice," said _____.
   ○ Mop   ● Bob   ○ Pan

2. His whole body looked _____.
   ○ rest   ○ said   ● sad

3. "You _____ practice your violin," said his mother.
   ○ find   ● must   ○ lack

4. He went back to _____ his music.
   ● get   ○ tell   ○ mix

5. He played _____ a number of times.
   ○ ill   ○ itch   ● it

6. He did not stop until it was _____ right.
   ○ jump   ● just   ○ bit

Reading 3A: "The Singing Knight," pp. 7-13, Lesson 2
Phonics: identifying short vowel sounds: /ă/, /ĕ/, /ĭ/, /ŏ/, /ŭ/; using letter-sound association for short vowels

Making Music

▶Match Them

Listen carefully to the story your teacher reads.
1. Draw a line to match each picture with the correct sentence.
2. Put the sentences in story order by writing a number on each note.

1 The violin maker must find the right piece of wood.

5 He carefully puts the four strings in the right places.

3 Special sandpaper is used on the outside of the violin.

4 A thin layer of varnish is carefully painted on the violin.

2 He then carves the scroll, neck, and body of the violin.

Reading 3A: "Music in Your Heart," pp. 14-17, Lesson 4
Comprehension: recalling a logical sequence

Musical Hearts

▶**Make Some**

Read the digraph in each music note. Draw a line through each group of letters on the heart that does not go with the digraph to make a word. The first one is done for you.

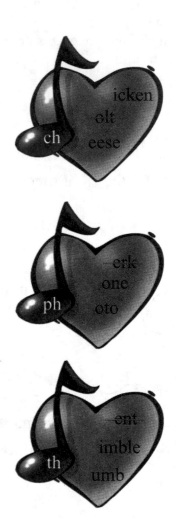

▶**Write Some**

Choose a word from the hearts to write in each sentence.

1. The king climbed the steps to his _____ *throne / chair* _____.

2. He posed for a _____ *photo* _____ with the queen.

3. Her pet _____ *chicken* _____ sat on a chair nearby.

4. The royal _____ *shark* _____ swam in a tank in the background.

Reading 3A: "Music in Your Heart," pp. 14-17, Lesson 4
Phonics: using letter-sound association for *sh* as /sh/, *ch* as /ch/, *ph* as /f/, *th* as /th/, and *wh* as /hw/

6

The Making of a Violin

▶Look and Read

Read the parts of the violin. Look at where each arrow is pointing.

> **PSALM 150:4**
> *Praise him with stringed instruments.*

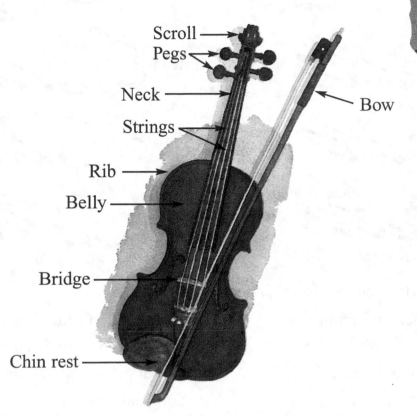

Scroll ⟶
Pegs ⟶
Neck ⟶
Strings ⟶
Rib ⟶
Belly ⟶
Bridge ⟶
Chin rest ⟶

Bow ⟵

▶Write It

Use the diagram of the violin to help you find the parts and write the answers.

1. Where would the violinist place his fingers?

   neck / strings

2. What part would help the violinist to keep his instrument steady?

   chin rest

3. What part is the body of the violin?

   belly

4. What can be turned to tune the violin?

   pegs

5. What does the violinist draw across the strings to make beautiful music?

   bow

Reading 3A: "Music in Your Heart," pp. 18-23, Lesson 5
Study skills: reading a diagram

Weather Trouble

►Color Them

If the word has a short *e* sound, color the cloud beside it.
If it has a short *u* sound, color the lightning bolt.

young   *color*

head   *color*

Doug   *color*

instead   *color*

ready   *color*

trouble   *color*

►Write Them

Write one of the words from above in each space to complete the rhyme.

1. I rolled away a rock and found
   A roly poly bug.
   I gently took it home at once
   To show my brother ___.

   Doug

2. I have two ears, a chin, some hair
   (a lovely shade of red),
   A nose, a mouth, a brow, two eyes;
   I keep them on my ___.

   head

3. My sister Kay and I are twins.
   We enjoy being double.
   We do get tired of hearing folks
   Call us double ___.

   trouble

4. I'll tell you a little secret—
   I sleep with a stuffed teddy.
   I'll act grown up and throw him out
   Someday when I am ___.

   ready

5. I poked a bee upon a flower.
   The bee—it quickly stung.
   I learned that I should not poke bèes
   When I was very ___.

   young

6. My parents asked me if I'd like
   A brother to call Ted.
   I sweetly smiled and told them that
   I'd like a pet ___.

   instead

Reading 3A: "Music in Your Heart," pp. 18-23, Lesson 5
Phonics: using letter-sound association: *ea* as /ĕ/ in *bread ou* as /ŭ/ in *touch*;
supplying rhyming words

God Gives Guidance and Victory

Name

▶Color Some
Color the pitcher beside each true sentence.

color 1. Gideon knew that the man was an angel of the Lord.

color 2. The people were angry that Gideon had destroyed the idols.

3. The first morning after Gideon prayed, the sheepskin and the ground were dry.

4. After God told Gideon to send some men home, only one hundred were left to fight.

color 5. The soldiers of the enemy army were confused.

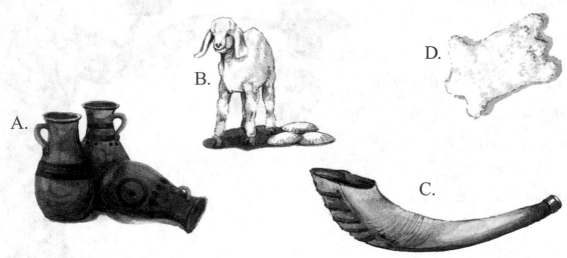

A. B. C. D.

▶Match Them
Write the letter of the picture that matches each sentence.

__B__ 1. Gideon made an offering of these.

__C__ 2. Gideon blew a call to war on this.

__A__ 3. Gideon's army hid their torches inside these.

__D__ 4. Gideon wrung out a bowlful of water from this.

Reading 3A: "Trumpets and Pitchers," pp. 29-33, Lesson 8
Comprehension: recalling facts and details

11

A Child Finds Gold

> Some words like *child*, *find*, *most*, and *gold* have long vowel sounds even though they are in closed syllables.

▶Find the Rhyme

Circle the word in each sentence that has the same vowel sound as the word in the green box.

1. kind

Rick made up his (mind) to play on the apple tree in the field.

2. bold

The tree was (old,) and its limbs were twisted and easy to climb.

3. wild

Rick enjoyed the (mild) breeze that blew through the branches.

4. post

Rick spent (most) of his time looking around.

5. scold

He slipped when he forgot to (hold) on.

6. fold

His hand touched something hard and (cold) in a bird's nest.

7. mold

It was his mother's (gold) chain that she lost last year!

Reading 3A: "Trumpets and Pitchers," pp. 29-33, Lesson 8
Phonics: reading words with long vowels in closed syllables: /ō/ as in *gold*, /ī/ as in *mind*

Climbing Higher

▶ Read and Decide

Read the sentence that tells what happened. Fill in the circle beside the character's feeling and action.

> **PHILIPPIANS 4:19**
> But my God shall supply all your need according to his riches in glory by Christ Jesus.

What Happened	Character Feeling	Character Action
1. Isobel looked at the mules carrying their belongings.	Isobel felt ○ happy. ● worried. ○ sad.	Isobel ○ sang. ○ cried. ● prayed.
2. The muleteer saw how dangerous the trail was.	The muleteer felt ● unhappy. ○ relieved. ○ joyful.	The muleteer ○ prayed. ● said to go back. ○ left.
3. Isobel pointed out rugged mountains and deep canyons to her daughter.	Isobel felt ● excited. ○ homesick. ○ angry.	Isobel ○ cried. ○ made Kathryn go back. ● squeezed Kathryn's hand.
4. The muleteer told John they should go back.	John felt ○ sick. ○ puzzled. ● determined.	John ● said to go on. ○ said to turn back. ○ scolded the man.
5. God spoke to Isobel's heart.	Isobel felt ○ proud. ● ashamed. ○ alarmed.	Isobel ○ sang. ○ cried.
6. The Kuhns' new home was gloomy and cold.	Isobel felt ● discouraged. ○ excited. ○ angry.	○ ○ wrote ● trusted God

Reading 3A: "An Instrument for God," pp. 34-37, Lesson 10
Comprehension: identifying characters' feelings and actions

"Note"able Words

/îr/

▸**Circle Some**

Circle the music note beside each word in which the letter *r* controls the vowel.

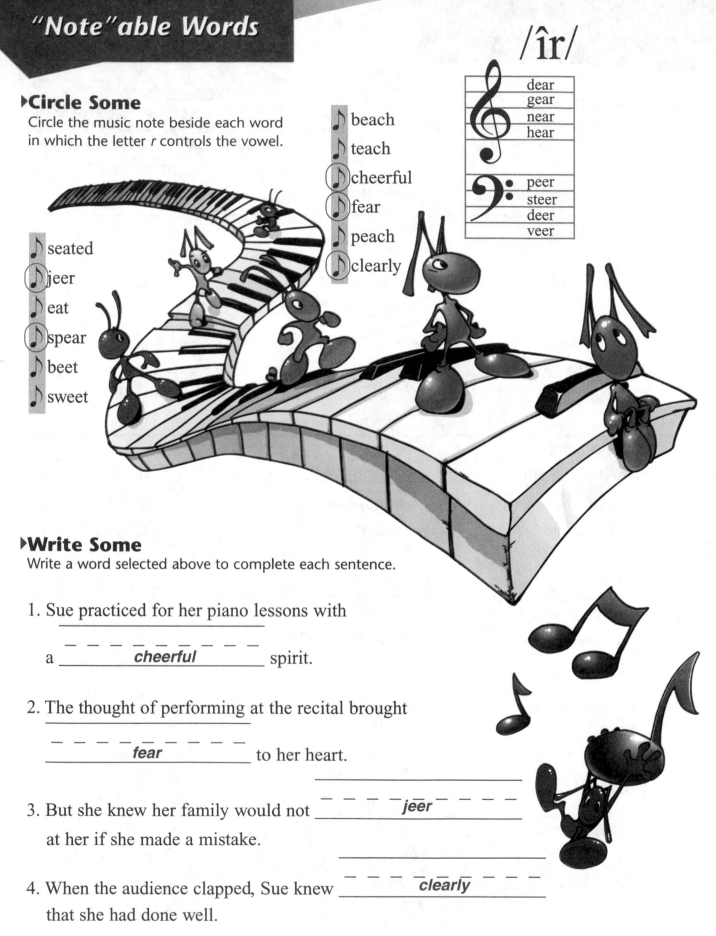

beach
teach
cheerful
fear
peach
clearly

seated
jeer
eat
spear
beet
sweet

dear
gear
near
hear

peer
steer
deer
veer

▸**Write Some**

Write a word selected above to complete each sentence.

1. Sue practiced for her piano lessons with

   a _____ *cheerful* _____ spirit.

2. The thought of performing at the recital brought

   _____ *fear* _____ to her heart.

3. But she knew her family would not _____ *jeer* _____
   at her if she made a mistake.

4. When the audience clapped, Sue knew _____ *clearly* _____
   that she had done well.

14

Reading 3A: "An Instrument for God," pp. 34-37, Lesson 10
Phonics: reading words with *r*-influenced vowels: /îr/ as in *fear, cheer*

Words of Faith

Name _____

▶Fill It In

Complete the story with words from the box. Write a letter in each space.

prayed	Pa-pa	baby organ	hut	missionaries
muleteer	Isobel	Salween	Lisu	Eldest	Kathryn

1. Isobel Kuhn played music on a _b_ _a_ _b_ _y_ _o_ _r_ _g_ _a_ _n_ .

2. The _L_ _i_ _s_ _u_ people loved music.

3. The Lisu lived along the _S_ _a_ _l_ _w_ _e_ _e_ _n_ River.

4. _I_ _s_ _o_ _b_ _e_ _l_ prayed for safety.

5. The Kuhn family were _m_ _i_ _s_ _s_ _i_ _o_ _n_ _a_ _r_ _i_ _e_ _s_ .

6. _K_ _a_ _t_ _h_ _r_ _y_ _n_ was the Kuhns' daughter.

7. The Kuhns _p_ _r_ _a_ _y_ _e_ _d_ for an unsaved Lisu girl.

8. Music brought _E_ _l_ _d_ _e_ _s_ _t_ Sister to church.

9. The name the Lisu believers gave John Kuhn was _P_ _a_ - _p_ _a_ .

10. The Kuhns lived in a _h_ _u_ _t_ .

11. A _m_ _u_ _l_ _e_ _t_ _e_ _e_ _r_ led the pack mules.

▶Use the Code

Use the matching colored boxes to find the correct letter to write in each space.

_M_ _y_ _G_ _o_ _d_ _s_ _h_ _a_ _l_ _l_ _s_ _u_ _p_ _p_ _l_ _y_

_a_ _l_ _l_ _y_ _o_ _u_ _r_ _n_ _e_ _e_ _d_ .

Reading 3A: "An Instrument for God," pp. 38-41, Lesson 11
Comprehension: recalling facts and details

Canyon Colors

▶**Color Some**
Color the parts of the canyon to match the mountain with the same vowel sound.

thorn
/or/

worm
/ûr/

worship
blue

horse
purple

purple
north

purple
shore

worse
blue

fork
purple

worm
blue

world
blue

morning
purple

purple
more

work
blue

blue worth

▶**Write Some**
Choose a word from a canyon above to complete each sentence.

1. Bryan has a _____ *horse* _____ named Rocket.

2. Every _____ *morning* _____ Rocket needs to be fed.

3. Some people say that having a horse is hard _____ *work* _____ .

4. Bryan loves Rocket more than anything in the _____ *world* _____ .

Reading 3A: "An Instrument for God," pp. 38-41, Lesson 11
Phonics: reading words with *r*-influenced vowels: /ûr/ as in *work* and /or/ as in *stork*

Songbirds

Name _____

▶Make a List

One good way to remember the facts and details you read
is to make a list. Write the name of a bird from the story
beside each fact on this list.

house sparrow   Carolina wren   mockingbird   blue jay   catbird

1. _____**Carolina wren**_____ sings "teakettle, teakettle"

2. _____**blue jay**_____ likes to tease cats

3. _____**mockingbird**_____ can sound like a whistle or a flute

4. _____**house sparrow**_____ cheers winter days with its "cheep, cheep"

5. _____**catbird**_____ cries "mew, mew"

▶More Lists

Put an *X* by two reasons that songbirds sing to each other.	Put an *X* by two reasons that songbirds cry to each other.
_X_ to call to their families	_X_ to warn of danger
___ to show that they can sing better	___ to say that they are sad
_X_ to find a mate	_X_ to signal the flock

Reading 3A: "Song Signals," pp. 42-47, Lesson 13
Comprehension: recalling and organizing facts and details

New Blue Raccoon

▶**Choose and Circle**

Circle the word in each row that has the same vowel sound as the blue word.

soon	(true)	sock	tub
blew	stump	(tooth)	chop
glue	(grew)	trod	hutch
flew	dust	(blew)	fox
broom	trust	shop	(chew)

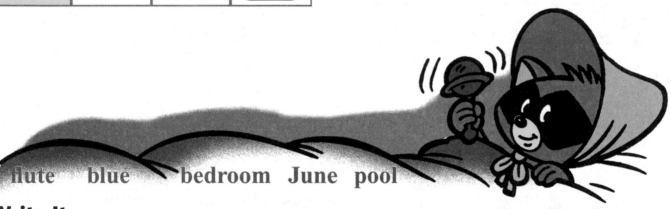

flute   blue   bedroom   June   pool

▶**Write It**

Complete each sentence with a word from the baby's blanket.

1. The raccoons do not mind that their new baby is _____ *blue* _____ .

2. He was born at the end of _____ *June* _____ .

3. They sometimes let him play in the _____ *pool* _____ .

4. He naps in his _____ *bedroom* _____ every afternoon.

5. His mother plays a tune on her _____ *flute* _____ to help him sleep.

Reading 3A: "Song Signals," pp. 42-47, Lesson 13
Phonics: using letter-sound association: /o͞o/ as *oo* in *room, ew* in *flew,* and *ue* in *blue*

Whistle a Happy Tune

Name

▶Read and Think

You are going to teach someone to whistle. There is only one problem. He comes from a place where no one has ever whistled before. He does not even know what whistling is!

What would you tell him about whistling? What directions would you give him?

▶Write It

Write your directions here. If you need more space, use your own paper and attach it to this page.

Answers will vary.

Reading 3A: "Whistles," pp. 48-49, Lesson 14
Comprehension: responding to poetry
Composition: writing directions

19

Prison Praise

▶Solve It

Read each sentence. Choose a word from the box and write it in the correct space in the puzzle.

ACROSS

3. "No, we are still here," ____ one of the men.

5. Everyone would say it was his ____.

6. Suddenly the jail ____ shook, and the doors opened.

11. They had done no ____, but the men would not listen.

12. Paul and Silas ____ him that he must believe on the Lord Jesus Christ.

14. The prisoners' ____ dropped open when they heard men singing.

DOWN

1. ____ down before them, he said, "Sirs, what must I do to be saved?"

2. The jailer ____ them out of the cell.

4. Before ____ the jailer and his family became Christians.

7. The men's ____ showed that they were trusting Christ, even in jail.

8. Bad men said Paul and Silas had broken the ____ by preaching about the true God.

9. The jailer was sure that the men had ____.

10. What would ____ Paul and Silas to sing praises to God at midnight?

13. Paul and Silas had been beaten until their backs were ____.

jaws   called
cause   brought
song   falling
law   taught
wrong   dawn
raw
walls
gone
fault

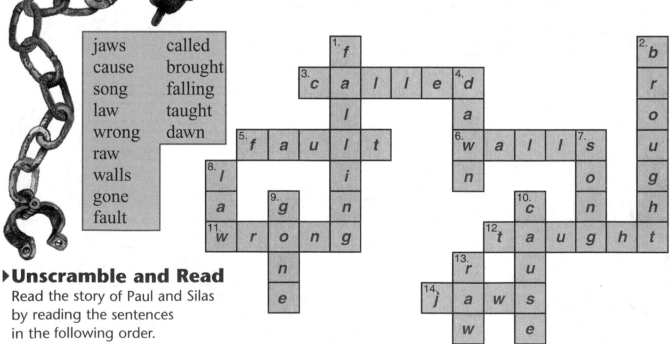

▶Unscramble and Read

Read the story of Paul and Silas by reading the sentences in the following order.

8   11   13   14   10   7   6   9   5   3   2   1   12   4

Reading 3A: "Whistles," pp. 48-49, Lesson 14
Phonics: reading words with *au, aw, o,* and *a(l)* as /ô/ in *Paul, claw, cost,* and *wall*

The Coyote's Story

Name

▶Read and Decide

This is a story about real coyotes, but some fanciful sentences have gotten mixed into it. Read the story. Find each sentence that is fanciful and put an X beside it.

_____ Coyotes are found in most parts of the United States and in Canada and Mexico.

_____ The coyote has large, pointed ears and a bushy tail.

_____ Coyotes are grayish brown in color.

✗ Coyotes talk to other animals and make friends with them.

_____ They hunt for small mammals, reptiles, and insects to eat.

_____ The voice of the coyote is a strangely sad howl.

✗ Other animals teach their songs to coyotes.

✗ Coyotes often take other animals home with them to sing to their families.

▶Match Them

Think again about the story "The Coyote's Song."
If the character trait describes Coyote, write a C beside it.
If it describes Locust, write an L.

_C_ 1. Quick to blame others   _L_ 3. Encouraging

_L_ 2. Helpful   _C_ 4. Discontent with what he had

Reading 3A: "The Coyote's Song," pp. 50-54, Lesson 16
Comprehension: distinguishing fantasy from reality; identifying characters by traits

21

Howl and Shout

▶Choose One

Choose a word from the fence to complete each sentence.

1. Mrs. Smith said I should open my __**mouth**__
   when I sing.

2. Our singing is much too __**loud**__ .

3. Mrs. Smith says we do not need to __**shout**__ .

4. She says our singing voices make lovely __**sounds**__ .

5. My dog Rover __**howls**__ along with my singing.

▶Add One

Write another word for each word family. Choose a word that helps to describe the picture.

frown

clown

_____

__**down**__

grouch

couch

_____

__**pouch**__

Reading 3A: "Coyote's Song," pp. 50-54, Lesson 16
Phonics: reading words with *ou, ow* as /ou/ in *couch* and *tower*

A New Song

▶Read It

Mr. Sankey's New Song

During a revival meeting, D. L. Moody startled Ira Sankey by asking him to sing about Jesus, the Good Shepherd. Mr. Sankey didn't have a song about the Good Shepherd. He did have a poem about a lamb lost in a storm, but he had not written any music for the poem. What should he do? How could he make up a song right away? He prayed, walked from the platform to the organ, and started playing and singing. At the end of the verse, he was afraid that he couldn't remember the same melody for the other verses. But again the Lord helped him with the music.

Songwriters often spend many hours writing one song. The Lord helped Mr. Sankey write the music for "The Ninety and Nine" in just a few minutes.

▶Answer Them

Write the answer to each question.

1. How do you know that Mr. Sankey had not planned to sing about the Good Shepherd?

   _ _ _ _ He was startled, or _ _ _ _ _
   he did not have a song.

2. What does a poem need to make it into a song?

   _ _ _ _ _ _ _ _ _ _ _
   music

3. How did Mr. Sankey feel after he sang the first verse?

   _ _ _ _ _ _ _ _ _
   afraid

4. What did Mr. Sankey do that showed he trusted God to give him a new song?

   _ _ _ _ _ _ _ _ _
   He prayed.

> **PSALM 33:1, 3**
> *Rejoice in the Lord. . . .*
> *Sing unto him*
> *a new song.*

Reading 3A: "The Coyote's Song," pp. 55-59, Lesson 17
Comprehension: recalling facts and details; making inferences

Joyful Noise

Make a joyful noise unto the Lord.

▶Add It

In each picture, add the thing that is named.

Roy practicing

a noisy toy

a royal crown

some boiling water

two coiled snakes

a moist starfish

Reading 3A: "The Coyote's Song," pp. 55-59, Lesson 17
Phonics: reading and illustrating words with *oi, oy* as /oi/ in *oil* and *toy*
Comprehension: illustrating phrases

Squeak Up, I Can't Hear You!

Name

▸ Choose and Color

Color the frame around each animal that was a character in the play.

Mouse

Rabbit

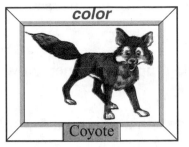

color

Coyote

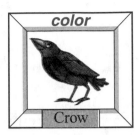

color

Crow

Frog

Cat

color

Pigeons

color

Horse

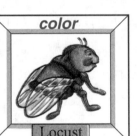

color

Locust

color

Gopher

color

Fish

▸ Choose and Write

Write the name of the character who said each sentence.

1. "My family would like to hear your song."   *Coyote*

2. "Don't startle us so!"   *Pigeons*

3. "Just sing the song you know."   *Crow*

4. "You are kicking dust into my home."   *Gopher*

5. "You are getting our water muddy."   *Fish*

6. "Listen carefully while I sing it again."   *Locust*

Reading 3A: "The Coyote's Song," pp. 60-61, Lesson 18
Comprehension: identifying characters; matching characters and dialogue

25

/oi/

oil
toy

/o͞o/

good
wood

/ou/

now
found

Lookout Point

▶Choose and Circle

Circle the word in the sentence that has the same vowel sound as the word on the oval.

look   1. Jon picked up the (wooden) clown toy.

out   2. He put it with a coin in his wool (pouch.)

point   3. He zipped his hood and ran down Mount (Joy.)

look   4. He started south and crossed the (brook.)

out   5. Kneeling on the moist (ground,) he took a sip of cool water before he went on.

point   6. Just before noon, Jon reached the house of the old (toymaker.)

look   7. ("Good) sir," said Jon, "my toy makes loud noise, not music."

out   8. The toymaker looked at the joints of the little (clown.)

point   9. "Some good (oil) will change the sound," he said.

point   10. When Jon heard the happy music, he held out his (coin.)

look   11. "No, thank you," said the old man. "Your smile is (good) pay for me."

Reading 3A: "The Coyote's Song," pp. 60-61, Lesson 18
Phonics: reading words with /oi/ as in *oil* and *toy*, /o͞o/ as in *good*,
and /ou/ as in *now* and *found*

Coyote Notes

▸Read and Decide

Write on each note the number of a phrase from below that tells about Coyote.

1. kicked dust into someone's home
2. was startled out of tall grass
3. lived in a tall tree
4. hunted every morning
5. did not want muddy water
6. forgot songs
7. lived in a hole in the ground
8. wanted to sing for his family

9. practiced singing
10. blew bubbles
11. explained the story
12. went home wet and tired
13. did not watch where he was going
14. wasted the whole day
15. sang his own song best

▸Choose One

Circle the phrase that tells the *most important* thing about Coyote.

Reading 3A: "The Coyote's Song," pp. 50-61, Lesson 19
Comprehension: identifying information relating to a character

A Happy Helper

▶**Match Them**

Draw a line from each word to the word in the box that follows the same rule.

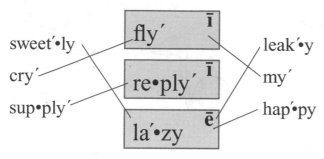

sweet′•ly

cry′

sup•ply′

| fly′ ī |
| re•ply′ ī |
| la′•zy ē |

leak′•y

my′

hap′•py

▶**Choose and Write**

Choose a word from above to complete each sentence.

1. Mrs. Pigeon looked very sad, as though she might
   _____
   _ _ _ _ _ _ _ _
   _____ **cry** _____ at any moment.

2. "What is wrong, _____ **my** _____ friend?"
   asked Mr. Gopher.

3. "The roof of my house is _____ **leaky** _____ ,
   and I cannot fix it myself," she replied.

4. "Well," said Mr. Gopher, "I have a large _____ **supply** _____ of wood.

5. I'd be _____ **happy** _____ to fix it for you!"

6. Grateful Mrs. Pigeon sang
   _____
   _ _ _ _ _ _ _ _
   _____ **sweetly** _____
   as she flitted away toward home.

Reading 3A: "The Coyote's Song," pp. 50-61, Lesson 19
Phonics: reading words with y as /ē/ in an unaccented syllable (*lazy*);
reading words with y as /ī/ in an accented syllable (*reply, fly*)

Name _____

▶Think and Decide

Draw a ♪ beside the sentence that answers the question.

1. Which sentence tells you why Wolfgang was an amazing child?

   ♪ By the age of five, he was even writing music.

   ____ Maria and Wolfgang visited many countries.

   ____ Wolfgang enjoyed listening to music.

2. Which sentence tells you that Wolfgang's father did not think he could play very well?

   ____ Wolfgang was given a violin as a present.

   ♪ "You must play so softly that no one can hear you," Papa told Wolfgang.

   ____ Papa and two friends sat down to practice.

3. Which sentence tells you that Wolfgang could play other instruments besides the harpsichord?

   ____ He began to take his children to other cities.

   ____ Papa brought some of his musician friends home.

   ♪ He also liked to play the violin.

4. Which sentence tells you an instrument that Wolfgang played?

   ____ Wolfgang climbed onto the bench.

   ♪ Wolfgang went to the harpsichord to play his music.

   ____ Wolfgang was invited to join a special music club.

Reading 3A: "The Amazing Mozart," pp. 62-70, Lesson 20
Comprehension: recalling facts and details

Famous Maker of Glorious Music

▶Read It
Read the story.

Wolfgang Mozart grew up in the **mountainous** country of Austria. As a very young child he was able to make **harmonious** sounds on the harpsichord. Slowly his family realized his **marvelous** talent for music. Wolfgang was **generous** in sharing his talent with people and never seemed **nervous** about performing. He wrote **numerous** pieces of music in his lifetime. Many people have enjoyed the music of this **famous** composer.

-ous
famous dangerous glorious

▶Choose One
Write one of the colored words in the story to complete each sentence.

1. Someone who is known by many people is ___*famous*___.

2. Willing to give to others is ___*generous*___.

3. Having many mountains is ___*mountainous*___.

4. Something that is amazing is ___*marvelous*___.

5. Upset or easily excited is ___*nervous*___.

6. Large in number is ___*numerous*___.

Reading 3A: "The Amazing Mozart," pp. 62-66, Lesson 20
Phonics: using letter-sound association: *-ous* as /əs/ in unaccented syllables as in *famous*
Vocabulary: determining word meaning from context

Musical Minds

When Mozart's talent was discovered, his whole family began performing together. News of his genius spread quickly as they traveled abroad.

▶Read and Choose

Read the following sentences and color the note with the correct answer.

1. At the age of 5, Mozart wrote a beautiful song, but he could not play it because it was too difficult. Mozart felt

   excited 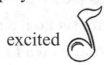   frustrated *color*   tired

2. When Mozart played the violin perfectly without any instructions, his father felt

   surprised *color*   angry   sad

3. Mozart performed before King George III and Queen Charlotte when he was only seven years old. His parents felt

   lonely   proud *color*    confused

4. Wolfgang and his sister had just finished a long, difficult concert. They had performed well and felt

   disappointed   careful   relieved *color*

5. The audience watched as Mozart played a song with a cloth draped over the keys. They felt

   amazed *color* 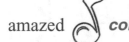   funny   terrified

A Grand Concert

/shən/

Percussion instruments must be tuned often to function properly.

▶Color and Complete

1. Read each word in the list and circle the letters that make the *schwa* sound spelled *sion* or *tion*.
2. Read each sentence. Choose a word from the list and write it in the correct spaces in the puzzle.

man s i o n
loca t i o n
opera t i o n
mis s i o n ary
punctua t i o n
permis s i o n
carna t i o n
salva t i o n
na t i o n

ACROSS

2. Father gave Mother a pretty pink ____ for Valentine's Day.

4. A question mark is an example of ____ .

6. Adoniram Judson was a ____ to Burma.

8. ____ is a free gift from God.

9. The governor lives in a beautiful ____ .

DOWN

1. Kendra got ____ to go to her friend's slumber party.

3. Matthew had an ____ to fix his broken leg.

5. We needed a map to find the ____ of the bus stop.

7. The United States is a free ____ .

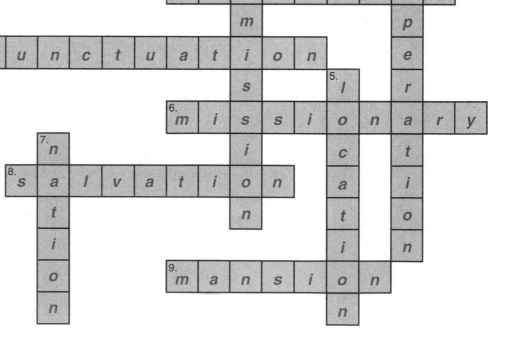

Reading 3A: "The Amazing Mozart," pp. 67-70, Lesson 21
Phonics: using letter-sound association: *-tion, -sion* as /shən/ in unaccented syllables
as in *function, percussion*; noting the sound of schwa

Gullah

This page should be completed with teacher direction.

▸Learn About It

Read silently as your teacher reads aloud about a dialect spoken in the United States.

It is believed that the Gullah culture may be traced back to western African slaves. These slaves arrived in the coastal areas of South Carolina and Georgia during the early 1600s.

The Gullah dialect blends English and several African languages. It is spoken rapidly and in a rhythmic pattern.

The words *goober* (peanut), *gumbo* (okra), and *yam* (sweet potato) are from Gullah.

Dialects are different ways a language is spoken by different groups of people.

dy	the
farruh	father
heh-wm	heaven
oonuh	you
ow-uh	our
resplain	explain
tebl tappa	preacher
troot ma-wt	truthful person
wedduh	rain, storm

▸Think and Write

Use the word bank to answer the questions.

1. How would you write "our father" in Gullah?

   ow-uh farruh

2. How would you write "the storm" in Gullah?

   wedduh

3. Are you a "troot ma-wt"?

   Answers may vary.

4. Where does a "tebl tappa" work?

   possible answer: in the church

5. Write your favorite Gullah word from the word bank and write the English word next to it.

   Answers may vary.

Reading 3A: "A Song in the Night," pp. 71-75, Lesson 23
Comprehension: recognizing the use of dialect

Gentle Gerbils and Nice Mice

▶Find Them

Read the words on the cotton balls.
Find and write the soft *c* and soft *g* words.

soft *c*	soft *g*
celery	edge
place	cage
mice	page

soft *c* = /s/
soft *g* = /j/

clock
celery

guard
edge

gopher
compass

place
cage

call

page
mice

▶Use Them

Use the words you wrote above in these sentences.

1. Cerise found two white _____ mice _____ .

2. She keeps them in a tall _____ cage _____ .

3. She feeds them _____ celery _____ .

4. The little one sits on the _____ page _____ while she reads.

5. It also likes to hang over the _____ edge _____ of the book.

6. This makes it hard for Cerise to keep her _____ place _____ .

Reading 3A: "A Song in the Night," pp. 71-75, Lesson 23
Phonics: reading words with soft *c* before *e, i,* and *y* as in *cent, city,* and *cyclone;*
reading words with soft *g* before *e, i,* or *y* as in *gem, giant,* and *gym*

34

Name

▶Read and Choose

After you read, fill in the circle next to the sentence that tells the main idea of the paragraph.

The Underground Railroad was not underground, and it was not a railroad. It got this name because of the swift, secret way slaves escaped. Along the way, friendly people, both black and white, allowed the escaping slaves to hide and rest in their houses and barns. These places were known as "stations." The helpers were known as "conductors."

- ○ The Underground Railroad went to Canada.
- ○ Escaped slaves hid in houses and barns.
- ● The Underground Railroad was an escape route.

Escaping slaves traveled on back roads and paths, mostly through Ohio, Indiana, and western Pennsylvania. They went from there to Canada by way of Detroit, Michigan, or Niagara Falls, New York. Some sailed across Lake Erie to Ontario, Canada. A few stopped in the states along the way, but they were in danger of being captured and returned to their owners. Most kept on until they were beyond the reach of slavery.

- ● There were many paths to freedom.
- ○ The Underground Railroad was dangerous.
- ○ Some escaped slaves became sailors.

Reading 3A: "A Song in the Night," pp. 76-80, Lesson 24
Comprehension: identifying the unstated main idea of a paragraph

35

Pack Up! Be Very Quiet!

knuckle   knife
wrestle   wrist
knight   wrong
wrench   knob
kneel   knee
right   walk

▶ Choose and Write
Write the words that belong on each bundle.

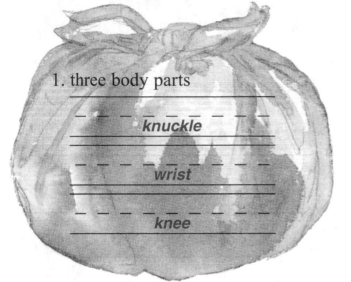

1. three body parts

_ _ _ _ _ _ _ _
knuckle

_ _ _ _ _
wrist

_ _ _ _
knee

2. two tools

_ _ _ _ _
knife

_ _ _ _ _ _
wrench

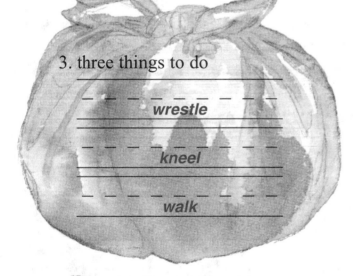

3. three things to do

_ _ _ _ _ _ _
wrestle

_ _ _ _ _
kneel

_ _ _ _
walk

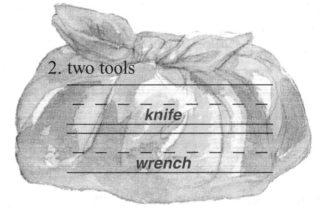

4. one part of a door

_ _ _ _
knob

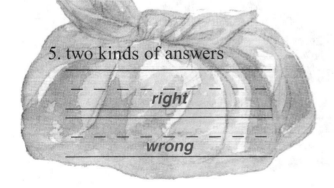

5. two kinds of answers

_ _ _ _ _
right

_ _ _ _ _
wrong

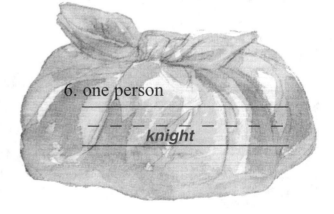

6. one person

_ _ _ _ _ _
knight

Reading 3A: "A Song in the Night," pp. 76-80, Lesson 24
Phonics: reading words with silent consonant patterns: *lk, wr, kn, gh* (*igh* as /ī/)

Why?

▶Choose One

Fill in the circle beside the sentence that tells **why**.

1. Zoe stayed awake all night. Why?
   - ○ Her baby brother was noisy.
   - ● She was worried about what would happen.
   - ○ She had a long nap during the day.

2. Zoe's grandmother did even more baking than on a holiday. Why?
   - ○ They were having company.
   - ○ She liked to bake.
   - ● They needed food for the journey.

3. Zoe's family ran away. Why?
   - ● Her father was going to be sold.
   - ○ They did not want to work anymore.
   - ○ Her grandmother made them go.

4. Zoe's family traveled at night. Why?
   - ○ They had to work during the day.
   - ● They did not want to be seen.
   - ○ They needed moonlight to see.

> **PSALM 101:1**
> Unto thee, O Lord,
> will I sing.

▶Think and Write

Why do people sing? Make a list of reasons you can think of.

Answers will vary.

Night Neighbors

▶Fill It In

Write a word from one of the stars in each sentence.

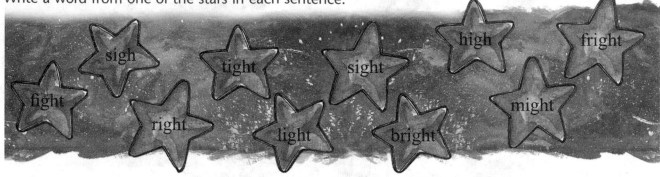

sigh · tight · sight · high · fright · fight · right · light · bright · might

1. The nearest star is not very __*bright / light / high*__ .

2. We can barely see its __*light*__ without a telescope.

3. The star-filled sky is a __*sight*__ to remember.

▶Connect Them

Draw a line from one star to another, following the clues.

1. word for 8
2. something kings do
3. used for a snowy ride
4. stated in pounds
5. cargo
6. four times two equals

eight

sleigh   weight

freight   reign

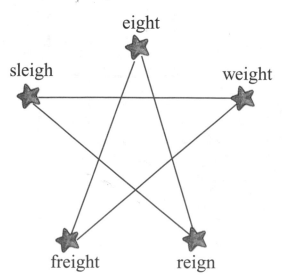

Reading 3A: "A Song In the Night," pp. 81-86, Lesson 25
Phonics: reading words with silent consonant patterns: *igh* as /ī/ in *light; eigh* as /ā/ in *eight*

Busy As a Bee

Name

▸Finish It

Complete each phrase by writing the letter of the picture
in the space where it belongs.

A. **B.** **C.** **D.** **E.**

1. sweet as _F_

2. cold as _H_

3. quick as a _A_

4. hard as a _E_

5. waddle like a _C_

6. big as a _J_

7. pretty as a _I_

8. strong as an _G_

9. sing like a _D_

10. sharp as a _B_

F. **G.** **H.** **I.** **J.**

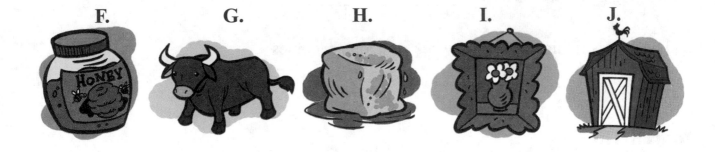

▸Think Again

Choose two of the phrases above and write new endings for them. ***Answers will vary.***

1. _____

_____

2. _____

Reading 3A: "The Spelling Window," pp. 88-95, Lesson 26
Comprehension: using and writing phrases for similes

A Christmas Chorus

▶Choose and Write

Write a word from the box to complete each sentence.
One word will not be used.

ached	chorus
Christ	echoed
chord	Christian

1. The shepherds heard a _____ **chorus** _____ of angels singing.

2. Tidings of joy _____ **echoed** _____ over the plains.

3. Every _____ **chord** _____ of music praised the Savior.

4. We sing about the birth of _____ **Christ** _____ too.

5. The angels rejoice in heaven when someone becomes a _____ **Christian** _____ .

▶Match Them

Write the letter of the correct word beside each definition.

__C__ 1. used to keep ships from floating away

__A__ 2. a person in a story, book, or play

__D__ 3. three or more different musical notes played at the same time to produce a pleasant sound

__B__ 4. a pain in the area of the body above the neck

__E__ 5. a person skilled in repairing machines

A. character
B. headache
C. anchor
D. chord
E. mechanic

Reading 3A: "The Spelling Window," pp. 88-95, Lesson 26
Phonics: reading words with *ch* as /k/ in *Christmas*

We Can!

Many inventions make it possible for people with handicaps to work and play in ways that would not be possible without them.

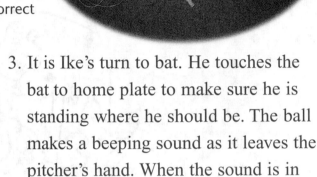

▶Read and Choose

Read each paragraph. Fill in the circle beside the correct answer.

1. Mrs. Britten's boss has asked her to make some calls. She dials a phone that is attached to a special machine. When Miss Leland says "good morning," her greeting appears on a screen. Mrs. Britten types questions on her keyboard and waits to read the answers.

Mrs. Britten cannot

○ see.
● hear.
○ use her legs.
○ use her hands.

2. Mr. Allison is finishing an ad for a new product. He adds color by touching the computer screen with a wand he holds in his mouth. He changes where the figures are placed on the ad using a "mouse" that he moves with his foot.

Mr. Allison cannot

○ see.
○ hear.
○ use his legs.
● use his hands.

3. It is Ike's turn to bat. He touches the bat to home plate to make sure he is standing where he should be. The ball makes a beeping sound as it leaves the pitcher's hand. When the sound is in the right place, Ike swings. Home run!

Ike cannot

● see.
○ hear.
○ use his legs.
○ use his hands.

4. Molly is racing today. She lines up with the other boys and girls. The signal to start is given. Molly presses a button on the side of her chair. Zoom! All the wheels are moving fast. Molly finishes second, but she has lots of fun.

Molly cannot

○ see.
○ hear.
● use her legs.
○ use her hands.

Reading 3A: "The Spelling Window," pp. 96-100, Lesson 27
Comprehension: making inferences based on embedded text clues

Dog Hog

▶Read and Rhyme

Write a word from List 1 with a rhyming word from
List 2 to complete each sentence.

/ōō/

WANTED:
MORE PUPPIES!!

List 1

broom
blue
June
rude
cool
cute
loose
true

List 2

food
fruit
moose
clue
pool
stew
room
tune

1. A chilly swimming hole is a ___cool___ ___pool___ .

2. A pretty banana is a ___cute___ ___fruit___ .

3. A summer song is a ___June___ ___tune___ .

4. A sky-colored soup is a ___blue___ ___stew___ .

5. An impolite lunch is a ___rude___ ___food___ .

6. An escaped beast is a ___loose___ ___moose___ .

7. A sweeper closet is a ___broom___ ___room___ .

8. A correct hint is a ___true___ ___clue___ .

Reading 3A: "The Spelling Window," pp. 96-100, Lesson 27
Phonics: using letter-sound association: /ōō/ as in *cool, blue, flew, fruit,* and *tune;* choosing rhyming words

Organize It

Many of the sentences and paragraphs you read have
more than one part that tells about the main idea.
A good way to remember what you read is to organize
those parts. Use only a few words to tell about each part.

▸Place Them

Read the question below the window. Find the parts that would
answer the question and write them on the window panes.

loud noises

flashing clocks

born that way

illness

sign language

aging

dogs

special telephones

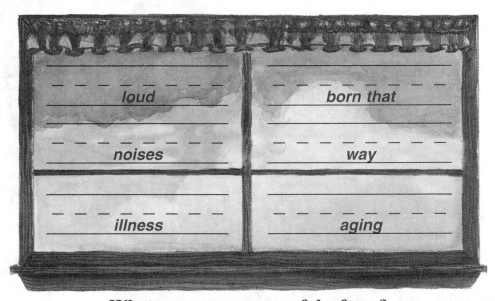

loud

noises

born that

way

illness

aging

What are some causes of deafness?

flashing

clocks

sign

language

dogs

special

telephones

What are some things that help deaf people?

▶Divide It

Draw a dot between the consonants that are not alike to divide each word into syllables.

b a s•k e t
e n•g i n e
a b•s e n t
m a s•t e r

i n•s e c t
w i n•d o w
i n•v i t e
c i r•c u s

> Divide words into syllables between unlike consonants.
> **W O N • D E R**

▶Read and Divide

Read the story. Draw a dot to divide the colored words between the two syllables.

This story is told in the **G o s•p e l** of Mark. A **c e r•t a i n** man who could not hear and whose speech was not clear was brought to Jesus. Jesus took him away from the **c e n•t e r** of the crowd. He put his **f i n•g e r s** in the man's ears. He **a l•s o** touched the man's tongue and said, "Be opened." A look of **w o n•d e r** came into the man's eyes. All the new noises must have sounded like a **t e m•p e s t** around him. It was **a l•m o s t** more than he could believe! He could hear and speak. His heart could scarcely **c o n•t a i n** his joy! Jesus said to the **c i r•c l e** of people, "Don't tell anyone." They were so full of surprise that they had to tell. What could **c o m•p a r e** with what Jesus had done with a gentle touch?

(Mark 7:32-37)

Daydreams

© 2000 BJU Press. Reproduction prohibited.

Name _____

▶Read and Choose

Circle *True* or *False* for each sentence.

1. Alex dreamed of being a spy.	True	(False)
2. An enemy general ordered Alex's family to bring food.	(True)	False
3. Alex bought a drum with his own money.	True	(False)
4. Alex was eager to deliver the food to the enemy.	True	(False)
5. Colonel Tarleton was an enemy to Alex and his family.	(True)	False
6. Alex was able to do what his father told him to do.	(True)	False

▶Tell About It

Write your answers in the thought cloud. **Answers will vary.**

PSALM 139:1-2
*O Lord,
thou hast searched me,
and known me. . . .
Thou understandest
my thought afar off.*

What do you dream of doing?

_____

_____

_____

_____

_____

What would you have to learn before you could do this?

_____

_____

_____

_____

Reading 3A: "Alex, the Drummer Boy," pp. 106-11, Lesson 30

Comprehension: recalling story events; relating personal experience to the message of the story

Composition: writing about an idea

Giant Celebration

▶Listen and Color

Color around each puff of smoke that has the same beginning sound as *giraffe* or *cent.* Color yellow the letter after each soft *g* or soft *c.*

soft *c*
soft *g*
followed by
e, i, y

goat

color gym

gallon

games

color gem

cover

color giraffe

gerbil *color*

city *color*

color celery

germ *color*

color gentle

cotton

center *color*

guard

color general

color circus

cash

carpet

curtain

gate

color centipede

color cyst

e

i y

Reading 3A: "Alex, the Drummer Boy," pp. 106-11, Lesson 30
Phonics: using letter-sound association: *c* as /s/ in *cent, g* as /j/ in *giraffe;* reading words with soft *c* or *g* before *e, i, y*

Sign of a Simile

"Alex's heart pounded like a hammer."

▸Match Them

The phrases below are often used in similes.
Complete each phrase by writing the best word on the line.

1. light as a _____ *feather* _____

2. swims like a _____ *fish* _____

3. rough as _____ *sandpaper* _____

4. runs like a _____ *deer* _____

5. flies like a _____ *bird* _____

feather

sandpaper

fish

bird

deer

▸Think and Write

Write your own similes to describe each of the following.

Answers will vary.

1. A very large dog _____

   That dog is as big as a _____ .

2. A very fast runner _____

   He runs like a _____ .

A **simile** uses *like* or *as* to compare two things that are different but have something in common.

Reading 3A: "Alex, the Drummer Boy," pp. 112-18, Lesson 31
Comprehension: using and writing similes

Alex Meets the General

▶Read and Circle

Circle each word that has the same sound
as *g* in *giraffe* or *c* in *cent*.

1. A (gentle) rain began to fall as Alex entered the camp.

2. The tent stood in the (center) of the enemy camp.

3. Alex was not (certain) that he could find out what his

   father wanted to know.

4. He learned all he could about King (George's) troops.

5. Alex's father took him to see (General) Daniel Morgan.

▶Choose One

Complete each sentence with a word that you circled above.

1. Alex was _____ **certain** _____ that he would be unable to speak clearly.

2. The _____ **general** _____ told him about the scar on his face.

3. He spoke to Alex in a _____ **gentle** _____ voice.

4. Alex sat up straight in the _____ **center** _____ of the table.

5. Alex spoke slowly as he told about the plans of King

   _____ **George's** _____ army.

Reading 3A: "Alex, the Drummer Boy," pp. 112-18, Lesson 31
Phonics: using letter-sound association: *c* as /s/ in *cent* and *g* as /j/ in *giraffe*;
reading words in context with soft *c* or soft *g* before *e, i,* or *y*

Do You Mean It?

▶Read and Match

Match each sentence with what the writer wants you to know by writing the correct letter in the space.

__D__ 1. Alex listened carefully to each signal.

__E__ 2. "On this ground I will defeat the British or lay my bones."

__B__ 3. Alex shivered as he marched beside the soldiers.

__A__ 4. "We will give Bloody Tarleton a good fight."

__C__ 5. Alex's father lay in the high grass with the rest of the riflemen.

__F__ 6. When the smoke cleared, fifteen of the horsemen had fallen from their saddles.

A. We will fight the best we can.

B. The weather was cold.

C. It is harder to hit a man who is lying down than one who is standing up.

D. Alex tried hard to be a good drummer.

E. I will win the battle or die trying to win.

F. A number of the enemy had been hit by rifle fire.

Reading 3A: "Alex, the Drummer Boy," pp. 119-25, Lesson 32
Comprehension: inferring the author's purpose

The Battle of Cowpens

▶Read the Map Key

Read the information on the map key.
Find each symbol on the map.

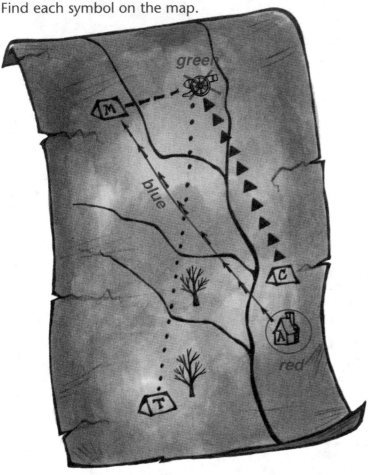

KEY

The map key helps you locate places on a map. A map often has symbols instead of names.

M   General Morgan's camp

T   Tarleton's camp

C   Cornwallis's camp

A   Alex's house

    Cowpens Battlefield

→ →   Alex and his father

• • •   Tarleton's army

– – –   Morgan's army

▶ ▶ ▶   Cornwallis's army

▶Follow the Directions

1. Draw a red circle around Alex's house.

2. Use a blue crayon to trace the path Alex and his father took to General Morgan's camp.

3. Put a green *X* on the Cowpens battlefield.

4. Write the name of the person. _____

His camp was closest to Alex's house. _____ *Cornwallis* _____

His camp was closest to the battlefield. _____ *Morgan* _____

His army marched farther than either of the others. _____ *Tarleton* _____

Reading 3A: "Alex, the Drummer Boy," pp. 119-25, Lesson 32
Study skills: interpreting place relationships on a map; reading a map key

Reading What Isn't There

Name

▸Read and Think

Put an X beside the correct answer.

> A story writer tells you many things without actually saying them. The clues you are given help you to know these things.

1. Alex and his father rode through bare forests and rushing creeks. Cold wind and rain followed them all the way.

   The season of the year was probably
   ____ summer.
   _X_ winter.
   ____ spring.
   ____ fall.

2. Alex and Jake carried red drums the color of Alex's heavy coat.

   Alex's coat was
   _X_ red.
   ____ yellow.
   ____ blue.
   ____ green.

3. Alex saw the general limp into the woods. "Where is the general going?" he asked. "General Morgan always prays before a battle," answered Jake.

   General Morgan was going
   ____ home.
   ____ to battle.
   _X_ to pray.
   ____ for a walk.

4. Alex saw British horsemen in green uniforms and soldiers in bright red coats.

   Alex could tell that
   ____ none of the British soldiers had uniforms.
   ____ all of the British soldiers had the same uniform.
   _X_ the British soldiers had different kinds of uniforms.

5. Two hundred British horsemen broke through the lines and galloped away. Many of the British soldiers threw down their guns and begged for mercy.

   When the battle was over
   ____ all British soldiers got away.
   _X_ some British soldiers got away.
   ____ no British soldiers got away.

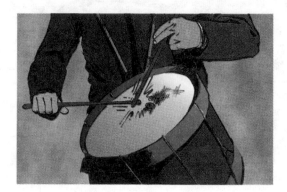

Reading 3A: "Alex, the Drummer Boy," pp. 126-30, Lesson 33
Comprehension: inferring unstated facts and details

Classified Information

▶Choose One

Circle the one in each group that does not belong.

1. bread   taters   (knife)   meat

2. (Jake)   cabin   field   British camp

3. rifle   knife   (soldiers)   musket

4. mittens   stockings   (woods)   quilt

5. Mrs. McDonald   Alex   (cannon)   Colonel Tarleton

▶Choose and Write

Write each of the words from the box beside the correct drum.

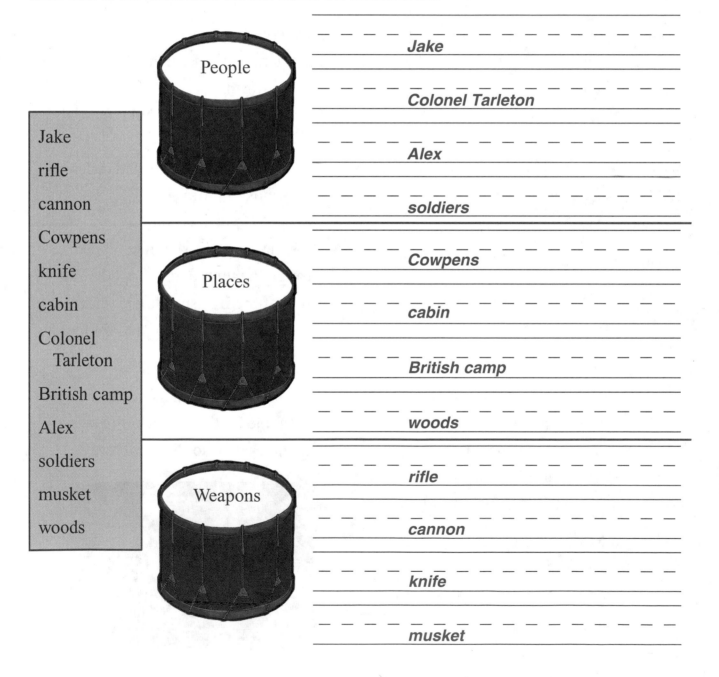

Jake
rifle
cannon
Cowpens
knife
cabin
Colonel Tarleton
British camp
Alex
soldiers
musket
woods

People

Jake

Colonel Tarleton

Alex

soldiers

Places

Cowpens

cabin

British camp

woods

Weapons

rifle

cannon

knife

musket

Reading 3A: "Alex, the Drummer Boy," pp. 126-30, Lesson 33
Comprehension: identifying irrelevant words; classifying words into categories

As Is

Name _____

▶**Choose and Write**

Complete each sentence with a word from the **red** list.

dark	football
bird	high
write	ankle

1. **Bike** is to **ride** as **pen** is to __*write*__.

2. **Goal** is to **soccer** as **touchdown** is to __*football*__.

3. **Day** is to **night** as **light** is to __*dark*__.

4. **Tank** is to **fish** as **cage** is to __*bird*__.

5. **Hand** is to **wrist** as **foot** is to __*ankle*__.

6. **Right** is to **left** as **low** is to __*high*__.

▶**Choose and Write Again**

Complete each sentence with a word from the **blue** list.

| red |
| hand |
| dog |
| taste |
| lake |
| player |

1. **Bridle** is to **horse** as **leash** is to __*dog*__.

2. **Nose** is to **smell** as **tongue** is to __*taste*__.

3. **Shoe** is to **foot** as **glove** is to __*hand*__.

4. **Go** is to **green** as **stop** is to __*red*__.

5. **Teacher** is to **student** as **coach** is to __*player*__.

6. **Bike** is to **street** as **boat** is to __*lake*__.

Reading 3A: "One of a Kind," pp. 131-37, Lesson 35
Comprehension: finding relationships between pairs of words

Bits and Pieces

Divide compound words into syllables between the base words.

d r i v e•w a y

Divide words into syllables between like consonants or unlike consonants.

w h i s•p e r   p u z•z l e

▶Divide Them

Follow the racetrack and put a dot between each syllable.

START

s t r a w•b e r•r y   h u m•m i n g•b i r d   b a s•k e t

l u m•b e r   b a s e•b a l l

g r a s s•h o p•p e r   s u n•r i s e   y e l•l o w

FINISH

t h u n d e r   b u t•t e r•c u p

Reading 3A: "One of a Kind," pp. 131-37, Lesson 35
Structural analysis: dividing compound words into syllables between the base words;
dividing words into syllables between like and unlike consonants

Like This

▶Think and Write

Name

Read the phrase in the yellow space.

Choose one of the following words that tells about the person. Write it in the green space.

faithful   **impatient**   **thrifty**
kind   **cooperative**   **careful**

In the blue space, write the name of a person from the story. Choose one of the following:

Roger   **Pete**   **Mr. Cord**

Each name can be used more than once. Note that a character trait may apply to more than one character. Allow for different choices of character trait if answers are logical.

If a person does this . . .	We might call him this . . .	Name **one** character in the story who is like this.
1. saves his money	thrifty	Roger or Mr. Cord
2. does things for someone else	kind	Mr. Cord or Roger
3. stays with a job until it is done	faithful	Mr. Cord or Roger
4. works well with others	cooperative	Roger or Pete or Mr. Cord
5. wants to do things right	careful	Mr. Cord or Roger
6. does not want to wait	impatient	Pete

Reading 3A: "One of a Kind," pp. 138-42, Lesson 36
Comprehension: identifying character traits
Study skills: organizing information in a table

Do It Right

▸Solve It
Use words from the box
to solve the puzzle.

ACROSS

2. Roger's parents could not _____ to buy him a bike.

3. Mr. Cord said the bike was for a _____ boy.

6. Roger thought the bike should be painted _____ .

7. Roger began to _____ with paper and pencil.

9. Roger missed soccer _____ .

11. Mr. Cord said Roger could _____ the bike.

DOWN

1. Mr. Cord said it would not take as long as he thought to _____ the bike.

2. Roger bought school supplies from his _____.

4. Mr. Cord wanted each part to fit _____ .

5. Roger was _____ about who would get the bike.

7. Mr. Cord said "_____ it right" a lot.

8. Roger wanted a bike called the _____ Streak.

10. The boys used sandpaper to _____ off the old paint.

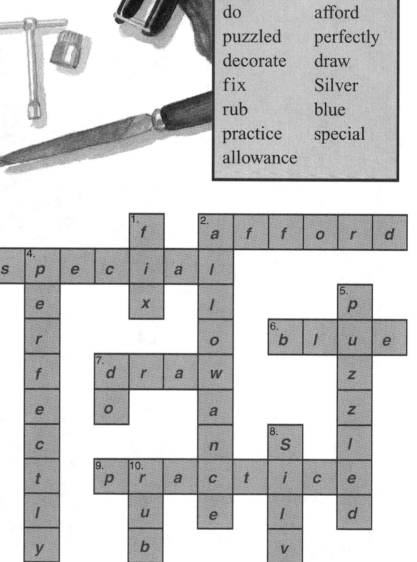

do	afford
puzzled	perfectly
decorate	draw
fix	Silver
rub	blue
practice	special
allowance	

Crossword solution:

1. f
2. afford
3. special
4. p
5. p
6. blue
7. draw
8. S
9. practice
10. r
11. decorate

Down words spelled out: serfectly, exlow, draonb, practiceld, blue, pzzle...

56

Reading 3A: "One of a Kind," pp. 138-42, Lesson 36
Comprehension: recalling facts and details
Vocabulary: determining appropriate words from context

The Brain-Boggling Bike Ride

▶Think About It

How do you know whether what you read makes sense?
Ask yourself these questions:

> Is it true to what I know already?
> Does it fit the story I am reading?
> Do the words fit the sentences?
> Is it in order?

▶Read and Think

Read the following story and think about the questions above.

1. Brian sped out of the driveway at turtle speed.

2. Cats, dogs, zebras, and small children jumped out of his path.

3. Cabbage first grew as a wild plant on the seacoasts of Europe.

4. All five wheels of his bike left the ground as he turned the corner.

5. Brian waved to his mother as he mounted his bike.

6. Officer Speedy stopped him. "Young man! Your bike has a
   burned-out (hillgatti!")

7. "I want you to turn around and ride slowly home, and don't
   let me catch you on this ship again!"

▶Find It

Write your answers in the spaces.

1. Write the number of the sentence above that does not belong. ____ *3* ____

2. What is not true in sentence number 4 about bikes?

   _____
   _
   Bikes do not have 5 wheels.

3. Circle the word in sentence number 6 that is not a real word. _____

4. Write the number of the sentence that is not in order with the others. ____ *5* ____

5. Which word in sentence number 7 does not belong? ____ *ship* ____

6. Which word in sentence number 1 does not fit the action? ____ *turtle* ____

Which He Could He Be?

▶Write It

Write the name that the underlined word refers to.

Mr. Cord

Roger

Pete

1. Pete stretched and put down <u>his</u> tattered sandpaper.

   <u>His</u> refers to _____*Pete*_____ .

2. Mr. Cord and Roger stopped to admire the bike.
   "Time for <u>us</u> to eat," Mr. Cord said.

   <u>Us</u> refers to _____*Mr. Cord*_____ and _____*Roger*_____ .

3. As Pete left, Roger watched <u>him</u> pedal down the street.

   <u>Him</u> refers to _____*Pete*_____ .

4. Pete rode up on <u>his</u> bike to remind Roger of the soccer game.

   <u>His</u> refers to _____*Pete*_____ .

5. Mr. Cord just grinned as <u>he</u> began picking up the tools.

   <u>He</u> refers to _____*Mr. Cord*_____ .

6. Roger spun the bike's wheels as <u>he</u> turned into the driveway.

   <u>He</u> refers to _____*Roger*_____ .

Reading 3A: "One of a Kind," pp. 143-48, Lesson 37
Word work: identifying pronoun referents

Greatest Gold

Poets often **pick** words that start with the same or similar sounds and use them close together to add interest to their poems.

▶Find and Circle

Circle the words that begin with the same or similar sounds in each of these lines from Proverbs. The first one is done for you.

1. I have taught thee in the (way) of (wisdom.) (Proverbs 4:11)

2. How long wilt thou (sleep,) O (sluggard?) (Proverbs 6:9)

3. For the commandment is a (lamp;) and the (law) is (light.) (Proverbs 6:23)

4. To do (justice) and (judgment) is more acceptable to the Lord than sacrifice. (Proverbs 21:3)

5. The (fear) of the Lord is a (fountain) of life. (Proverbs 14:27)

▶Think and Write

Write a describing word that begins with the same sound as each of these words. *Answers will vary.*

_____   _____

_____ frog   _____ bird

_____ slipper   _____ mountain

▶Compose It

Use one of your word pairs in a sentence.

_____

Answers will vary.

_____

_____

Reading 3A: "Jim," p. 149, Lesson 39
Comprehension: recognizing and creating alliteration

Don't Host Germs

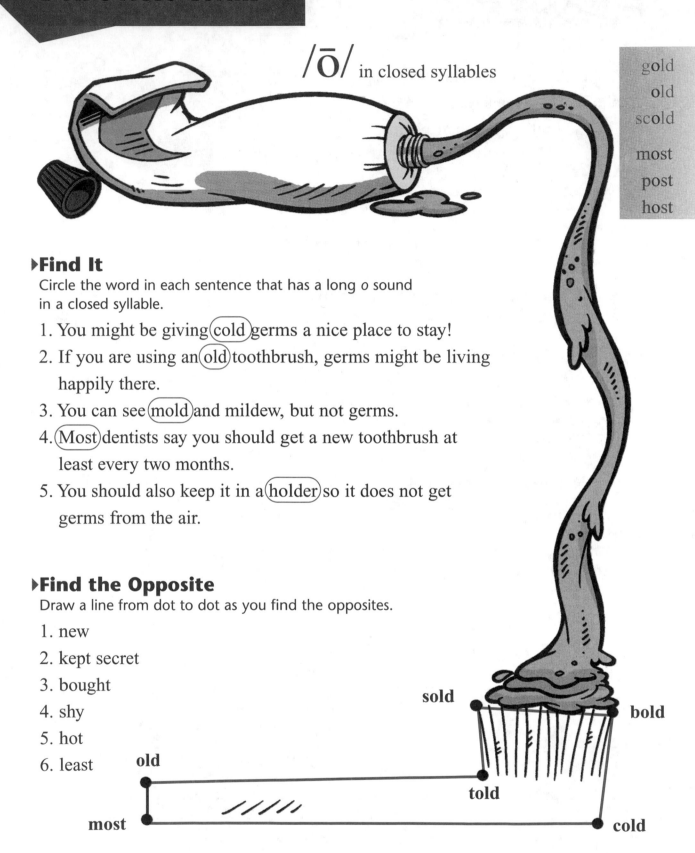

/ō/ in closed syllables

gold
old
scold

most
post
host

▶Find It

Circle the word in each sentence that has a long *o* sound in a closed syllable.

1. You might be giving (cold) germs a nice place to stay!
2. If you are using an (old) toothbrush, germs might be living happily there.
3. You can see (mold) and mildew, but not germs.
4. (Most) dentists say you should get a new toothbrush at least every two months.
5. You should also keep it in a (holder) so it does not get germs from the air.

▶Find the Opposite

Draw a line from dot to dot as you find the opposites.

1. new
2. kept secret
3. bought
4. shy
5. hot
6. least

old
most

sold
bold
told
cold

Reading 3A: "Jim," p. 149, Lesson 39
Phonics: reading words with /ō/ in closed syllables
Vocabulary: recognizing antonyms

Sure As a Shootin' Star

Name _____

▶Read and Choose

Write the letter of the correct answer in the space in the sentence.

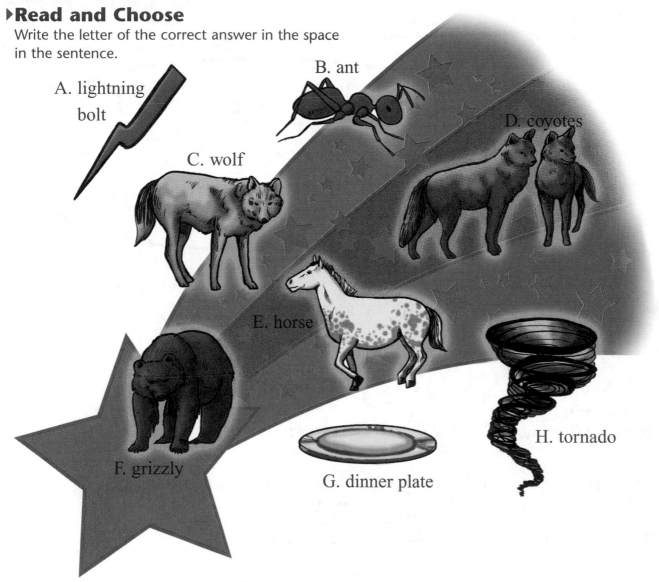

A. lightning bolt

B. ant

C. wolf

D. coyotes

E. horse

F. grizzly

G. dinner plate

H. tornado

1. Pecos Bill was raised by __*D*__ .

2. He could outhowl a __*C*__ .

3. Pecos watched an __*B*__ crawl.

4. Pecos Bill could outfight the meanest __*F*__ .

5. He could outrun the fastest __*E*__ .

6. Pecos rode a __*A*__ straight down.

7. Widow Maker's hoofprint was as big as a __*G*__ .

8. Pecos Bill rode a __*H*__ until his head spun.

Reading 3A: "Pecos Bill," pp. 150-54, Lesson 40
Comprehension: recalling facts and details

Howdy, Neighbor!

▶Choose Them

Pecos Bill wants to say only *neighborly* words.
Circle the ones that have the long *a* sound.

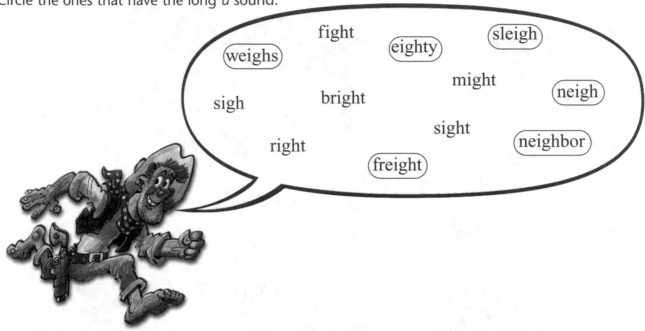

fight   eighty   sleigh

weighs

sigh   bright   might   neigh

right   sight   neighbor

freight

▶Write Them

Complete each sentence with one of the words you circled.

1. Pecos Bill bought a ranch that has _____ *eighty* _____ thousand acres.

2. It is many miles from the nearest _____ *neighbor* _____ .

3. When it snows, he hitches eight or ten longhorn steers

to a _____ *sleigh* _____ .

4. They pull the sleigh as if it _____ *weighs* _____ nothing at all.

5. Widow Maker follows the sleigh with a toss of his head and

a _____ *neigh* _____ .

6. Off they go to get their supplies at the _____ *freight* _____ station.

Reading 3A: "Pecos Bill," pp. 150-54, Lesson 40
Phonics: reading words with *eigh* as /ā/ in *neighbor*

This Tale Shore Is Tall!

Name _____

▶Solve It

Use the words in the box below to complete the puzzle.

DOWN

1. Any other man would have been _____ flat when Widow Maker rolled in the dirt.
2. Pecos Bill and Widow Maker set out to _____ the West.
4. Widow Maker snapped Pecos Bill's rope like a banjo _____.
5. Pecos Bill chased Widow Maker for _____ days.
6. Widow Maker kicked hard enough to send any man except Pecos Bill to the top of _____ Peak.
8. Anyone except Pecos Bill would have hit the ground hard enough to make another Grand _____.
10. Anyone except Pecos Bill got a quick _____ to Pikes Peak if he tried to ride Widow Maker.

ACROSS

3. Pecos Bill drank from a _____.
5. Widow Maker was _____ as tall as the mares.
7. It would be a long walk home if Widow Maker _____ a man to Pikes Peak.
9. Pecos Bill is _____ a true story.
11. This tale is as tall as a _____!

crushed
Canyon
cactus
kicked
mountain
not
Pikes
string
three
trip
twice
tame

Reading 3A: "Pecos Bill," pp. 155-59, Lesson 41
Comprehension: recalling story details

Lasso Fierce Fearsome Steers

/îr/ in
deer near here fierce

▶Circle Them

Draw lassoes around eight words that have the vowel sound you hear in *steer*.

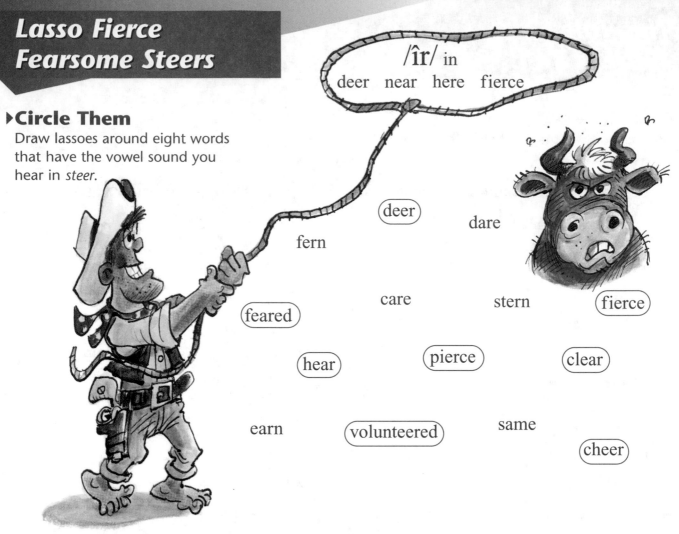

deer

fern

dare

care   stern   fierce

feared

hear   pierce   clear

earn   volunteered   same

cheer

▶Write Them

Complete each sentence with one of the words you circled.

1. Pecos Bill _____**volunteered**_____ to tame the West.

2. It was _____**clear**_____ to all that Pecos Bill was the fastest man around.

3. Widow Maker could run faster than a _____**deer**_____ .

4. All the people _____**feared**_____ riding Widow Maker.

5. Bill could _____**hear**_____ Widow Maker whinnying.

6. Pecos Bill tamed Widow Maker's _____**fierce**_____ spirit.

Reading 3A: "Pecos Bill," pp. 155-59, Lesson 41
Phonics: reading words with /îr/ as in *deer, near, here, fierce*

Spinning Splendor

▶Number Them

Number the sentences in each set in the order that they occurred in the story.

 2 David gave his mother his wages.

 3 The storekeeper sold David a Latin book.

 1 David went to work for the first time.

 3 David accepted Christ as his Savior.

 1 David began collecting herbs and rocks.

 2 David read a book that helped him understand that science and the Bible agree.

▶Read and Choose

If the sentence is true, color the book in the *true* column. If it is false, color the book in the *false* column.

	TRUE	FALSE
1. David did not like school, so he did not mind going to work instead.		color
2. David fixed thinning threads at a cotton factory.	color	
3. David could not read his book at first.	color	
4. David got angry when the other boys knocked his book down.		color
5. David found out that the Bible and true science agree with each other.	color	

Reading 3A: "David Livingstone: Man of Determination," pp. 160-64, Lesson 42
Comprehension: sequencing events; identifying statements as true or false

65

Spool Proof

© 2000 BJU Press. Reproduction prohibited.

Riddle: If the consonant plus *le* run away, what is left?

ma- ple
lit- tle

▶Divide and Decode

1. Draw a dot to divide each word into syllables.
2. Color the spools that have an open syllable green.
3. Color the spools that have a closed syllable yellow.

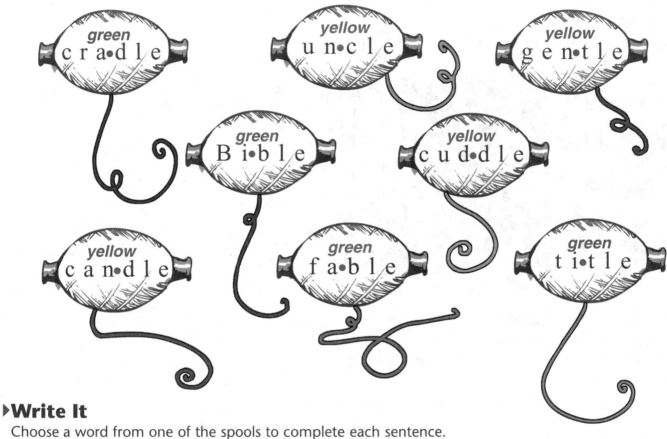

green
c r a • d l e

yellow
u • n c l e

yellow
g e n • t l e

green
B i • b l e

yellow
c u d • d l e

yellow
c a n • d l e

green
f a • b l e

green
t i • t l e

▶Write It

Choose a word from one of the spools to complete each sentence.

1. The wax from my _____*candle*_____ dripped down on my sandal.

2. My favorite _____*Uncle*_____ Duncle lives on Buncal Street.

3. The _____*title*_____ of the tale was "Tiny Tim's Tiger."

4. The _____*gentle*_____ giraffe had a cute little laugh!

Reading 3A: "David Livingstone: Man of Determination," pp. 160-64, Lesson 42
Structural analysis: dividing into syllables words that end in a consonant + *le* before the consonant
Phonics: identifying words with long vowel open syllables as /bī/ in *Bi•ble;*
identifying words with short vowel closed syllables as /lĭt/ in *lit•tle*

Smoke Signals

▶Choose and Draw

Choose the best answer for each question. Draw a smoke signal around the correct answer.

1. The night before he left, Dr. Livingstone wanted to talk all night because he _____ .

   A. couldn't sleep   B. liked to talk   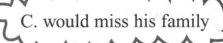 C. would miss his family

2. When Mr. Moffat spoke of the "smoke of a thousand villages," he was speaking of villages in _____ .

   A. Australia   B. India    C. Africa

3. The verse "The Lord shall preserve thee from all evil; He shall preserve thy soul" gave Dr. Livingstone a feeling of _____ .

    A. comfort   B. forgiveness   C. sadness

4. The African people listened and got saved because of _____ .

   A. the magic lantern   B. the chief    C. the Holy Spirit

▶Match Them

Draw a line to match the quote with the person.

1. "Why do you come? I have heard of white men who come for ivory or slaves."

2. "Africa needs the Word of God."

3. "Lord, show me what to do."

Mr. Moffat

Dr. Livingstone

chief

Reading 3A: "David Livingstone: Man of Determination," pp. 165-70, Lesson 43

Comprehension: inferring ideas not explicitly stated; matching characters and dialogue

Determined to Find the Key

▶Color It

Use the map and map key to follow the directions below.

A map key shows what the symbols represent on a particular map.

KEY	
desert	⠂⠄⠂
grasslands	ᴡ ᴡ ᴡ
mountains	⋀⋀⋀ ⋀
Victoria Falls	∼⊢⊬∿

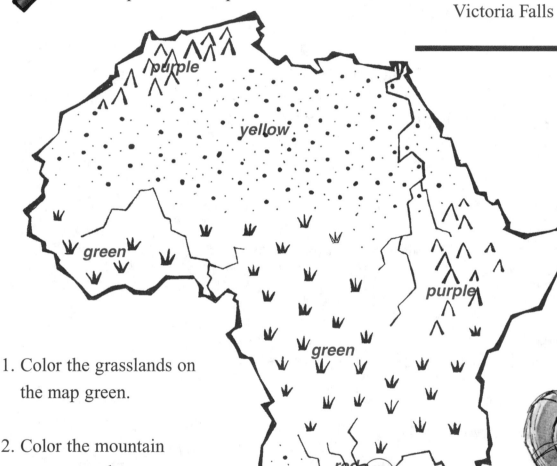

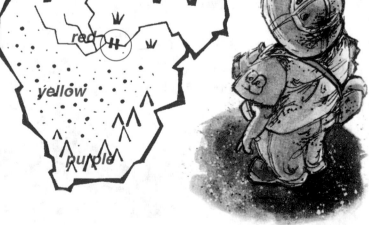

1. Color the grasslands on the map green.

2. Color the mountain ranges purple.

3. Circle Victoria Falls in red.

4. Color the deserts on the map yellow.

68

Reading 3A: "David Livingstone: Man of Determination," pp. 165-70, Lesson 43
Study skills: interpreting a map key; reading symbols on a map

Map It Out

Name _____

▶Think and Choose

Read each sentence. Choose the chapter title in which you would find the sentence. Write the letter of the title in the blank.

__A__ 1. David Livingstone went to school at night.

__C__ 2. For years Dr. Livingstone explored Africa to find a place to build a mission.

__B__ 3. A puzzled chief could not understand why a white man would come to Africa to help the natives.

Chapters

A. A Book I Can Study
B. The Smoke of a Thousand Villages
C. Up River

▶Order Them

Read the paragraph, tracing the trip on the map. Number the following sentences in story order.

Tallah had wanted to explore Africa for a long time. He gathered supplies and began his trip on foot in Serowe, Botswana. He soon arrived at Victoria Falls. From there he traveled by boat to Kabalo, Zaire. Once again he went on foot, going west to Kananga. He traveled north by camel to the Congo River where he caught a boat to Kinshasa. At the market, Tallah hired a man to guide him through Angola and back into Botswana. Once home, Tallah paid the guide his wages and ran to tell his family of his adventures.

__3__ Tallah traveled from Kananga to the Congo River by camel.

__2__ Tallah rode on a boat from Victoria Falls to Kabalo, Zaire.

__1__ Tallah began his trip on foot in Serowe, Botswana.

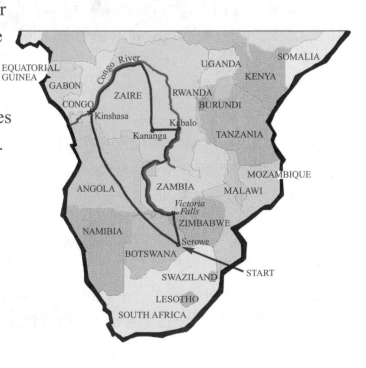

Reading 3A: "David Livingstone: Man of Determination," pp. 171-76, Lesson 44
Comprehension: relating facts and details to a chapter title; sequencing events

69

Rescue Upriver

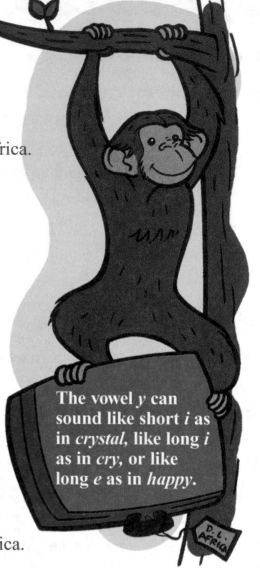

▶Find It

Read the sentence and look at the underlined word. Then circle the word below that has a *y* with the same sound as the *y* in the underlined word.

1. Dr. Livingstone explored the river <u>systems</u> in Africa.
   - Ⓐ crystal
   - B. sky
   - C. laundry

2. He did <u>try</u> to make maps for other missionaries.
   - A. many
   - B. mystery
   - Ⓒ dry

3. Dr. Livingstone spent many nights in <u>dusty</u> huts.
   - Ⓐ country
   - B. syllable
   - C. fry

4. Dr. Livingstone was <u>happy</u> to see Mr. Stanley.
   - A. symptom
   - B. pry
   - Ⓒ boundary

The vowel *y* can sound like short *i* as in *crystal*, like long *i* as in *cry*, or like long *e* as in *happy*.

▶Choose and Mark

Read each sentence. Put an *X* in the blank if the word in color has a *y* that sounds like a long *e* as in *happy*.

<u>X</u> 1. David Livingstone was a missionary to Africa.

___ 2. He went a long way into the African jungle.

Read each sentence. Put an *X* in the blank if the word in color has a *y* that sounds like short *i* as in *gym*.

___ 3. The natives eagerly watched the "magic lantern" slide pictures.

<u>X</u> 4. They listened to the hymns he sang.

Read each sentence. Put an *X* in the blank if the word in color has a *y* that sounds like long *i* as in *cry*.

___ 5. Lions had killed many animals and even people.

<u>X</u> 6. "Why don't you kill the lions?" David asked.

He Said—She Said

▸Decide and Write

What a character says often shows what he is like or how he feels.
Read each quotation and fill in the circle beside the correct answer.

1. "Send away Queen Vashti? But who will be our queen?"

   Esther was—

   ○ excited ● surprised ○ thankful

2. "You know much better than I what would please the
   king. I will wear what you choose to give me."

   Esther was—

   ● humble ○ wicked ○ proud

3. "What is this? Servants are plotting to kill me?
   I am the most powerful king on earth, and they
   plot to kill me?"

   King Ahasuerus was—

   ● proud ○ happy ○ thoughtful

4. "You honor your king. You have helped to save my life."

   King Ahasuerus was—

   ○ surprised ○ angry ● grateful

▸Think and Write

What do you think would have happened to the Jewish nation if
Esther had not gone before the king?

Answers will vary.

Reading 3A: "Esther, the Queen," pp. 177-81, Lesson 46
Comprehension: inferring character traits and emotions from dialogue

Scenes from the Palace

b climb   h hour   c scent   t whistle

▶Choose and Color

1. Read the sentence. Choose the word with the silent consonant to complete the sentence.
2. Color the crown of the correct word yellow.

1. Confusion was everywhere. Hegai felt _____.

tired   numb *color*

2. The maidens _____ about the palace.

flew   bustled *color*

3. "I must wear the king's favorite _____," insisted one girl.

 scent *color*    garment

4. Esther was as gentle as a _____.

 kitten   lamb *color*

5. Esther chose to _____ to Hegai's advice.

 obey    listen *color*

6. "Surely you will win the highest _____," he said.

 award    honor *color*

Reading 3A: "Esther, the Queen," pp. 177-81, Lesson 46
Phonics: reading words with silent consonants: *c* as in *scent*, *h* as in *hour*, *t* as in *whistle*,
and *b* as in *climb*

Which Is It?

> **JOHN 15:13**
> *Greater love hath no man than this, ...*
> *that a man lay down his life for his friends.*

great   greater   greatest

Use -er to compare two things.

Use -est to compare three or more things.

▶Choose One

Circle the word that best completes each sentence.

1. Of all the powers in the kingdom, the king's power was the (stronger, (strongest)).

2. Mordecai was a (noble, (nobler)) man than Haman.

3. Of all the girls in the land, Esther was the ((prettiest,) prettier) one.

4. "I am (great, (greater)) than Mordecai," boasted Haman.

5. Esther showed the (sweeter, (sweetest)) spirit of all the women.

▶Write One

Choose the correct form that best completes each sentence.

1. Esther was the _____*loveliest*_____ of all the women
   (lovely, lovelier, loveliest)

   brought before King Ahasuerus.

2. Mordecai seemed _____*taller*_____ than Haman
   (tall, taller, tallest)

   when the wicked prince passed by.

Reading 3A: "Esther, the Queen," pp. 182-87, Lesson 47
Comprehension: using comparative and superlative forms correctly

73

The Journal of Her Majesty

journal	firm
learn	her
nurse	work

/ûr/

▶Read and Circle

Circle the letters in each word that make the /ûr/ sound.

ch(ur)ch   b(ir)d   f(er)n   c(ou)rage   h(ear)d

w(or)m   b(ur)st   d(ir)ty   s(er)ve   w(or)ship

▶Choose and Circle

1. Read the journal below, which is similar to one Queen Esther may have kept.
2. Choose and circle one word from each pair of colored words that has the same vowel sound you hear in *bird*.

The first day of the month Adar, 480 B.C.

Living like a queen is so different from living with Cousin Mordecai. There are some things that I enjoy greatly, such as the beautiful flowers that (flourish, grow) in the big gardens. Oh, yes, the food is abundant and delicious too. My maidens usually bring my meals to my room and the (spices, herbs) fill the place with delightful scents! I also love my new bed. It is very soft and warm, unlike the (hard, firm) mattress at Mordecai's home. I do not feel (worthy, good) enough to have all these wonderful things!

I think it quite (absurd, unusual) that I have to bathe so often. The funny thing is that I rarely see my husband, the king. I often feel very lonely and have the (desire, urge) to run home to Mordecai. However, I will do my very best to be a good wife and queen. Who knows? Maybe the Lord put me here for a special purpose.

▶Think and Write

Imagine that you were a king or queen for one day. On your own paper, write a short journal entry telling about what your day as royalty was like.

Reading 3A: "Esther, the Queen," pp. 182-87, Lesson 47
Phonics: reading words with /ûr/ as in her, firm, nurse, journal, learn, and work
Composition: writing a description

▸Match Them

Look at the words in each crown. Draw lines to match the antonyms.

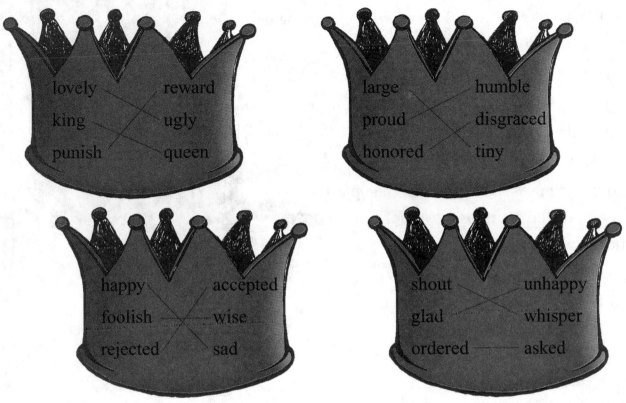

lovely — reward
king — ugly
punish — queen

large — humble
proud — disgraced
honored — tiny

happy — accepted
foolish — wise
rejected — sad

shout — unhappy
glad — whisper
ordered — asked

▸Correct It

Read the note below. Correct the mistakes in the note by writing an antonym for each word in color. Use the words from the crowns above.

Dear Mordecai,

I feared for my life as I approached the queen. But he rejected me. How happy I was.

I invited him to a tiny feast. I asked Haman to come as well. He was unhappy, for he thought he was being disgraced.

Love,
Esther

1. _____ *king* _____

2. _____ *accepted* _____

3. _____ *large* _____

4. _____ *glad* _____

5. _____ *honored* _____

Reading 3A: "Esther, the Queen," pp. 188-92, Lesson 48
Vocabulary: matching antonyms; using antonyms correctly in sentences

75

What's the Meaning of This?

court•yard | **kôrt′** yärd′ | —*noun* An open space surrounded by walls or buildings.

chron•i•cle | **krŏn′** ĭ kəl | —*noun* A chronological record of historical events.

de•cree | dĭ **krē′** | —*noun* An official order; a law.

gal•lows | **găl′** ōz | —*noun* A frame from which criminals are hanged.

sack•cloth | **săk′** klôth | —*noun* A rough cloth of camel's hair, goat hair, hemp, cotton, or flax worn as a symbol of mourning.

scep•ter | **sĕp′** tər | —*noun* A rod or staff held by a king or queen as a symbol of authority.

If the meaning of a word in a sentence is not clear, use the glossary.

▸Choose and Write

Read the following sentences. In each blank write a word from the glossary above. Check your work by reading the definitions.

1. The king wrote a _____ **decree** _____ to destroy all those who did not keep his laws.

2. Mordecai stood outside the king's gate in _____ **sackcloth** _____ and ashes.

3. The king held out the golden _____ **scepter** _____ for the queen to touch.

4. Haman commanded a tall _____ **gallows** _____ to be built on which to hang Mordecai.

Reading 3A: "Esther, the Queen," pp. 188-92, Lesson 48
Study skills: using definitions from the glossary to locate the word that best fits in the sentence

Who's Who?

▶Match Them
Draw a line from each word to the picture of the person it describes.

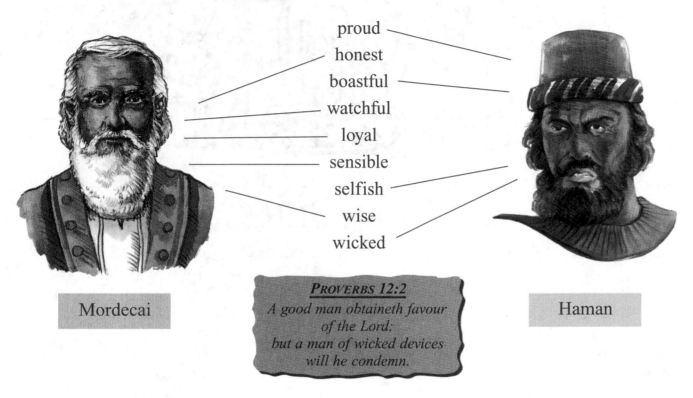

proud
honest
boastful
watchful
loyal
sensible
selfish
wise
wicked

Mordecai

PROVERBS 12:2
*A good man obtaineth favour
of the Lord:
but a man of wicked devices
will he condemn.*

Haman

▶Choose and Write
Read each sentence. Write the name of the speaker in the blank.

Esther   Mordecai   Haman   the king

1. "I worship only the one true God."   *Mordecai*

2. "Whatever you want, I will give you."   *the king*

3. "If I perish, I perish."   *Esther*

4. "Do not tell anyone that you are a Jewess."   *Mordecai*

5. "I will kill Mordecai."   *Haman*

Reading 3A: "Esther, the Queen," pp. 193-200, Lesson 49
Comprehension: identifying character traits; matching story characters and dialogue

77

Contraction Construction

▶**Find and Write**

Underline the contraction in each sentence.
Write the two words from which the
contraction is made.

1. "You've been made queen for
   such a time as this."

   You + *have*

2. Esther could've been put
   to death.

   could + *have*

3. "I've been sent to remind you
   of the queen's banquet."

   I + *have*

4. Haman would've hanged
   Mordecai on the gallows.

   would + *have*

5. Esther bowed low to the king and
   said, "We've been plotted against."

   We + *have*

▶**Match Them**

Draw lines to match each contraction with the correct words.

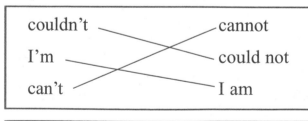

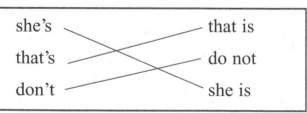

Reading 3A: "Esther, the Queen," pp. 193-200, Lesson 49
Structural analysis: demonstrating understanding of contractions formed with *have*;
reading contractions formed with *have, not, am,* and *is*

A Jewish Tradition

▶Read and Think

As you read each paragraph, think about the main idea.

A. When God brought His people out of Egypt, He gave many ways for them to show that they were true to Him. He told His people to do certain things to help them remember to worship only the one true God and to keep His commandments. He told them to put His commandments where they could be seen often.

B. A small rectangular box called a *mezuzah* was attached to the door frame of the house or to the gate of the yard. The box contained a small piece of parchment on which were written two passages from Deuteronomy. One passage was God's words to the people. The other passage listed blessings to those who kept His commandments and the punishment for those who did not.

C. Many Jewish families still honor the commandments of God by placing *mezuzahs* on the entrances to their homes. Some place a small reminder box at the entrance to every room in the house. Every member of the family pauses to touch the *mezuzah* when entering or leaving the home.

> **DEUTERONOMY 6:6, 9**
> And these words, which I command thee this day, shall be in thine heart: And thou shalt write them upon the posts of thy house, and on thy gates.

▶Decide and Match

Write the letter of the correct paragraph beside each main idea.

1. __B__ A mezuzah contains two Scripture passages from Deuteronomy about keeping God's commandments.

2. __A__ God told His people to show that they were true to Him.

3. __C__ Jewish people still have mezuzahs today.

Reading 3A: "New Year in a New Land," pp. 202-6, Lesson 50
Comprehension: inferring the main idea of a paragraph

The Misplaced Story

mis—
wrong
or
bad

re—
again
or
back

un—
not
or
opposite

▸Circle and Choose

1. Circle the prefix in each colored word below.
2. Put an *X* on the line beside the words that mean the same thing
   as the colored word.

1. Kathy (mis)placed the story
   that she had written.
   ____ put in place again
   _X_ put in the wrong place
   ____ put in place

2. She needed to (re)write
   the story before class.
   _X_ write the story again
   ____ write the story the first time
   ____ not write the story

3. Kathy knew she had found many
   (mis)spelled words in her story.
   ____ spelled again
   ____ spelled correctly
   _X_ spelled the wrong way

4. She did not want to have
   to (re)check all her spelling.
   _X_ check again
   ____ check the wrong story
   ____ check the first time

5. She sat down to (re)read the library
   book she liked best.
   ____ not read at all
   ____ read the first time
   _X_ read again

6. When Kathy opened the book,
   something (un)expected fell out.
   ____ expected again
   _X_ not expected
   ____ expected the first time

7. "What an (un)usual place to
   find my story," she said.
   ____ usual
   ____ usual again
   _X_ not usual

8. "Now I don't have to (re)do
   my story," she exclaimed.
   _X_ do again
   ____ not do
   ____ do the first time

Reading 3A: "New Year in a New Land," pp. 202-6, Lesson 50
Word work: identifying the meaning of prefixes *mis-, re-, un-;* identifying prefixes in words

Sonya and the New Year

Name _____

▶Read and Choose
Circle *True* or *False* for each statement.

1. The Tallmans had just moved to Russia.	True	(False)
2. Sonya missed her friends in Russia.	(True)	False
3. Sonya wanted to celebrate the Jewish New Year.	(True)	False
4. The Kuril family was saving money to buy a house.	True	(False)
5. Mr. Tallman could not pay the children early.	True	(False)
6. Mr. Tallman helped the children because he was Jewish.	True	(False)
7. Sonya could not read English.	True	(False)

▶Choose One
Fill in the circle beside the sentence that tells why.

1. Sonya cried when she heard that they could not celebrate the New Year.
   - ○ Sonya did not like to celebrate the New Year.
   - ● Sonya liked to celebrate the New Year.

2. Sonya asked if she could take her apple home.
   - ● Sonya wanted to save the apple for the New Year.
   - ○ Sonya did not like the taste of apples.

3. Mr. Tallman asked if Sonya could read English.
   - ○ Mr. Tallman wrote in Russian.
   - ● Mr. Tallman wrote in English.

▶Write About It
On a separate sheet of paper, write a short explanation of how the author let us know that Sonya was starting to like the new land.

Reading 3A: "New Year in a New Land," pp. 207-11, Lesson 51
Comprehension: recalling facts and details; making inferences

81

Going Shopping

▶Circle and Write

Circle the abbreviations on the windows of Mr. Tallman's store.
Write each one beside the correct word on the list below.

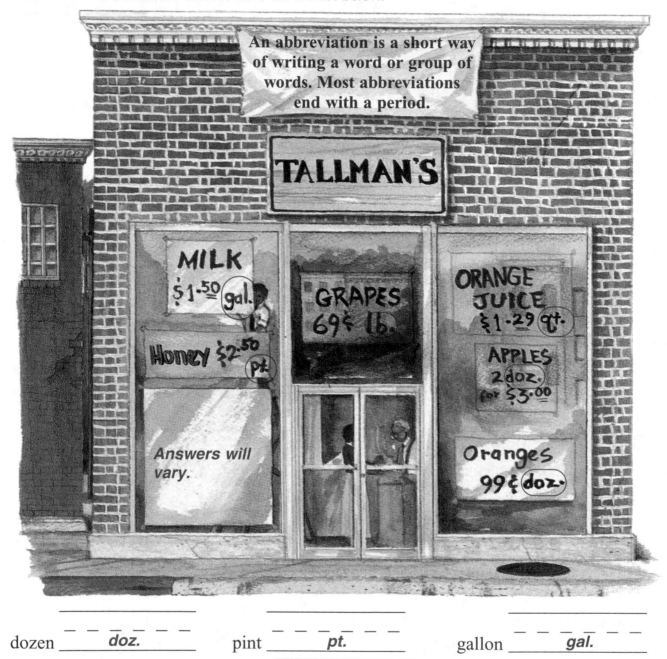

An abbreviation is a short way of writing a word or group of words. Most abbreviations end with a period.

TALLMAN'S

MILK $1.50 gal.

Honey $2.50 pt.

GRAPES 69¢ lb.

ORANGE JUICE $1.29 qt.

APPLES 2 doz. for $3.00

Answers will vary.

Oranges 99¢ doz.

dozen ___*doz.*___   pint ___*pt.*___   gallon ___*gal.*___

pound ___*lb.*___   quart ___*qt.*___

▶Write One

On the blank sign in Mr. Tallman's window, advertise a different
sale item using one of the abbreviations.

Reading 3A: "New Year in a New Land," pp. 207-11, Lesson 51
Word work: using abbreviations
Composition: composing an advertisement

Flying High

▶Choose One

Color the circle of the phrase that completes each sentence correctly.

1. Before 1783, people could not travel in the air because _____.

   ○ they had never tried
   ○ they didn't want to
   ● they hadn't yet invented anything that could fly

2. Joseph Montgolfier got his idea for making hot-air balloons by watching _____.

   ● clouds
   ○ birds
   ○ airplanes

3. The king of France ordered that no one was to ride in the balloon because _____.

   ● a rider might get hurt
   ○ the law said only animals could ride
   ○ he wanted to ride first

4. The rooster had a broken wing when it returned because _____.

   ○ the balloon crashed
   ● the sheep kicked it
   ○ the balloon crushed it when it landed

5. Two men rode in the next balloon because _____.

   ○ the king ordered them to
   ○ they needed the money
   ● they were eager to try out the balloon

6. The balloon began to fall because _____.

   ○ it was too high
   ○ the men were afraid
   ● the men were enjoying the view, not fueling the fire

7. The balloon rose again because _____.

   ○ the wind carried it
   ● the men fed the fire
   ○ the men threw supplies overboard to lighten the load

Reading 3A: "Up in the Air," pp. 212-17, Lesson 52
Comprehension: recalling cause-and-effect relationships

83

Free Floating

▶Circle and Number

1. Circle the base word of the word in the balloon. Think about the last sound of the base word.
2. Write on the basket the number of syllables in the whole word.

If a base word ends with a *d* or *t* sound, the suffix *-ed* will be a separate syllable.

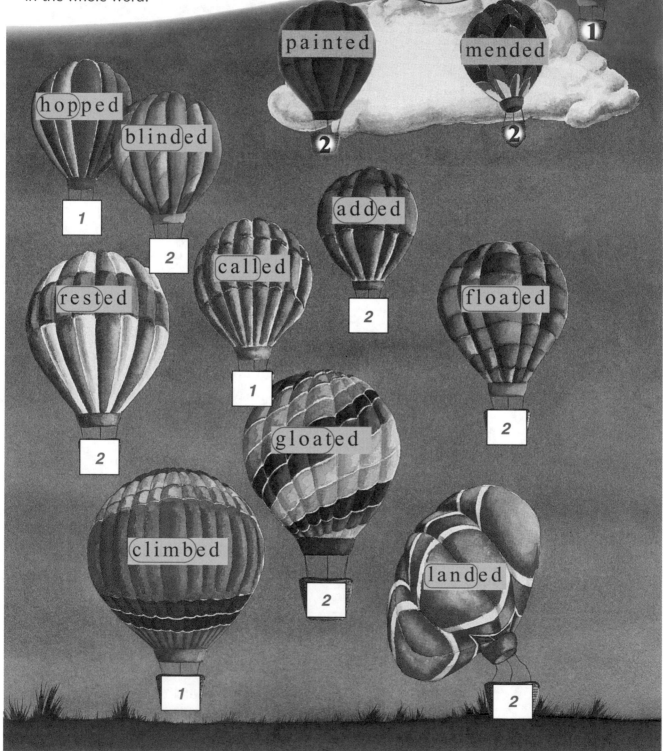

soared — 1

painted — 2

mended — 2

hopped — 1

blinded — 2

added — 2

called — 1

rested — 2

floated — 2

gloated — 2

climbed — 1

landed — 2

Reading 3A: "Up in the Air," pp. 212-17, Lesson 52
Structural analysis: recognizing that *-ed* is a separate syllable after /d/ and /t/ (floated, landed, hopped)

Ski Season

▶Think About It

Read each story carefully and color the ski next to the correct answer.

The two girls rode the ski lift up the hill. Jill tried to coax Jennifer to look at the skiers flying down the slope beneath them. "It's so beautiful," said Jill, leaning forward. Jennifer would not even open her eyes.

As the chair lift neared the top, Jill grasped her poles and slid off the chair onto the top of the hill. She turned around and was surprised to find Jennifer riding the chair lift back down the hill.

Jennifer missed getting off the lift because

- she was busy watching the scenery.
- she had her eyes closed.
- she was stuck to the chair.

Brian and Steve were racing near the ski lodge. Brian tried to slow down, but he plowed right into a rack of skis.

Steve tried to grab a ski as it shot past him, but he was too late.

The skis on the rack

- broke into pieces.
- fell on top of Brian.
- went sliding down the hill.

Reading 3A: "Danger on the Mountain," pp. 218-20, Lesson 54
Comprehension: inferring cause-and-effect relationships

Up the Mountain

▶Read and Think

Read the words in the box.
What sound does the *tain* make?

mountain
captain
chieftain
fountain

mountain
/ moun´•tən /

▶Choose One

Choose a word from the list above
to complete each sentence.

1. The _____*captain*_____ led his army
   through the deep valley.

2. Slowly they marched to the top of the _____*mountain*_____ .

3. The captain was alarmed when he met the Indian _____*chieftain*_____ .

▶Write Some

Write at least two sentences using words from the box above.

Answers will vary.

Reading 3A: "Danger on the Mountain," pp. 218-20, Lesson 54
Phonics: reading words with schwa syllable *-tain* as /tən/ in *mountain*

Sentence Sense

Name _____

▶Think and Write

Write your answers on the lines below the questions.
Use complete sentences.

1. Why did Hansel live with his grandparents?

   _____

   _
   Answers will vary but should include idea that he is an orphan.

   _____

   _____

2. What was the name of Hansel's friend?

   _____

   _
   Markus was Hansel's friend.

3. How will the boys get to school when there is a lot of snow?

   _____

   _
   They will ski to school.

4. What did Hansel name his puppy?

   _____

   _
   He named him Bear.

5. What are two things that might make the mountain dangerous?

   _____

   _
   possible answers: ice, snowstorms, rocks, cliffs, avalanches

   _____

   _

   _____

Reading 3A: "Danger on the Mountain," pp. 221-24, Lesson 55
Comprehension: making inferences; recalling facts and details

Contraction Action

▶Read and Find

Read the story and underline the contractions.

"Come ski with us," called Bill.

"I <u>don't</u> know how," Bob replied. "Would you teach me?"

"I <u>can't</u> teach you, but if <u>you'll</u> go to the bunny hill <u>you'll</u> find the ski instructor. <u>He'll</u> teach you."

"The bunny hill?" Bob looked at Bill with a puzzled expression.

"The bunny hill is a small hill where you can practice. The ski instructors are over there, and <u>they're</u> giving free lessons today."

"Great," said Bob as he picked up his skis. "<u>I'm</u> on my way!"

▶Match Them

Draw a line from each contraction to the words that make up that contraction.

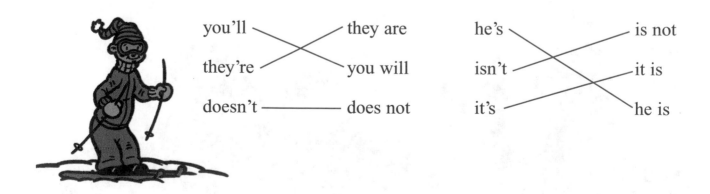

you'll — they are

they're — you will

doesn't — does not

he's — is not

isn't — it is

it's — he is

Reading 3A: "Danger on the Mountain," pp. 221-24, Lesson 55
Word work: reading contractions formed with *are, will, is,* and *not*; identifying contractions

How Did You Guess?

▸Match Them

Read the sentence on the hat. Find the activity on the mittens below that matches it. Write the number in the circle on the hat.

The teakettle whistled as we eagerly shed our boots and coats. **5**

Mark took careful aim and sent the puck speeding across the ice—*SWISH!* **3**

Huffing and puffing, we ran back up the snowy hill. **1**

Shawn dressed warmly and took a carrot, a scarf, and some sticks out into the snow. **4**

We prepared our ammunition and ducked behind the snowy wall. **2**

1. Going sledding

2. Having a snowball fight

3. Making a hockey goal

4. Building a snowman

5. Drinking hot cocoa

Reading 3A: "Danger on the Mountain," pp. 225-27, Lesson 56
Comprehension: drawing conclusions

Birthday Sleigh

sleigh
obey
rein
ā

▶Read and Circle

Read the story. Circle the words in the story that have the long *a* sound spelled like the words in the sleigh above.

Will's (Eighth) Birthday

"When a boy turns (eight,) he deserves a special (sleigh) ride," Grandpa told Will.

Will watched excitedly as Grandpa hitched Max to the big red (sleigh.) Then Will climbed into Grandpa's lap. He helped hold the (reins) to guide Max down the icy road.

"We'll pull in here for a rest," Grandpa said as they stopped at a (neighbor's) farmhouse.

"Hi there, Will," called the (neighbor.) "There's something for you behind the barn. Please go get it."

Will hurried to (obey.) He couldn't believe what he saw.

"Is it—is it for me?" he stammered.

Grandpa came up and patted his shoulder. "Yes, it's your very own pony and (sleigh.)"

"Oh, thank you, Grandpa!" Will exclaimed. "You're the best grandpa in the world!"

"When we get home, we'll give the best pony in the world some oats," Grandpa said.

"And I'll brush his coat till it shines," Will added.

"(Neigh,)" the pony seemed to agree.

Will laughed. "I think he just said thank you, too!"

▶Think and Choose

Read the sentence. Look at the underlined word. Circle the letter of the best definition for that word.

1. The <u>skein</u> of geese flew over the pond.

    a. ball   (b.) flock   c. honking

2. The men moved the <u>freight</u> from the loading platform to the train.

    a. falling   b. freedom   (c.) cargo

Reading 3A: "**Danger on the Mountain,**" pp. 225-27, Lesson 56
Phonics: using letter-sound association: /ā/ as *ey* in *obey*, *eigh* in *eight*, and *ei* in *rein*
Vocabulary: analyzing context to determine word meaning

Lost and Found

▶Number Them

Number the sentences in each set in story order.

 2 Hansel named the puppy Bear.

 1 Grandfather came in carrying a big basket.

 4 The boys walked together to the school in the valley.

 3 Hansel, Markus, and Bear spent many hours racing along the green slopes of the mountain.

 4 Grandfather and Bear found the boys huddled under the rocks.

 1 Hansel and Markus skied down the mountain to school.

 3 The boys prayed that the Lord would help Grandfather find them.

 2 Markus was down on one knee, holding his ankle.

▶Choose Two

Put an *X* in the box of each correct answer.
Each question will have two answers.

1. What were the dangers on the mountain that the boys faced?
   ☒ snowdrifts   ☐ lightning   ☒ sudden storms

2. Who came to the rescue?
   ☒ Bear   ☒ Grandfather   ☐ the police

3. What were the lessons the boys learned?
   ☐ to wait in the school   ☒ to trust the Lord   ☒ to be a good friend

Reading 3A: "Danger on the Mountain," pp. 228-31, Lesson 57
Comprehension: sequencing events in story order; recalling facts and details

91

Search the Scriptures

▶Underline It

Underline the parts of the words in the box that have the same sound as *tion* in *location*.

temptation   redemption

creation   instruction

nation   salvation

possession

▶Find and Read

Find and read in your Bible each Scripture verse below.
Complete each verse with a word from the box.

1. Matthew 6:13 And lead us not into _____**temptation**_____,
but deliver us from evil.

2. Proverbs 8:33 Hear _____**instruction**_____, and be wise, and
refuse it not.

3. Psalm 33:12 Blessed is the _____**nation**_____ whose God
is the Lord.

4. Acts 4:12 Neither is there _____**salvation**_____ in any other:
for there is none other name under heaven given among men,
whereby we must be saved.

5. Romans 1:20 For the invisible things of him from the
_____**creation**_____ of the world are clearly seen.

Reading 3A: "Danger on the Mountain," pp. 228-31, Lesson 57
Phonics: reading words with unaccented syllables *-tion* as /shən/ in *nation* and *-sion* as /shən/ in *mission*
Study skills: locating Scripture verses

Find the Facts

▶**Hunt It**

The words in the box below are hidden on the courthouse steps.
Find and circle each one.

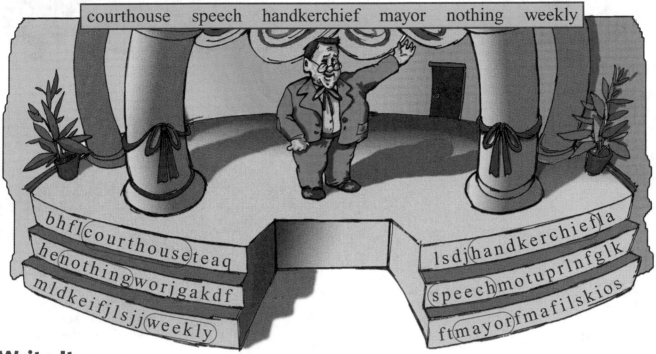

courthouse　speech　handkerchief　mayor　nothing　weekly

bhfl courthouse teaq
he nothing worjgakdf
mldkeifjlsjj weekly

lsdj handkerchief la
speech motuprlnfglk
ft mayor fmafilskios

▶**Write It**

Choose a word from the steps to answer the question
and write it in the blank.

1. Professor Plumcott was elected to what office? _____ *mayor*

2. Where did the townspeople gather? _____ *courthouse*

3. What did the townspeople expect to hear? _____ *speech*

4. How often was the mayor expected to speak? _____ *weekly*

5. What did the mayor wipe his brow with? _____ *handkerchief*

6. What did the mayor have to say? _____ *nothing*

Reading 3A: "Professor Plumcott's Problem," pp. 232-37, Lesson 58
Comprehension: recalling facts and details

Puzzle Power

▶**Fill It In**

honey
monkeys
double
trouble

Work the puzzle. Use the words from the purple box below.

ACROSS

1. January, June, and July are ____.
3. The day after Sunday is ____.
4. An animal that swings by
   its tail is a ____.
6. A father calls his boy ____.
7. When you don't obey, you
   get in ____.
9. The first person in line
   is at the ____.
11. Someone who is not
    old is ____.
12. America is our ____.

DOWN

2. Bees use the nectar from
   flowers to make ____.
4. Dollar bills and coins
   are kinds of ____.
5. If someone does not
   have anything,
   he has ____.
8. Someone who is starving
   does not have ____ to eat.
10. You feel things with your
    sense of ____.

country   enough   front   honey
Monday   money   monkey   months
nothing   Son   touch   trouble   young

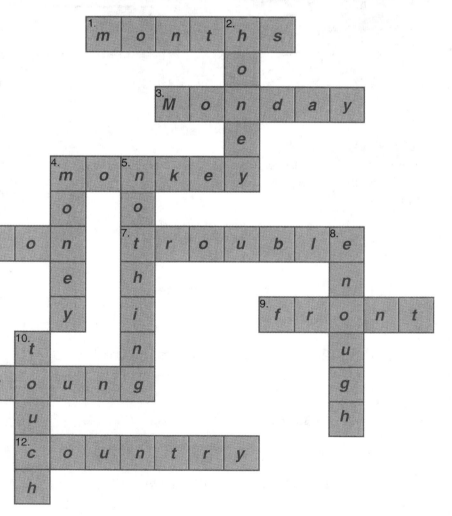

Reading 3A: "Professor Plumcott's Problem," pp. 232-37, Lesson 58
Phonics: using letter-sound association: /ŭ/ as *ou* in *country* and *o* in *Monday*
Vocabulary: developing vocabulary

Poor Professor Plumcott!

Name _____

▸Write It
Answer the questions about the story.

1. The last time that Mayor Plumcott asked
   the people what they had to say, what did they say?

   _____

   –
   _____ *They said nothing.* _____

2. How often did the mayor decide he would give speeches?

   _____

   –
   _____ *whenever he had something to say* _____

▸Figure It Out
Write what the author wanted you to think.

1. Why didn't the people of Plumville answer Mayor
   Plumcott's question?

   – – – – *Answers will vary but should include the idea that when* – – – –
   _____ *they had answered him, the mayor did not give a speech.* _____

2. Why did he have nothing to say to the crowd but something
   to say to each person?

   _____

   –
   _____ *Answers will vary.* _____

   _____

   –

   _____

▸Think About It
Answer with your own idea.

Do you think a mayor should give a speech every week?
Give a reason for your answer.

_____

– –
_____ *Answers will vary.* _____

_____

– –

_____

Reading 3A: "Professor Plumcott's Problem," pp. 238-40, Lesson 59
Comprehension: recalling story details; making inferences; thinking critically

Plumville's Pet Predicament

▶ Read and Think

Read the story. Notice the groups of words with the same beginning sounds.

In Plumville everything that anybody owns starts with the same letter as his name. All the names of Andy's things start with *a*. All the names of Billy's things start with *b*. And so it goes down through the alphabet.

One day a mean man came to Plumville. He wanted to mix everybody up. So that night he traded all the toy pets in Plumville. He exchanged Billy's buffalo with Sammy's skunk. He traded Paula's pig with Frank's fish. From house to house he went, mixing up the pets and laughing his evil laugh.

In the morning panic spread through Plumville. "Hey!" yelled Wilbur. "Where is my walrus?" Down the street Zelda wondered why a walrus was in her zebra pen. It was a disaster!

All the children brought the misplaced pets to Professor Plumcott. He quickly straightened out the situation and returned the proper pet to its proper owner. Everyone in Plumville went home pleased.

Add an *apostrophe* and an *s* to the name of a person, place, or thing to make it possessive.

▶ Write Them

Match each pet owner with his pet. Write each name with an apostrophe and an *s.*

Sammy

Paula

Frank

Billy's	buffalo
Frank's	fish
Paula's	pig
Sammy's	skunk
Wilbur's	walrus
Zelda's	zebra

Zelda

Billy

Wilbur

Reading 3A: "Professor Plumcott's Problem," pp. 238-40, Lesson 59
Word work: reading and writing possessives
Literature: noting the author's use of alliteration

Name

▶Number Them

Number each set of events in story order.

___3___ Jesus came to Bethany after Lazarus died.

___4___ At Bethany one sister ran to meet Jesus first.

___1___ Mary and Martha sent Jesus
a message concerning Lazarus.

___2___ Jesus stayed where He was for two days.

___3___ Mary saw Jesus and fell down at His feet.

___2___ Martha told Mary that Jesus had come.

___1___ Jesus told Martha that Lazarus would rise again.

___4___ Jesus wept.

___2___ Jesus prayed to His Father.

___1___ The stone was rolled away from the cave.

___4___ Lazarus was unbound from his graveclothes.

___3___ Lazarus came forth from the dead.

Reading 3A: "Raised from the Dead," pp. 241-48, Lesson 61
Comprehension: recalling sequence of events

Moving Day

▶Read and Circle

Read the story. Circle the base word in each colored word.

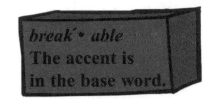

break • able
The accent is
in the base word.

On moving day we drove the big truck to our new house.
Dad un(lock)ed the door and we began un(load)ing the
many heavy (box)es. Mom told me to be (care)ful with her
box of (dish)es. She did not want to have to re(place) any
broken pieces. I gently put the box down and Mom began
un(pack)ing. As I was walking back to the truck I saw a
boy my age (jump)ing on a trampoline next door. He called
to me to join him. Dad let me take a break to meet the
(friend)ly boy. I knew I was going to like my new neighbor.

▶Divide and Mark

Divide the words into syllables using dots. Place an accent mark
above the last letter in each base word.

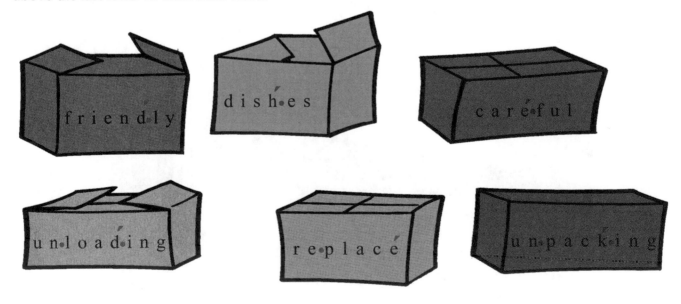

friendly

dish•es

care•ful

un•load•ing

re•place

un•pac•king

Reading 3A: "Raised from the Dead," pp. 241-48, Lesson 61
Structural analysis: identifying base words; dividing into syllables words with prefixes and suffixes;
identifying accented syllables in words with prefixes and suffixes

Character Counts

Name

▶Read It

This story takes place before Lazarus' death and resurrection. Read the story.

Jesus Visits Two Sisters

Mary and Martha could hardly wait. Each one was eager to see Jesus.

When Jesus came to their house, the sisters ran to meet Him. Then Martha hurried back to the kitchen. She had a lot of food to fix for supper!

Mary sat down to listen. She wanted to hear everything Jesus had to say.

While Mary sat quietly listening to Jesus, Martha began to grumble. "It isn't right that I have to work all by myself," she murmured. Finally she complained to Jesus. "Send Mary to help me," Martha demanded.

Then Jesus kindly rebuked Martha. "Mary has made a good choice," Jesus replied. "You are worried about other things and have no time to listen," He said.

▶Mark It

Mark an *X* in the correct column.

	Mary	Martha
1. Which sister prepared the meal?		X
2. Which sister sat and listened?	X	
3. Which sister did not grumble?	X	
4. Which sister complained and wanted the other to help with the meal?		X
5. Which sister did Jesus rebuke?		X
6. Which sister did not take time to listen to Jesus?		X

Reading 3A: "Raised from the Dead," pp. 241-48, Lesson 62
Comprehension: observing character actions; identifying character traits

A Weekend Picnic

an´hill

▶Circle and Mark

1. Read the story. Circle each base word in every compound word.
2. Place an accent mark above the correct syllable or base word.

This past week´end we went on a picnic. We spread a blanket out on a hill´top near the play´ground. I ate two drum´sticks and a slice of straw´berry pie. While my brothers played foot´ball, I watched some ants carry our crumbs to their ant´hill. At sun´set we repacked our basket and went home.

> **Compound Words: The accent is in the first base word.**

▶Write and Color

Solve the puzzles. Write the word on the line. Put an accent mark above the last letter of the accented syllable.

1. 🍵 + 🍰 = __*cup´cake*__

2. 🏔 + 📐 = __*hill´top*__

3. 🐖 + 🖊 = __*pig´pen*__

4. 🐈 + 🐟 = __*cat´fish*__

Reading 3A: "Raised from the Dead," pp. 241-48, Lesson 62
Structural analysis: identifying base words in compound words; marking accented syllables in compound words

Blast Off!

▸Read and Write

Read the record of the astronauts' activities. Then answer the questions.

4:10 A.M. The astronauts woke up.

7:07 A.M. They arrived at Mission Control.

7:12 A.M. They stepped into the spacecraft.

9:00 A.M. *Gemini IV* was expected to blast off (held up for repairs).

10:16 A.M. *Gemini IV* blasted off.

10:21 A.M. The second stage dropped off.

2:45 P.M. Major White started his space walk.

3:06 P.M. Major White finished his space walk and crawled back into the spacecraft.

1. What time did the astronauts wake up?

They woke up at 4:10 A.M.

2. What happened at 7:12 A.M.?

They stepped into the spacecraft.

3. What time did Major White start his space walk?

He started his walk at 2:45 P.M.

4. When did Major White complete his space walk?

He completed his walk at 3:06 P.M.

5. What time did *Gemini IV* blast off?

It blasted off at 10:16 A.M.

6. What time did the astronauts arrive at Mission Control?

They arrived at 7:07 A.M.

Reading 3A: "Space Walk," pp. 249-55, Lesson 63
Comprehension: perceiving time relationships
Study skills: reading a schedule; reading A.M. and P.M. abbreviations

Space Explorers

▶Read and Circle

Circle two words on each star that have the same vowel sound you hear in *search*.

▶Write Them

Use some of the words you circled to complete the sentences.

1. The astronauts went on a _____ **journey** _____ into space.

2. They wanted to _____ **learn** _____ more about space travel.

3. From the spacecraft, the _____ **earth / world** _____ looked like a tiny ball.

4. Mission Control _____ **heard** _____ the voices of the excited astronauts.

5. The president thanked the astronauts for the _____ **courage** _____ they showed during their mission.

Reading 3A: **"Space Walk,"** pp. 249-55, Lesson 63
Phonics: using letter-sound association: /ûr/ as *ear* in *heard*, *our* in *courage*, and *(w)or* in *work*

Don't Forget

Name _____

▶Read and Circle

Read the calendar about the Zander family's activities.
Circle the correct answer to each question.

November						
Sunday	Monday	Tuesday	Wednesday	Thursday	Friday	Saturday
			1	2	3 David's trumpet solo in chapel	4
5 Bible Memory Contest	6 parent-teacher meeting—7:30	7 David's trumpet lesson—4:15	8	9 book fair	10	11 Sally's birthday party—2:00
12	13	14 David's trumpet lesson—4:15	15 Bill's book report due	16	17	18
19	20 Grandma comes to visit	21 David's trumpet lesson—4:15	22	23 Thanksgiving Day	24	25 Bill's soccer game—3:30
26 Bible Memory Contest	27	28 David's trumpet lesson—4:15	29	30		

1. How many times each week does David have a trumpet lesson?

   (one)   two   three

2. If Mark gets Sally a book from the book fair for her birthday,
   how long will he have to wait to give her the book?

   two weeks   (two days)   five days

3. On which Thursday does Thanksgiving Day fall?

   the first   (the fourth)   it doesn't fall on a Thursday

4. Today is the parent-teacher meeting. How long will it be before
   Grandma comes to visit?

   eight days   twelve days   (two weeks)

5. On what day of the week is Bill's book report due?

   (Wednesday)   Monday   Thursday

6. What is the date of Bill's soccer game?

   November 15   (November 25)   November 18

Reading 3A: "Thanksgiving Day," pp. 256-57, Lesson 64
Study skills: reading a calendar

Imagine That!

▶Read and Color

Further teaching of this page is found in the lesson.

Read the poem. Read it again one stanza at a time. Label each stanza with the kind of images the author uses in those lines.

Images
sight
sound
taste
touch
smell

_____

_____ **sight** _____

Wild or tame,
Strawberries hardly
Look like their name:
Red as valentines,
Beaded with seeds,
Like rubies on vines.

Straw?berries?
by Dawn Watkins

_____

_____ **smell** _____

Wild or tame,
Strawberries hardly
Smell like their name:
A whiff of spring
In a basketful,
To make your heart sing.

_____

_____ **taste** _____

Wild or tame,
Strawberries hardly
Taste like their name:
Juicy and sweet,
Better than candy,
A shortcake treat.

_____

_____ **sound** _____

Wild or tame,
Strawberries always
Call my name:
From 'way in the field,
They call me to come,
And I always yield.

_____

_____ **touch** _____

Wild or tame,
Strawberries hardly
Feel like their name:
Sticky and plump,
They squish in your mouth,
Make your tastebuds jump!

Reading 3A: "Thanksgiving Day," pp. 256-57, Lesson 64
Literature: recognizing the author's use of imagery

What a Character!

▶Read and Color

Read the sentences. Circle the rabbit tracks beside the character trait that best fits the person in the sentence.

1. Colin divided his candy bar and gave each of his friends a piece. "Thank you," they said. Colin is

   greedy   jealous   (generous)

2. When Maria was sick, her mother brought her hot soup and read a book to her. Maria's mother was

   weak   (kind)   loyal

3. Mrs. Lewis was very busy, so her children dusted the furniture and washed the dishes. The children were

   honest   content   (helpful)

▶Match the Facts

Read each phrase on the left. Write the number of the phrase beside the matching word or phrase on the right.

1. what Abe's dog chases	_5_ fresh water
2. where the Lincolns are going	_3_ spring
3. the season in which they travel	_6_ turkeys
4. what knocks over Mrs. Lincoln's pot	_7_ wagon
5. the sign of a good camping place	_4_ Abe's dog
6. something the men shoot	_2_ Illinois
7. how the Lincolns travel	_1_ rabbits
8. where the Lincolns came from	_8_ Indiana

Reading 3A: "The Trail West," pp. 258-65, Lesson 65

Comprehension: observing character traits; recalling facts and details

The Chase Is On!

▶Find and Follow

Abe's dog is chasing a scared rabbit again. Help the rabbit escape by drawing a line to only those words that have the vowel sound you hear in *gear*.

/îr/ clear
      steer
      severe
      pierce

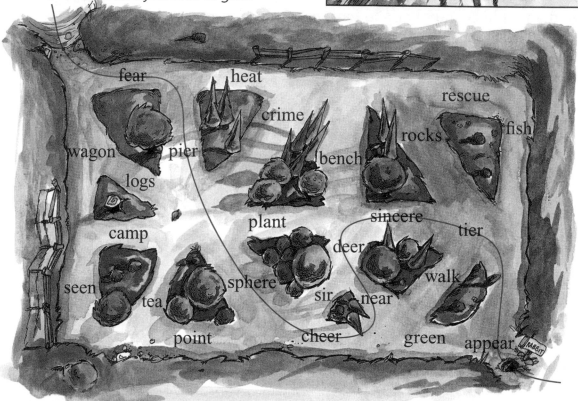

▶Write Them

Fill in the blanks using the words on the path you followed above. Do not use any words more than once.

The rabbit sat still on the _____ **pier** _____. When he peeked

over the edge, he saw his face _____ **appear** _____ in the water. "That horrible dog will never find me here. I have nothing to

_____ **fear** _____." But then he noticed another face drawing very

_____ **near** _____. Suddenly a loud bark sounded behind him!

▶Finish the Story

On your own paper, write a creative ending to the story above.

Reading 3A: "The Trail West," pp. 258-65, Lesson 65
Phonics: reading words with /îr/ as *ear* in *fear*, *ere* in *here*, *ier* in *fierce*, *eer* in *deer*
Composition: writing a story ending

Cross Carefully

▶Find the Word

Fill in the blank using a word from an ice piece.

Mr. Lincoln

shirt

Mrs. Lincoln

dog

nothing

numb

1. The children said _____*nothing*_____ as they crossed the stream.

2. The _____*dog*_____ wasn't in the wagon.

3. _____*Mr. Lincoln*_____ said, "We can't take a wagon back."

4. Abe put the dog in his _____*shirt*_____ as he crossed the stream.

5. Abe's feet felt _____*numb*_____ .

6. _____*Mrs. Lincoln*_____ put a blanket around Abe.

▶Write About It

Answer the following question with one or more complete sentences.

After reading about a family that traveled west in a covered wagon, how would you feel about doing the same thing with your family?

Answers will vary.

Reading 3A: "The Trail West," pp. 266-71, Lesson 66
Comprehension: recalling facts and details; identifying with a story character

▸Read and Mark

Read the story, following the directions carefully.

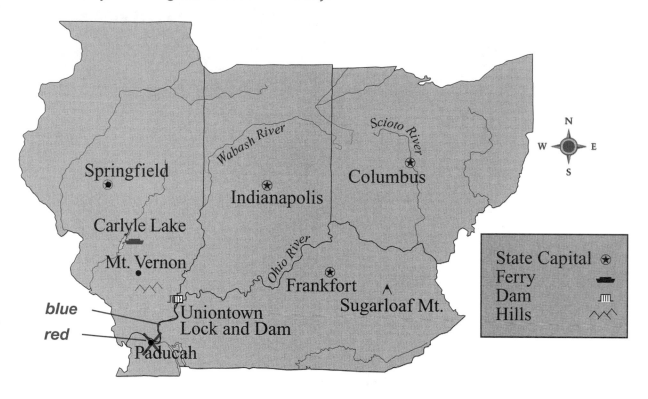

Trailing a Hero

A good way to learn more about Abraham Lincoln might be to follow some of the trails that Lincoln followed as a young man. Imagine you are planning such a trip and mark the map to chart your course. You will leave from Paducah, Kentucky. *(Put a red X at your starting point.)* From there you will need to travel by riverboat up the Ohio River to the Uniontown Lock and Dam in Illinois. *(Use a blue crayon to trace the section of the Ohio River you will follow; then use your pencil to draw the dam symbol at the Uniontown Lock and Dam.)* From there you will have to leave the river and travel over the hills to Mount Vernon. *(Draw the hills symbol below Mount Vernon.)* Once you get to Mount Vernon, you will head northwest until you reach Carlyle Lake, where you will take a ferry across the lake. *(Draw the ferry symbol beside the lake.)* From the lake you will travel on to Springfield, the capital of Illinois. *(Draw the state capital symbol below the letter r in Springfield.)*

Reading 3A: "The Trail West," pp. 266-71, Lesson 66
Comprehension: translating information in narrative form to markings on a map
Study skills: reading a physical map; using a map key

That's the Ticket!

Name _____

▸Read and Choose

Read the paragraph. Color the ticket of the best title for that paragraph.

1. The lion tamer cracked his whip. The huge lions stood on their hind legs and roared loudly. He blew his whistle, and the biggest beast leaped through a ring of fire. Finally, at the tamer's command, the lions formed a ring around the cage and rolled over to the audience's delight.

Ferocious Kittens

The Lion Tamer
color

A Delightful Audience

2. The crowd went wild as the clowns tripped, skipped, and drove into the ring. The funny driver took the big box off the truck. When the side of the box fell open, everything got quiet. The clown inside had no legs and was sitting in a wheelchair. He began juggling and then walking on his hands. The crowd roared with applause. This was definitely a special kind of clown.

The Funniest Clown

A Wild Crowd

A Special Clown
color

3. High atop Queen, the largest circus elephant, sat a brave young lady. She smiled fearlessly as Queen lowered her to the ground on her trunk. Next to Queen the lady looked very small. However, the little lady ruled the ring. The elephants obeyed every command perfectly. At the end of the show they all kneeled in front of her.

Giant Elephants of Africa

The Ride of a Lifetime

A Mighty Little Leader
color

Reading 3A: "A Ticket to the Circus," pp. 272-76, Lesson 68
Comprehension: relating facts and details to titles

A Quarter's Worth

▶Pick Some

Richy has only a quarter. Help him decide what he wants to see.
Put a check beside the attractions with words that have the vowel
sound you hear in *warn*.

_____ ✓ a swarm of bees

_____ ✓ a clown with a wart

_____ an army of monkeys

_____ ✓ a warbling gypsy

_____ an artistic giraffe

_____ a bear with a harp

_____ ✓ a warm zebra

▶Pick Some More

Richy saw more special sights. Color the circle beside each phrase
in which any letter *i* has the long *e* sound.

The letter *i* in the middle of a word can sound like long *e*.

per•i•od
rad•i•o

● a sunny patio

○ a calico cat

● a cheering audience

● an Indian brave

○ a toothless alligator

● an obedient bear

● a runaway chariot

● an automatic piano

Reading 3A: "A Ticket to the Circus," pp. 272-76, Lesson 68
Phonics: reading words with *ar* after *w* as /or/ in *swarm*;
reading words with *i* in an unstressed open syllable as /ē/ in *radio*

The "Write" Idea

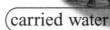

▶Choose One

Circle each correct answer.

1. What did the boys do at the circus?

   took tickets   fed animals   (carried water)

2. What did Richy do?

   helped put up tents   fed horses   (took a letter to Lou)

3. Why was Richy late to pick up his ticket?

   He was too short.   (He was practicing on the unicycle.)

4. Why didn't the ticket man see Richy?

   (Richy was too short.)   The booth was closed.   The ticket man was sleeping.

▶Choose and Write

Circle a main character, a setting, and an action from the boxes below. Write a short story including the items you have circled.

main character	setting	action
clown	circus ring	falling from the trapeze
acrobat	lion cage	juggling water balloons
lion tamer	the trapeze	losing his whip

Answers will vary.

Reading 3A: "A Ticket to the Circus," pp. 277-83, Lesson 69
Comprehension: recalling facts and details
Composition: writing a short story

111

Wildly Shaking Cages

Divide words between the base word and the suffix.

shak•ing

feed   ing

▶Divide Them

Divide the words in the cages into syllables by placing a dot between the base word and the suffix.

jump•ing
fly•ing
laugh•ing

pay•ment
treat•ment
pave•ment

dark•ness
fair•ness
sad•ness

▶Make a Word

Read the pairs of sentences. Use the colored word and a suffix from the box to complete the second sentence.

| est |
| less |
| ful |
| ly |
| es |
| ed |

1. Sunday is supposed to be full of rest.

   _____

   Sunday should be _____ *restful* _____ .

2. We did load the trailer with more than one box.

   _____   _____

   We _____ *loaded* _____ the trailer with many _____ *boxes* _____ .

3. Of all the athletes, Mark jumped the most high.

   _____

   Of all the athletes, Mark jumped the _____ *highest* _____ .

Reading 3A: "A Ticket to the Circus," pp. 277-83, Lesson 69
Structural analysis: dividing words into syllables between the base word and the suffix;
demonstrating the meanings of suffixes by using them to form words

112

▸Cross It Out

Read the story. Draw a line through one sentence in each paragraph that does not belong.

In the Big Tent

Soon Richy would be called to enter the big tent. He wiped his hands on his pants and swallowed hard. ~~I have some pencils for you~~. Would he be able to stay on the unicycle?

Richy began watching the acts. Far above the crowd, an acrobat swung on a trapeze. His partner on the other trapeze swung toward him. ~~Elephants like peanuts~~. Up, up went the acrobat; then he turned loose. Over and over and over he

flipped. The crowd gasped. The acrobat reached for his partner's hands. He was safe!

Richy had been holding his breath. He let it out in a low whistle. What fun it would be to work on the trapeze! ~~Alan wanted pizza for supper~~. Richy wondered if he could learn someday.

Next came the clowns. Richy was chuckling along with the crowd. One of the clowns was driving a tiny car. ~~He hadn't had breakfast~~. Both his legs hung over the sides of the car.

The clown stopped at the foot of a tall ladder. The ladder reached to the window of a cardboard house on stilts. Another clown opened the door of the house. He started to step out; then he saw how high the house was. ~~Our dog's house is very little~~. The clown tried different ways to get out of the house.

Richy was laughing so hard that he almost didn't see his signal. ~~Alan fed the horses~~. It was time for Richy to join the act. He took a deep breath and pedaled. Richy was in the circus.

Get in the Act

▶Read and Decide

Read the glossary. Then follow the directions at the bottom of the page.

ac•ro•bat | **ăk′** rə băt | —*noun*
A person who is skilled in performing on a trapeze, walking a tightrope, and tumbling.

cart•wheel | **kärt′** hwēl | —*noun*
A somersault or handspring in which the body turns over sideways with the arms and legs spread like the spokes of a wheel.

me•nag•er•ie | mə **năj′** ə rē | —*noun*
A collection of live wild animals on exhibition.

midg•et | **mĭj′** ĭt | —*noun*
An extremely small person who is otherwise normally proportioned.

ring•mas•ter | **ring′** măs tər | —*noun*
A person in charge of the performances in a circus.

u•ni•cy•cle | **yoo′** nĭ sī kəl | —*noun*
A vehicle made of a frame built over one wheel and usually propelled by pedals.

Put an *X* on the ringmaster.

Draw a funny hat on the clown in the car.

Draw spokes on the unicycle.

Draw a trainer to take care of the menagerie.

Draw shoes on the midget doing cartwheels.

Draw a balancing pole for the acrobat.

funny hat

pole

shoes

spokes

trainer

Reading 3A: "A Ticket to the Circus," pp. 284-87, Lesson 70
Study skills: using the glossary to build vocabulary

Round 'Em Up

▶Pick an Ending
Draw a lasso around the correct ending to each sentence.

1. Slim was well known for his ability to _____.
   a. tie strange knots
   b. tell tall tales
   c. make horseshoes

2. The cowboys went on a _____.
   a. safari
   b. roundup
   c. wild goose chase

3. The stallion brought the mares to the arroyo for _____.
   a. security
   b. shade
   c. food and water

4. A dry wash is _____.
   a. a dried-up stream bed
   b. like dry cleaning
   c. an uncovered cave

5. Slim knew the horses were coming when he saw _____.
   a. the whites of their eyes
   b. a tornado
   c. a trail of dust

6. It was easy to tell the stallion from the mares because the stallion's _____.
   a. scent was different
   b. tail was longer
   c. coat was red

▶Complete It
Use your imagination. Fill in the blanks. Then finish the story on your own paper. **Answers will vary.**

My name is _____. I live on a ranch called _____. When I turned _____ years old, I went on my first roundup. We left the ranch at _____ A.M. and headed for the desert. We had been riding for about _____ hours when . . .

Reading 3A: "The Beast of the Desert," pp. 288-95, Lesson 71
Comprehension: recalling facts and details
Composition: composing a story ending

Prospecting for Gold

ar•roy•o | ə **roi′** ō |—*noun*
A deep gully cut out by a stream that comes and goes with the rains; dry gulch.

can•yon | **kăn′** yən |—*noun*
A deep valley with steep cliffs on both sides. Often a stream runs through it.

me•sa | **mā′** sə |—*noun*
A flat-topped elevation with one or more clifflike sides.

mes•quite | mĕs **kēt′** | —*noun*
A thorny shrub or tree of southwestern North America.

▶Find and Write

1. Read the words and definitions in the glossary above.
2. Use the glossary words to label the areas identified on the prospector's map.

mesa

mesquite

canyon

arroyo

Reading 3A: "The Beast of the Desert," pp. 288-95, Lesson 71
Study skills: using words and definitions in a glossary to develop vocabulary relating to desert geography

Ride 'Em Cowboy!

Name _____

▶Pick a Word

1. Read the clues below.
2. Choose a word from the lists that fits the clue.
3. Write the word on the blanks.

If your answers are correct, the first letter of each answer will form a special word for a cowboy.

Orly
beast
echoed
canyon
ranchers
stallion
branches
unfolded
tall tales

rope
opening
nose

1. _b_ _e_ _a_ _s_ _t_   another name for a camel

2. _r_ _o_ _p_ _e_   used to catch the camel

3. _O_ _r_ _l_ _y_   name of Mr. Sloan's grandson

4. _n_ _o_ _s_ _e_   part of the camel where Slim put the leather

5. _c_ _a_ _n_ _y_ _o_ _n_   where the cowboys went to look for the horses

6. _o_ _p_ _e_ _n_ _i_ _n_ _g_   part of the arroyo the horses ran through

7. _b_ _r_ _a_ _n_ _c_ _h_ _e_ _s_   used to block one end of the dry wash

8. _u_ _n_ _f_ _o_ _l_ _d_ _e_ _d_   what the camel did with his legs

9. _s_ _t_ _a_ _l_ _l_ _i_ _o_ _n_   the red horse

10. _t_ _a_ _l_ _l_   _t_ _a_ _l_ _e_ _s_   what Slim told often

11. _e_ _c_ _h_ _o_ _e_ _d_   what the camel's roar did in the canyon

12. _r_ _a_ _n_ _c_ _h_ _e_ _r_ _s_   who went looking for the wild horses

Reading 3A: "The Beast of the Desert," pp. 296-301, Lesson 72
Comprehension: matching words and story details

Pickle Power

▶**Think About It**

A. When a word ends in a consonant plus *le*, divide the word into syllables before the consonant.

bu•gle

sim•ple

B. When a word ends in *ck* plus *le*, divide the word into syllables after the *ck*.

pick•le

▶**Mark It**

Write the letter of the rule that was used to divide each word.

_B_ buck•le   _B_ shack•le   _A_ pur•ple

_A_ cir•cle   _A_ whis•tle   _B_ freck•le

_B_ sick•le   _A_ cra•dle   _A_ gur•gle

_B_ chuck•le   _A_ crum•ble   _A_ Bi•ble

_A_ bub•ble   _B_ tack•le   _B_ cack•le

_A_ sam•ple   _B_ heck•le   _A_ sta•ple

_B_ tick•le   _A_ ea•gle   _A_ ti•tle

Reading 3A: "The Beast of the Desert," pp. 296-301, Lesson 72
Structural analysis: dividing into syllables words that end with a consonant + *le*;
dividing into syllables words that end with *ck* + *le*

Be a Missionary!

Did you know that there are stories of missionaries in the Bible? Probably the most famous missionary of all time was the apostle Paul. The stories below tell of experiences he had on the mission field.

Teacher direction is recommended for this page.

▶Read and Circle
1. Read each paragraph.
2. Read the choices for main ideas at the right.
3. Circle the main idea that fits the paragraph.

Paul and Silas were in prison once again. Even in prison, they were a good testimony for the Lord. They sang hymns through the night and witnessed to the guards. When God caused an earthquake to set them free, they were able to lead the chief guard to the Lord.

- Paul and Silas were a good testimony.
- Paul and Silas liked to sing hymns.
- God sent an earthquake.

Finally Paul had the opportunity for which he had been praying. He was called to give his testimony before the highest judge in the land and all his counselors. He bravely told them what the Lord had done for him and how He could save them also. He then invited them to accept Christ into their hearts.

- Paul gave his testimony.
- People die without being saved.
- The judge was Paul's friend.

Every missionary needs a quiet place where he can rest and recover from his hard work. Paul found a resting place in the home of his good friends Aquila and Priscilla. While he stayed with them, he helped them stitch tents. As they worked they sang and talked of Paul's journeys. When he left, Paul felt refreshed and ready to continue his work for the Lord.

- Stitching tents is hard work.
- Aquila and Priscilla felt refreshed.
- Paul rested at the home of Aquila and Priscilla.

Reading 3A: "Mission over Mexico," pp. 302-5, Lesson 73
Comprehension: identifying the main idea of a paragraph

The Unfinished Letter

enough   atmosphere

▶Listen and Color

Using a yellow crayon, color the letters in the words below that make the /f/ sound.

biography   dolphins   Philadelphia   Ralph

elephants   trophy   Joseph   photocopy

phone   photograph   trough   rough

▶Choose and Write

Choose one word from above to fill in each blank.
The words will be used only one time.

Dear Joseph,

I am having fun visiting my cousin _____ *Ralph / Joseph* _____ .

The flight from Phoenix to _____ *Philadelphia* _____ was long.

I read a _____ *biography* _____ of the Wright brothers.

We went to the zoo and fed peanuts to the _____ *elephants* _____ .

I got splashed by _____ *dolphins* _____ .

I accidentally dropped my zoo map in the pig's _____ *trough* _____ .

Mom made a _____ *photocopy* _____ of her map for me.

I will tell you more when I get home.

Your friend,
Stephan

Reading 3A: "Mission over Mexico," pp. 302-5, Lesson 73
Phonics: reading words with /f/ as *ph* in *phone* and *gh* in *laugh*

Painting Pictures with Words

"like a brown shoelace"

▸Read and Choose

Read each sentence starter. Circle the answer that uses a simile to complete the sentence.

1. Eric walked outside and saw that the sky was

     A. dark and gloomy.

     (B.) as black as the inside of a cave.

> Similes compare two things that are different but have something in common. They use the words *like* or *as*.

2. On the runway sat his new plane

     (A.) as shiny as a new nickel.

     B. shining in the sunlight.

3. The plane rose into the air

     (A.) like a mighty eagle.

     B. very fast.

4. The desert below him looked

     A. very hot and dry.

     (B.) as hot as bread fresh from the oven.

5. He lined his plane up with the runway for a landing

     A. that was smooth and careful.

     (B.) as smooth as whipped cream.

Reading 3A: "Mission over Mexico," pp. 306-11, Lesson 74
Comprehension: identifying similes used to create imagery

"Plane" Talk

▶Choose and Write

1. Read the definition and choose a word from the box that matches the definition. You may refer to the reader page or use a dictionary.
2. Write the word in the blanks beside the correct number.
3. The name of the island the missionaries were flying to will appear in the colored strip.

1. <u>r</u> <u>u</u> <u>n</u> <u>w</u> <u>a</u> <u>y</u>

2. <u>c</u> <u>o</u> <u>r</u> <u>k</u> <u>s</u> <u>c</u> <u>r</u> <u>e</u> <u>w</u>

3. <u>v</u> <u>e</u> <u>e</u> <u>r</u> <u>i</u> <u>n</u> <u>g</u>

4. <u>s</u> <u>t</u> <u>a</u> <u>b</u> <u>i</u> <u>l</u> <u>i</u> <u>z</u> <u>e</u> <u>r</u>

5. <u>a</u> <u>l</u> <u>t</u> <u>i</u> <u>t</u> <u>u</u> <u>d</u> <u>e</u>

6. <u>v</u> <u>a</u> <u>l</u> <u>v</u> <u>e</u> <u>s</u>

7. <u>g</u> <u>a</u> <u>u</u> <u>g</u> <u>e</u> <u>s</u>

8. <u>r</u> <u>u</u> <u>d</u> <u>d</u> <u>e</u> <u>r</u>

9. <u>a</u> <u>i</u> <u>r</u> <u>p</u> <u>o</u> <u>r</u> <u>t</u>

altitude	airport
valves	stabilizer
rudder	veering
runway	gauges
corkscrew	

1. A strip of level ground on which an aircraft takes off and lands (p. 310)

2. To move in a spiral course (p. 308)

3. Turning aside or swerving (p. 307)

4. A part of the tail that keeps the plane steady (p. 307)

5. A word that means height (p. 307)

6. Devices that regulate the flow of gases and liquids (p. 309)

7. Instruments for measuring (p. 309)

8. A device for steering an airplane to the left or right (p. 308)

9. A place where airplanes take off and land (p. 308)

Reading 3A: "Mission over Mexico," pp. 306-11, Lesson 74
Vocabulary: matching words and definitions to expand vocabulary

Details, Details, and More Details

▶Read and Choose

Read the sentences and write the letter of the chapter title that best fits those sentences.

> A. Mission Begun
> B. Mission Interrupted
> C. Mission Accomplished

1. __A__ "We should make good time. There's nothing in our way to slow us down."

   Mr Pruden eased onto the runway and waited for the "all clear" on the radio.

2. __B__ "Look out! It's coming right through the windshield."

   "Lord, help us. You can control this plane."

3. __C__ "God wanted us to live so that we could come here to tell you how much He loves you."

   Mr. Pruden, Jason, and Matt knelt with them and thanked God for another miracle.

▶Color It

Read the sentence and color the compass needle red if the sentence is true.

1. The missionaries knew the pilots were coming.

4. The pilots said they were lucky to be alive.

2. The boys prayed while Mr. Pruden flew.

5. All ten men got saved.

3. The engine quit before they landed.

6. The pilots gave the men copies of John and Romans.

Reading 3A: "Mission over Mexico," pp. 312-16, Lesson 75
Comprehension: relating facts and details to chapter titles; identifying true and false statements

123

Where in the World?

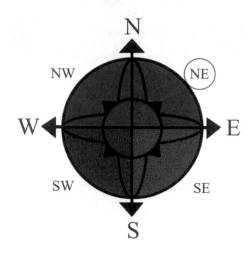

▶Look and Answer

Use the **compass rose** to answer the following questions.

1. What color is the northwestern

   area? _____ _blue_

2. Circle the abbreviation for northeast.

3. The yellow area falls between the south

   and the _____ _east_ . It

   is called the _____ _southeast_ .

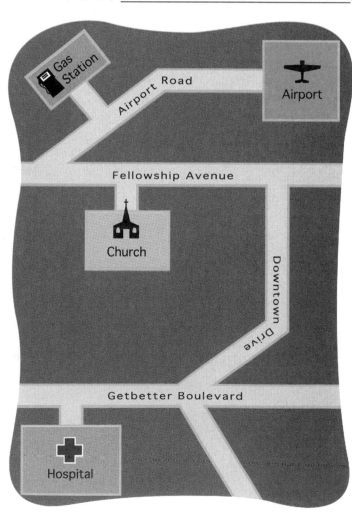

4. What does the abbreviation SW represent?

   _____ _southwest_

▶Use the Map

Use the **map** and the abbreviations on the **compass rose** to answer the following questions.

1. The hospital is __SW__ of the airport.

2. The church is directly __S__ of Fellowship Avenue.

3. The gas station is __NW__ of the church.

4. The hospital is __SW__ of the church.

5. Downtown Drive is __SE__ of the gas station.

6. The airport is __NE__ of the church.

7. To get to Downtown Drive from the church, you must go __E__ on Fellowship Avenue.

Reading 3A: "Mission over Mexico," pp. 312-16, Lesson 75
Study skills: using a compass rose to read a map

As Round As a Tortilla

Name _____

▶Choose and Write

Some descriptive phrases are used often in similes. Write
the best word from the pictures to complete each description.

pancake

bell

log

deer

glove

diamonds

bone

roses

1. clear as a ___*bell*___

2. slept like a ___*log*___

3. run like a ___*deer*___

4. cheeks like ___*roses*___

5. dry as a ___*bone*___

6. sparkled like ___*diamonds*___

7. fits like a ___*glove*___

8. flat as a ___*pancake*___

▶Find and Write

Look in the story to find what the author
is describing with a simile.

1. (page 2) like a dark, shiny blanket

   ___*Rosalina's hair*___

2. (page 5) like flapping blackbird wings

   ___*Juan's hair*___

3. (page 6) like saucers of hot chocolate

   ___*Juan's eyes*___

Reading 3B: "**The Best Kind of Love,**" pp. 2–6, Lesson 76
Comprehension: demonstrating understanding of similes
Literature: noting the author's use of similes

125

Sh! We're Working!

▶Listen and Color

Read each word below. Color the letters yellow that make the /sh/ sound in each word.

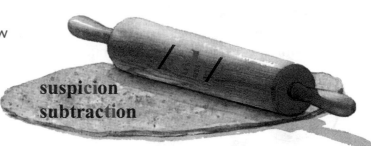

suspicion
subtraction

deli**ci**ous	spe**ci**al	na**ti**on
fa**ci**al	pa**ti**ent	addi**ti**on
tempta**ti**on	gra**ci**ous	physi**ci**an

▶Choose and Write

Choose the correct word from the box to write in each blank.

1. The nurse sat by the ____**patient**____ until he became conscious.

2. The American flag is a symbol of our ____**nation**____ .

3. These sugar cookies are ____**delicious**____ .

4. God assures us that we don't have to give in to ____**temptation**____ .

5. During math class Mike worked seven ____**addition**____ problems in three minutes.

6. The ____**physician**____ examined me to be sure I did not have the flu.

7. Our salvation is a ____**special**____ gift from God.

Reading 3B: "The Best Kind of Love," pp. 2-6, Lesson 76
Phonics: reading words with /sh/ as *ci* in *precious* and *ti* in *nation*

Can You Describe It?

I brush my dog's hair.

I enjoy brushing my big dog's thick brown and white hair.

▶Circle the Phrase

An author often uses adjectives to paint a good mental picture for the reader. Answer each question below by circling the phrase that paints the best word picture.

1. Which phrase helps you see things most clearly in the story setting?
   a. a house in Mexico
   b. a small, adobe Mexican house
   c. on a long street

2. Which phrase best helps you see the fruits and vegetables at the market?
   a. different fruits and vegetables
   b. a lot of fruits and vegetables
   c. many brightly-colored fruits and vegetables

3. Which phrase best helps you picture Señora Gomez?
   a. a good tortillera
   b. sturdy woman flashed a wide smile as she kneaded dough
   c. a lady who made tortillas in town

4. Which phrase best helps you see the ribbon in the pretty lady's hair?
   a. a pretty white ribbon
   b. a silky white ribbon with threads of gold
   c. a long ribbon

▶Paint a Picture

Using good describing words, paint a word picture of the jewelry vendor on your own paper.

Reading 3B: "The Best Kind of Love," pp. 7-9, Lesson 77
Literature: noting the author's use of adjectives to paint word pictures
Composition: writing to paint a word picture

A Secret Party

▸Read and Circle
Read the story and circle the silent consonants in the colored words.

One ni(gh)t, Mr. Lopez had an idea. "My son Pedro is having a birthday soon. I need to throw a party!"

Mr. Lopez whis(t)led merrily as he filled out the party invitations. "We should have tacos," he whispered to his wife, "and burritos and enchiladas. We should have all of Pedro's favorite foods." But he didn't tell Pedro.

The party day came. Mrs. Lopez worked in the kitchen, (k)neading dough for tortillas. She cooked chili sauce and grated cheese. But Pedro was at school all day, so he didn't (k)now.

When Pedro walked in the door, he noticed his mother had flour on her thum(b)s. But she only smiled at Pedro.

Someone (k)nocked at the door. "I hope nothing's (w)rong," Mrs. Lopez said with a frown. "No one ever (k)nocks at this time of day. Pedro, open the door."

Pedro swung the door wide. There stood Mr. Lopez and all of Pedro's friends.

"Surprise!" they yelled. They came strai(gh)t through the door and into the hall, singing to Pedro.

Pedro's mouth dropped open and his hands flew to his face.

Mrs. Lopez handed him a taco. "Happy birthday. Eat up, son," she said. And Pedro thought it was the best taco he had ever tasted.

▸Write About It
Write a sentence to answer the question.
Why did Pedro's mouth drop open and his hands fly to his face?

_____

Answers will vary.

_____

_____

Reading 3B: "The Best Kind of Love," pp. 7-9, Lesson 77
Phonics: identifying silent consonants in words

Who's Who?

▶Match Them

Match the characters to the correct actions.

Mother

Rosalina

Ana

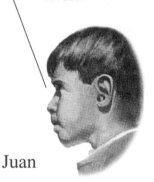

vendor

Juan

| brushed her long, black hair |
| couldn't keep a secret |
| used Mother's money to buy a gift |
| said, "The best kind of love—well, it loves *just because*." |
| sold beautiful jewelry and ribbons |

▶Think and Write

Who was your favorite character? What did this character do to make you like him or her? Write your answers.

Answers will vary.

_____

_____

_____

_____

Reading 3B: "The Best Kind of Love," pp. 10-14, Lesson 78
Comprehension: matching characters with plot action; evaluating the actions of characters

Action Packed!

▶Choose and Write

Choose the word that gives the best picture and write it in the blank.

1. Rosalina almost **_stumbled_** over Ana.
   (fell, stumbled)

2. Chico **_raced_** down the hill after Juan.
   (ran, raced)

3. Señora Gomez **_chatted_** with her customers.
   (chatted, talked)

4. Ana **_plunked_** down two of her mother's pesos.
   (plunked, put)

5. Ana heard a bird **_twittering_** and a bee buzzing.
   (singing, twittering)

6. Ana **_glanced_** toward Rosalina.
   (looked, glanced)

7. Rosalina's laughter **_floated_** through the room.
   (floated, was heard)

Reading 3B: "The Best Kind of Love," pp. 10-14, Lesson 78
Word work: selecting verbs that clarify meaning

Important Ideas

Name

▶Read and Choose

Read each paragraph from the story. Circle the sentence on the right that tells you the main idea of the paragraph.

1. Heat pressed down on the dry land like a blanket, smothering the thirsty ground. Elijah pulled his cloak of camel's hair over his head to protect himself from the burning sun.

   Elijah is tired.

   (Elijah is hot.)

   Elijah has far to go.

2. As he came closer to the city, he saw a woman gathering sticks. She was dressed in the clothes of a widow. "Ah," thought Elijah, "She must be the woman of whom God spoke."

   God provided food for the widow.

   The widow saw Elijah coming.

   (Elijah found the woman to whom God had sent him.)

3. The woman stopped and turned back to Elijah. "I am sorry, but I have not one cake. I have only a handful of meal in the bottom of my barrel and a little oil in a jar. I am gathering these sticks so that I may go in and cook for myself and my son. We are going to eat our last meal and die."

   The woman is gathering sticks.

   Elijah is hungry.

   (The woman doesn't have much food left.)

The Great Provider

▶Choose and Circle

Look at the colored guide words in each box. Circle the entry words that would be on a page with these guide words at the top.

Guide words show which entry words will appear alphabetically on that page.

Lord   provides
food
fraction
laugh
lizard
loaded
(lumber)
(money)
(nature)
(octagon)
(poster)

PSALM 37:25
I have been young, and now am old; yet have I not seen the righteous forsaken, nor his seed begging bread.

various   ways
truth
umbrella
upright
vacuum
(vary)
(vital)
(voice)
(walking)
(warped)
western

▶Think About It

In the lists above, find three things that the Lord provides and write them in the blanks below. Then think of three more things He has provided for you and write them in the other three blanks.   **Answers will vary.**

1. _____   4. _____

2. _____   5. _____

3. _____   6. _____

Reading 3B: "God Provides," pp. 15-18, Lesson 80
Study skills: using guide words on a dictionary or glossary page
Comprehension: thinking critically

Harvesting Ideas

▶**Choose and Underline**

In each of the following paragraphs, underline the
sentence that tells the main idea.

In Bible times it was important to gather
olives at just the right time. If the olives were
too green, the olive oil pressed from them would
be bitter. If they were too ripe, the oil would be
rancid, or rotten-tasting.

The olives were poured into an olive
press. There were several ways to press
the oil from the olives. One way was to
have the workers walk on the olives,
pressing the oil from the fruit with their
feet. Another way was to put a pole
through a wheel-like stone. Men or work
animals crushed the olives by rolling the
stone over the fruit.

Each pressing of the olives produced a different
grade of oil. The first oil pressed out of the olives
was used for special purposes—to burn in the
tabernacle lamps or to anoint a king. Lower
grades of olive oil were used for cooking and
for burning in household lamps.

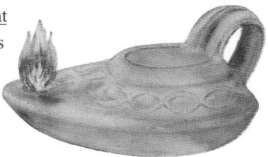

Reading 3B: "A Jar of Oil," pp. 19-21, Lesson 81
Comprehension: locating the sentence that states the main idea of a paragraph

133

Glossary Choices

crane | krān | —*noun* 1. A large bird with a long neck, long legs, and a long bill. Cranes usually live near water. 2. A large machine for lifting heavy objects. A crane has a long arm and uses cables to do the lifting.

cream | krēm | —*noun* 1. The yellowish part of milk that contains fat. It can be separated from milk and is used in cooking, with coffee, and to make butter. 2. The color of cream; a yellowish white: *We painted the bedroom walls cream.*

crib | krĭb | —*noun* 1. A child's bed, enclosed on four sides. 2. A small building for storing corn or other grain.

▸Choose and Write

1. Read each sentence and find the colored word in the glossary entries above.
2. Read both definitions of each entry word.
3. Write the number of the correct definition.

___2___ We spent the morning watching the crane lift steel beams to the top of the new building.

___2___ We found a raccoon feasting in the corn crib.

___1___ Whipped cream makes peaches taste delicious.

___1___ My dad built a crib for my baby brother.

___1___ We saw a large crane flying near the lake early in the morning.

___2___ We bought a cream couch to match our carpet.

Reading 3B: "A Jar of Oil," pp. 19-21, Lesson 81
Vocabulary: determining the meaning of words in sentences by using glossary entries

Secret Sentences

Name _____

▶Order and Write
Write the words in the correct order to make a sentence.

1. Elly secrets.   trouble had keeping

   Elly had trouble keeping secrets.

2. brothers Elly's let her wouldn't the loft.   in

   Elly's brothers wouldn't let her in the loft.

3. secret Father.   about knew a Elly

   Elly knew a secret about Father.

4. brothers.   to wanted her tell Elly

   Elly wanted to tell her brothers.

5. teeth.   Bruiser Amanda Lyn with tore his

   Bruiser tore Amanda Lyn with his teeth.

6. diamonds her Amanda Lyn.   in hid Mother

   Mother hid her diamonds in Amanda Lyn.

7. Yankee jewels.   wanted soldiers The

   The Yankee soldiers wanted jewels.

8. sick a had to Mother visit lady.

   Mother had to visit a sick lady.

Reading 3B: "Elly's Secret," pp. 22-28, Lesson 82
Comprehension: developing sentence sense; recalling facts and details

Predawn till Midday Chores

predawn

pre—"before"

midday

mid—"in the middle of"

▶ Circle Them

Circle the words with the prefix *pre-* or *mid-*.

During Civil War days no frozen dinners filled cooling units in big stores. No (precooked) foods lined the shelves. Since (prepackaged) foods weren't available, it took all morning to make the big (midday) meal. Housekeepers began cooking lunch right after breakfast.

Even making clothing wasn't easy. True, cotton grew right on the southern plantations. But if someone was (midway) through making a pair of pants and realized he had forgotten to (preshrink) the cotton cloth, this is what the pants would look like!

Today, when you buy cotton clothes, they usually have been (preshrunk.) However, don't forget to check the label to make sure!

▶ Make a Word

Read the definitions. Write a new word on the line by adding the *pre-* or *mid-* prefix to the underlined word.

in the middle of the <u>night</u>   *midnight*

wood that's been <u>cut</u> before going to the lumberyard   *precut*

food that's <u>packaged</u> before being sold   *prepackaged*

in the middle of the <u>stream</u>   *midstream*

food that's <u>cooked</u> before being packaged   *precooked*

Reading 3B: "Elly's Secret," pp. 22-28, Lesson 82
Word work: using prefixes *mid-* and *pre-*

Civil War Secrets

▶Pick One

Put a check mark beside the correct answer.

1. Why was Elly the only one who didn't know where things were hidden?
   ___ She was a girl.
   ___ She was in Atlanta.
   ✓ She was sick in bed when everything was hidden.

2. How did Elly know where Tom and Jake were hiding things?
   ___ Pearl told her.
   ✓ Elly saw the boys go into the cotton barn.
   ___ Elly was hiding in the barn.

3. What secret did Elly tell?
   ___ where the filigree box was hidden
   ✓ that Father was coming home
   ___ that Mother had baked cookies

4. When did Mother decide to put the jewels in Amanda Lyn?
   ___ when the cotton barn was burning
   ___ after the soldiers came
   ✓ when she was sewing the rip

5. Why did Mother leave?
   ___ to take the jewels to Atlanta
   ✓ to help a sick neighbor
   ___ to meet Father

6. How many people knew where the jewels were hidden?
   ___ everyone except Pearl
   ___ Elly, Jake, and Tom
   ✓ Elly, Mother, and the Lord

7. Why was the soldier searching the room?
   ✓ He was looking for money or jewels.
   ___ He was gathering papers.
   ___ He was looking for guns.

8. Why did Elly decide to tell her secret to the soldier?
   ___ The soldier hit her.
   ✓ She was afraid that the soldier might hurt Jake.
   ___ She liked to tell secrets.

9. Why did the soldiers leave?
   ___ Their horses ran away.
   ___ Elly frightened them.
   ✓ A Confederate regiment was coming.

10. Why was Elly's secret safe even though she told the truth?
    ✓ The soldier misunderstood her.
    ___ The jewels weren't in Amanda Lyn.
    ___ Amanda Lyn was upstairs.

Reading 3B: "Elly's Secret," pp. 29–35, Lesson 83
Comprehension: recalling facts and details; inferring supporting details about characters

Very Vital Vowels

This page is intended to be completed with teacher guidance. Students may write the words without using the markings.

▶Read and Color

Read the words below. Color the accented syllable yellow.

go´•ing   wig´•gle   cap´•tain   bu´•gle   dent´•ed   neat´•ly

rain´•ing   sta´•ple   un•load´   scat´•ter   rest´•ed   fill´•er

▶Write Them

List under each set of vowel characters the words that fit with them.
An example is given for each set of vowel characters.

h i d´ • d e n

_____

wiggle

_____

captain

_____

scatter

n e c k´ • l a c e

_____

dented

_____

rested

_____

filler

B i´ • b l e

_____

going

_____

staple

_____

bugle

p e a c h´ • e s

_____

raining

_____

unload

_____

neatly

Reading 3B: "Elly's Secret," pp. 29-35, Lesson 83
Structural analysis: classifying words according to vowel generalizations

Just Passin' Through

▸Read It

Read the story.

Farmer Brown dug a hole and put in some little seeds. "I wish something exciting would happen," he said. "Something to make me forget how hot the sun is."

Just then a pirate appeared with a map. "What ho, matey," he said. "There's treasure here, and I aim to find it!"

As the pirate began digging, a crook wearing a **mask** ran by. Behind him a police officer with a badge was crying, "Stop, thief!"

Before Farmer Brown could say a word, he was startled by a loud crash. A pilot was climbing out of his crumpled plane. "Sorry, chap," the pilot said. "I thought I could fly this plane as easily as I can drive a **car**."

Suddenly, another man appeared. "I'm sure one of you knows where to find my **clue**, or my name's not Detective Dick."

"You're right. I do," said the pilot. He led the detective toward his plane.

At that moment a parade marched into the field. "We've come to entertain you," said the band director, waving his **baton**. "We won't stay long."

After the parade a fireman appeared with a hose. He sprayed the farmer with **cold** water!

"That should cool you off," he said cheerfully. And he waved a friendly goodbye.

"Well, the sun doesn't seem as hot," Farmer Brown said. "And this morning *did* pass quickly. But I wonder. . . . Did all those people really pass through my field today?" He smiled, picked up his hoe, and went back to planting **little** seeds.

▸Finish the Sentence

Complete each sentence using the colored words above.

1. *Pirate* is to *map* as *detective* is to _____ clue _____.

2. *Fireman* is to *hose* as *band director* is to _____ baton _____.

3. *Police officer* is to *badge* as *crook* is to _____ mask _____.

4. *Tree* is to *big* as *seed* is to _____ little _____.

5. *Sun* is to *hot* as *ice* is to _____ cold _____.

6. *Fly* is to *plane* as *drive* is to _____ car _____.

Reading 3B: "Two Crooks and Two Heroes," pp. 36-40, Lesson 84
Comprehension: finding relationships between pairs of words

Sounds Like . . .

▶Listen and Write

Listen to the vowel sound in each word in the boxes. Write each
word under the word that has the same vowel sound.

| slow   crown   growl   flown | | beach   thread   health   meat |

grown	bread
slow	*thread*
flown	*health*
towel	leap
crown	*beach*
growl	*meat*

▶Rhyme Them

Use a word from List 1 and a rhyming word
from List 2 to complete each sentence.

1. A friendly bird is a

   pleasant pheasant .

2. Mr. *O* dries off with a

   vowel towel .

3. A rotten vegetable is a

   mean bean .

4. When it's raining violets, we have a

   flower shower .

List 1
pleasant
mean
flower
vowel

List 2
shower
pheasant
bean
towel

Reading 3B: "Two Crooks and Two Heroes," pp. 36-40, Lesson 84
Phonics: reading words with *ea* as in *bread* and *meat*, *ow* as in *show* and *now*

Hooray for Heroes!

▶Write Names

On the line, write the name of the speaker.

townsfolk	Mayor Setton
Mrs. Sullivan	Travis
Sheriff Ridgely	Shane

1. "Bye, Mom and Dad. Wave to me from the grandstand!"

Travis

2. "Catching bank robbers! Next thing I know one of you will be running for president of the United States."

Mayor Setton

3. "Grady, get those sacks of coins and put 'em by the door. I'll clean out the drawers up front."

Shane

4. "Boys, you're late! Get in your places. Here are your flags."

Mrs. Sullivan

5. "Come out with your hands up!"

Sheriff Ridgely

6. "Hip, hip, hooray! Hip, hip, hooray!"

townsfolk

▶Put in Order

Number the following sentences in order as they happened in the story.

1 The boys found Uncle Clem tied up like a horsefly in a spider's web.

3 Deputy Slim found Sheriff Ridgely.

2 The boys slid the crowbar through the door handles.

5 Uncle Clem drove the boys to the grandstand.

4 Sheriff Ridgely arrested the two crooks.

Reading 3B: "Two Crooks and Two Heroes," pp. 41-45, Lesson 85
Comprehension: matching characters with dialogue; sequencing events

141

Graphic Results

A graph is a good way to show information without writing a paragraph. Pretend that you have a savings account in the Porcupine Hollow Bank. The graph below shows the amount of money in your account each month.

Amount of Money in Your Savings Account

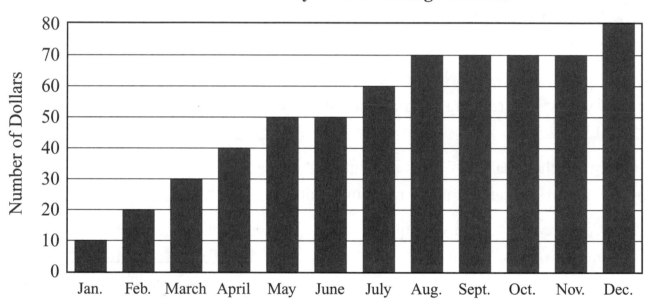

▶Think and Write
Use the graph to answer the questions.

1. In which month did your account have the most money?

   _____

   December

2. In which month did your account have the least money? How much money was in your account in that month?

   _____

   January

   _____

   10 dollars

3. How much money was in your account in June?

   _____

   50 dollars

4. How much money was in your account in March? In which month was there twice that amount of money in your account?

   _____

   30 dollars

   _____

   July

142

What Happened and Why?

Understanding why things happened can help you better understand a story. An **effect** is the result of something that took place in the story, and the **cause** tells why it happened.

▶Find and Write

Read the left side of the chart below. Then tell what event took place because of the cause.

Cause (Why)  **Effect** (What Happened)

Cause (Why)	Effect (What Happened)
1. Travis heard a noise inside Uncle Clem's truck.	*They looked in and found Uncle Clem tied up.*
2. The boys wanted to trap the bank robbers inside the bank.	*They used a crowbar to lock the door.*
3. Sheriff Ridgely didn't want the noisy band to scare the bank robbers away.	*They all tiptoed down the alley.*
4. Shane and Grady were disobeying the law.	*They were arrested and put in prison.*
5. The townsfolk were proud of the boys for saving the bank.	*They praised them and said, "Hip, hip, hooray!"*

Reading 3B: "Two Crooks and Two Heroes," pp. 36-45, Lesson 86
Comprehension: determining cause-and-effect relationships

Word Construction

We can find the correct spelling of a word by looking in the glossary or a dictionary.

▶Find and Write

Use your glossary to help you find the correct spelling of the word needed to complete the sentence. Write the word in the blank.

1. The missionaries built an ___**adobe**___ house in the desert.
(adobe, adabe)

2. Peter and John went down the ___**embankment**___ to get their fishing boat.
(embankmint, embankment)

3. Jesus was invited to ___**celebrate**___ a wedding at Cana.
(celebrate, celabrate)

4. The young girl at the well carried a ___**vessel**___ on her shoulders.
(vessel, vessul)

5. Grandma had to ___**knead**___ the dough before she baked the bread.
(kneed, knead)

6. The captain sent an ___**escort**___ to take Jesus to the palace.
(escart, escort)

7. In church the ___**congregation**___ stood up to sing.
(congrigation, congregation)

8. Cotton was an important crop on a southern ___**plantation**___ .
(plantation, plentation)

9. The German shepherd and the boy lay near the ___**hearth**___ .
(hearth, heirth)

Reading 3B: "Two Crooks and Two Heroes," pp. 36-45, Lesson 86
Study skills: using a glossary to increase vocabulary; recognizing a glossary as a tool for verifying spelling

Tender Loving Care

▶Find and Color
Find the rhyming words and color each set a different color.

After the Lights Go Out

I told them I don't need them
To tuck me in anymore—
Since I'm too old to be afraid
Of tigers on the floor.

But after all the lights go out
And I'm alone in bed,
Secretly, I'm glad that they
Ignored what I said.

—Eileen Berry

▶Choose and Write
1. Read each sentence, and then read the phrases in the box.
2. Choose a phrase to replace the colored words and write it in the blank.

- sounded as clear as a bell
- feel like a bird in a cozy nest
- felt like a soft wool blanket
- makes my eyes burn

1. My mother's singing **sounded beautiful.**

   sounded as clear as a bell

2. My father's coat **felt soft.**

   felt like a soft wool blanket

3. My Grandpa's taco sauce **tastes hot.**

   makes my eyes burn

4. My parents' love for me makes me **feel safe.**

   feel like a bird in a cozy nest

Reading 3B: "Andre," pp. 46-47, Lesson 88
Literature: noting the use of rhyme in poetry; using figures of speech to create imagery

145

"André" My Way

*See the lesson for
guided discussion.*

EXODUS 20:12
*Honour thy father and thy
mother: that thy days may
be long upon the land
which the Lord thy God
giveth thee.*

▶Think and Write

Read the poem "André" again. Write your version in story form.

_____

_____
_____
_____
_____
_____
_____
_____
_____
_____
_____
_____
_____
_____
_____
_____
_____
_____

Reading 3B: "Andre," pp. 46-47, Lesson 88
Composition: communicating ideas in writing; expanding the concise words of poetry into prose

Treasured Cloth

▶Read and Think
Read the story.

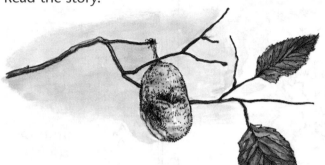

For many years, the Chinese kept the secret of silk-making to themselves. The people of western countries made many wrong guesses about how the beautiful silk cloth was made. Some thought it was spun from fleece that grew on special trees. Others thought it was spun from delicate fibers that grew underneath the bark of certain trees. Only the Chinese knew about the silkworm and how to make cloth from its cocoon.

Then two men smuggled silkworm eggs out of China. They told how the Chinese gathered silkworms and started silkworm farms. The silkworm farmers fed the worms mulberry leaves. When the silkworms began spinning cocoons, the farmers left them alone. If they bothered the silkworms, the worms would not make good silk. The silkworms might even die.

After the cocoons were spun, the farmers dropped them into bowls of hot water. The hot water softened the cocoons. All the tiny silk fibers loosened and untangled. Then the farmers twisted the fragile fibers together to make a strong silk thread. The thread was spun onto spools. The spools of thread were used to weave the beautiful silk cloth that amazed the rest of the world. At last the centuries-old art of making silk was no longer a secret.

▶Decide and Mark
Read each sentence. Write *F* if the sentence states a fact and *O* if it states an opinion.

1. **O** The Chinese people should not have kept this silk secret.

2. **F** Two men smuggled silkworm eggs out of China.

3. **F** The silkworms ate mulberry leaves.

4. **F** If the farmers bothered the growing cocoons, the worms would not make good silk.

5. **O** Silk is the best thread in the world.

Reading 3B: "Beautiful Feet," pp. 48-52, Lesson 89
Comprehension: discriminating between fact and opinion

What's China Like?

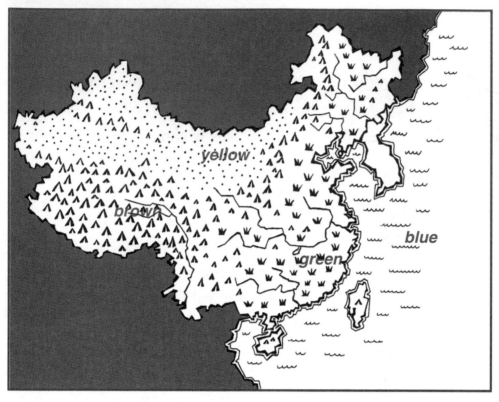

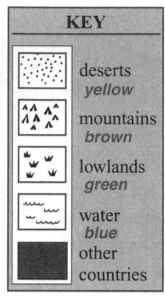

KEY

deserts *yellow*

mountains *brown*

lowlands *green*

water *blue*

other countries

▶Color, Draw, and Think

Study the map of China. Using crayons or colored pencils, follow the directions.

1. Complete the map by coloring it.

   a. Color the mountains brown.

   b. Color the lowlands green.

   c. Color the deserts yellow.

   d. Color the water blue.

2. In this box, draw the symbol used for mountains.

3. In this box, draw the symbol used for water.

4. Color the key to match the map.

5. Does China have a lot of mountains? ____*yes*____

6. Does China probably have a fishing industry? ____*yes*____

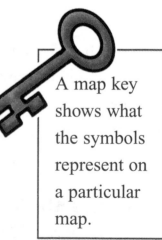

A map key shows what the symbols represent on a particular map.

Reading 3B: "Beautiful Feet," pp. 48-52, Lesson 89
Study skills: interpreting a map key that represents natural regions

First Things First

▶Read and Circle

1. Read the event in the box. Then read the eight events below it.
2. Circle the number for each of the five events from the story that happened before the event in the box.

> Ming-Chu married the young Chinese man.

(1.) Her mother bound Ming-Chu's feet to keep them tiny.

(2.) Ming-Chu packed her things to go home and prepare for her wedding.

(3.) The tailor measured Ming-Chu for her wedding dress.

4. Ming-Chu gave her little silk wedding shoes to the missionary as a gift.

(5.) Ming-Chu watched the missionary and the young Chinese man coach a baseball game.

6. Ming-Chu told her husband that he had beautiful feet because he carried the gospel to many people.

(7.) The tailor made the wedding shoes for Ming-Chu.

8. The missionary gave the wedding shoes to a little American girl.

ISAIAH 52:7

*How beautiful upon the mountains
are the feet of him
that bringeth good tidings,
that publisheth peace;
that bringeth good tidings of good,
that publisheth salvation;
that saith unto Zion,
Thy God reigneth!*

▶Think and Write

Where have your feet carried you to "publish peace"
and "bring good tidings"?

_____

Answers will vary.

_____

_____

_____

Reading 3B: "Beautiful Feet," pp. 53-57, Lesson 90
Comprehension: identifying time relationships; relating story content to personal experience

149

Ready and -able!

▶Choose One

Read the sentences. Underline the correct definition of each colored word.

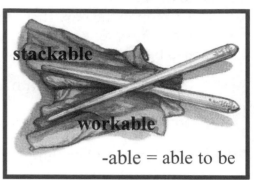

stackable

workable

-able = able to be

1. Monkeys are very trainable animals. (able to ride in a train, <u>able to be trained</u>)

2. The broken bicycle was fixable. (<u>able to be fixed</u>, able to fix)

3. These animal-shaped, chewable vitamins come in different flavors. (able to chew something else, <u>able to be chewed</u>)

4. Unlike wooden chopsticks, silver chopsticks are reusable. (<u>able to be reused</u>, able to use)

▶Choose and Write

Complete each sentence by using the best word from the fans.

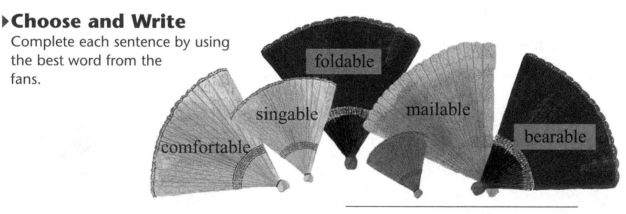

foldable

singable

mailable

comfortable

bearable

1. A Chinese lady's fan that can be closed is _____ *foldable* _____ .

2. A chair that gives comfort is _____ *comfortable* _____ .

3. A box that is not correctly wrapped is not _____ *mailable* _____ .

4. A song that has an easy melody to follow is _____ *singable* _____ .

5. The terrible noise from that howling dog is not _____ *bearable* _____ .

Reading 3B: "Beautiful Feet," pp. 53-57, Lesson 90
Word work: identifying the common meaning of the suffix -*able*;
reading words with the suffix -*able*

Laugh, Cry, Gasp, or Sigh?

An author does not always tell you just how a character feels. Sometimes he wants you to figure it out by noticing how the character reacts to things.

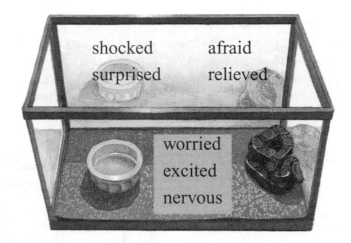

shocked   afraid
surprised   relieved

worried
excited
nervous

▶ Read and Respond

Read the clue the author gives. Write how you think the underlined character feels, using at least one word from the tank.

Clues From the Author	How the Character Feels
"Snakes?" Mr. Peroni stepped on the brake and turned to look at Lisa. "Snakes? Your mother agreed to let you keep a snake?"	*shocked*
"You don't know how glad I am to see you!" Mrs. Allen said. "I didn't know what I was going to do."	*Relieved. Also accept surprised or excited.*
Barney's tongue flickered as he moved closer to the glass. Mrs. Peroni took a quick step backward. "Beautiful, isn't he?" she said quietly.	*Afraid. Also accept worried or nervous.*
"Lisa said she would take good care of Barney, and I'm going to hold her to her word." Lisa's head flew up. "You mean . . ."	*Surprised. Also accept excited.*

Reading 3B: "A Snake in the House," pp. 67-70, Lesson 93
Comprehension: evaluating emotional responses of characters

Pet Shop Supplier

▶Write and Draw

You are the new supplier for a pet shop. You are responsible to supply the shop with healthy, well-behaved animals.

1. Write two words to describe how each animal looks and moves.
2. In the cages, draw a picture of each animal that fits your description.

How It Looks
                                                         Ways It Moves

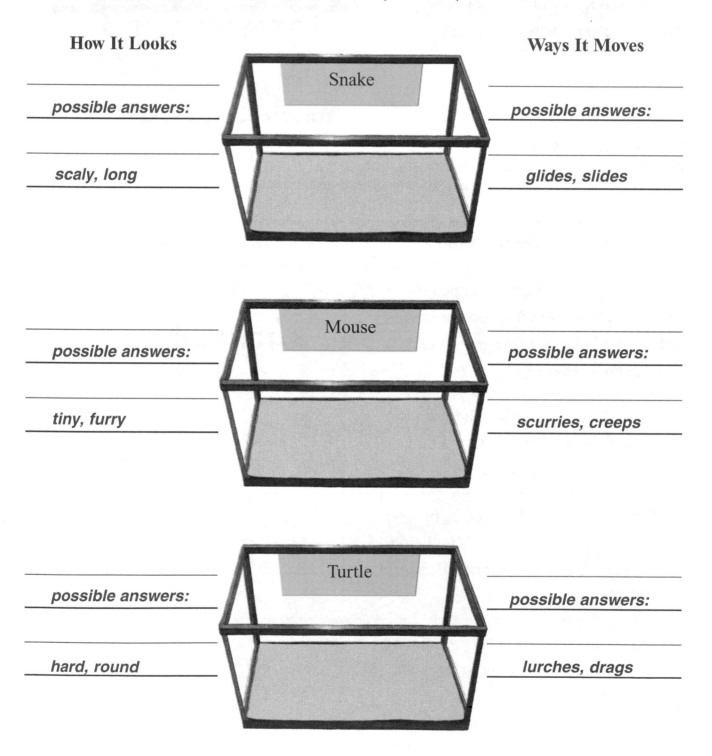

Snake

possible answers:

scaly, long

possible answers:

glides, slides

Mouse

possible answers:

tiny, furry

possible answers:

scurries, creeps

Turtle

possible answers:

hard, round

possible answers:

lurches, drags

Reading 3B: "A Snake in the House," pp. 58-66, Lesson 92
Word work: using descriptive words; using descriptive words to draw a picture

Jump In!

▶Choose and Write

Use the words from the box to complete the sentences.

| fascinated | poisonous | lukewarm | vacation | laboratories | ammonia |
| guest | boa | hamper | coax | vet | mites |

1. Boa constrictors are not _____ *poisonous* _____ snakes.

2. In their _____ *laboratories* _____ scientists raise mice to feed the snakes.

3. Lisa tried to _____ *coax* _____ Barney to eat.

4. Lisa put Barney back into his cage and took him to the _____ *vet* _____ .

5. Barney was sick. He had _____ *mites* _____ under his skin.

6. Barney's tank had to be cleaned with _____ *ammonia* _____ .

7. Barney had to be washed in _____ *lukewarm* _____ water.

8. Mother was _____ *fascinated* _____ as she watched Lisa bathe Barney.

▶Find and Circle

Find and circle in the tub all the words that are in the box above.

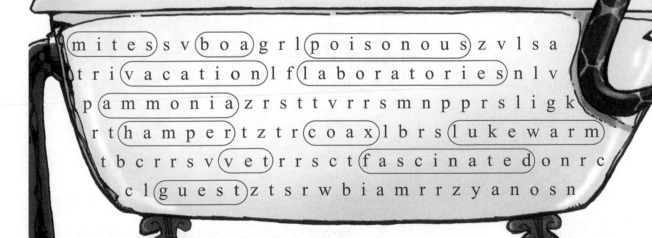

Reading 3B: "A Snake in the House," pp. 58-66, Lesson 93
Comprehension: recalling facts and details

Missssster Macron

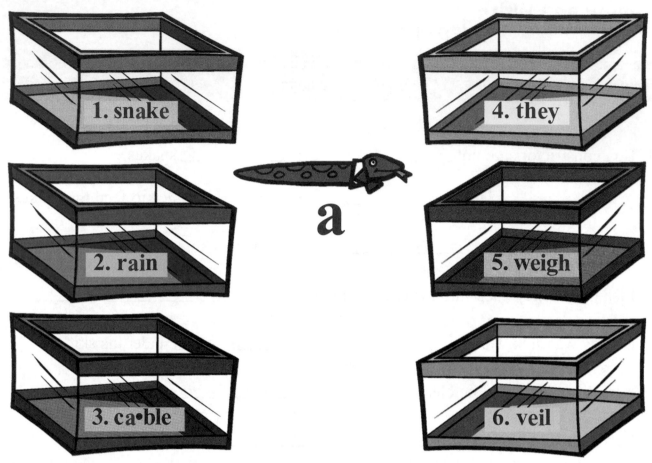

1. snake
2. rain
3. ca•ble
4. they
5. weigh
6. veil

a

▶**Choose and Number**

Help Mister Macron find his way to the right snake tank. Read each word and find a word in a snake tank that follows the same long *a* rule. Write the number of that tank in the blank.

__1__ bake	__4__ o•bey	__5__ freight
__2__ stain	__5__ eight	__1__ make
__2__ nail	__5__ neigh•bor	__5__ sleigh
__3__ la•dle	__2__ pail	__4__ con•vey
__3__ ta•ble	__1__ date	__3__ sta•ble
__6__ vein	__4__ sur•vey	__1__ in•take
__2__ gain	__3__ fa•ble	__3__ ma•ple

Reading 3B: "A Snake in the House," pp. 67-70, Lesson 93

Phonics: identifying different spellings of the long *a* sound as *a_e* in *snake*, *ai* in *rain*, *a* in *cable*, *ey* in *they*, *eigh* in *weigh*, and *ei* in *veil*

She, It, They, Him . . . Who?

▶Find and Circle

In each sentence, circle the character name that the colored word represents.

1. Mother told (Lisa) that she could keep a classroom pet for the summer.

2. (Mr. Peroni) asked why he hadn't been asked sooner about keeping the pet.

3. (Paul Bartlett) asked Lisa to keep Barney for him during the summer.

4. (Mrs. Peroni) looked into the cage and asked, "Can he smell me?"

5. "How fast does he grow?" Mrs. Peroni asked, watching (Barney) suspiciously.

6. When (Barney) changed his behavior, Lisa took him to the doctor.

7. The doctor said that (Barney) had mites under his skin.

8. (Lisa) gave Barney gentle baths in the large tub in her bathroom.

9. "Have you given (Barney) his bath yet?" Mother asked Lisa.

10. Lisa closed the door to the bathroom as the first (woman) drove up in her car.

11. "I could take the hamper to the garage," (Lisa) thought.

12. Lisa dashed after (Barney) as he disappeared under the couch.

13. "Yes," (Mrs. Peroni) said, "I had noticed."

14. Lisa grinned and said to (Barney,) "You just might not have to stay in the garage all summer after all!"

Reading 3B: "A Snake in the House," pp. 71-76, Lesson 94
Word work: identifying pronoun referents

At a Glance

Skimming is looking over new information to get the general idea. One way to do this is to read only the first and last sentences of each paragraph.

▶Underline It

Underline the first and last sentence of each paragraph in the following article.

The King Snake

① Few king snakes are actually giants. A snake must be twenty feet long to be called a "giant snake." The common king snake can be found in the eastern United States and can grow anywhere from 1½ to 6 feet long. The king snake's long, slender body is usually black with narrow, bright-colored bands across its back.

② The king snake, like its close relative, the boa, lives in tropical climates. Unlike its much larger cousin the anaconda, which is found in swamps and rivers of the Amazon, the common king snake does not live in the water. It is at home both on the ground and in trees.

③ King snakes, though excellent hunters, are harmless to people. However, because they are immune to snake venom, they will quickly attack and eat other snakes, including rattlesnakes. The king snakes hunt while hanging from trees. They attack small animals that pass under them. The strong snake coils itself around the victim and kills it, just like the boa constrictor. Then, stretching its jaws, it swallows its prey. King snakes cannot swallow horses, cattle, or other large animals. They feed mainly on small rodents.

▶Choose It

Read only the underlined sentences and circle the number of the paragraph that answers the questions.

Where do king snakes live?	1	②	3
What do king snakes look like?	①	2	3
What do king snakes eat?	1	2	③

Reading 3B: "A Snake in the House," pp. 71-76, Lesson 94
Study skills: skimming by reading the first and last sentences of a paragraph to get the general idea

A Serpent by the Sea

Name

▶Read and Cross Out

Read Paul's story. Cross out one sentence in each paragraph that does not belong.

As a minister of God, I suffered great persecution. However, the Lord protected and blessed me even through difficult times. ~~Our preacher lives near a lake.~~

Once I rode on a slave ship sailing to Italy. ~~They invented pizza in Italy.~~ We stopped for a few days in the city of Lasea. As we readied the ship to continue our journey, I began feeling uneasy. I feared that we would not arrive in Italy without great calamity and possibly even death.

I told a soldier my thoughts. He chose to ignore my warning and set sail. At first the wind blew softly, but then it came hard. Billowing and crashing, the waves tossed our ship like a cork in rapids. ~~Traveling in Africa can be dangerous.~~ The men tried frantically to control the ship, but to no avail.

It was during a sleepless night that the angel of God came to me. He assured me that not one of the 276 men aboard would perish. This news seemed to cheer the men. ~~Creating a newspaper is a long process.~~ On the fifteenth day our ship got stuck on the rocks, and the waves broke it in two. Miraculously, every man made it to shore alive.

Even here the Lord showed mercy. The kind natives of this island fed and sheltered us till we recovered. However, as I collected wood for a fire, I was bitten by a poisonous snake. ~~One time my ship sank.~~ The men watched to see what would happen as I began to pray. Again the Lord protected me. I never even felt faint. The men called me a god because I did not die. Perhaps now they will listen when I tell them of the one true God who can give them eternal life.

Computer Talk?
No, it's not a computer code. It's a way to study. First, turn a title into a **Q**uestion. Next, **R**ead to find the answer to your question. Once you find the answer, **R**ecite it, or write it down.

▶**Try It**
Study the following paragraph using the steps above.

1. **Q**uestion (Write a question from the title.)

_____

Are snakes blind? Why do snakes get blind? What kind of snakes are blind?

2. **R**ead

Blind Snakes

Blind snakes are a group of snakes that look like worms. They have teeth only on their upper jaw and feed mainly on ants and termites. They are called blind snakes because of the head scales that cover their eyes.

3. **R**ecite (Write the answer to your question.)   *Answers will vary.*

_____

_____

_____

_____

▶**Change Them**
Change these titles into questions.   *Answers will vary.*

1. The Molting Process   _____

    _____

2. The Speed of a Snake   _____

    _____

3. A Snake's Diet   _____

Reading 3B: "Just Plain Snaky," pp. 77-82, Lesson 95
Study skills: using the **Question**, **Read**, and **Recite** parts of the PQ3R method of study: forming a subheading into a question, reading to answer the formed question, reciting the answer to the formed question

Name

▶Read and Answer

Read the story and answer the following questions.

A Legend from Baghdad

One day, an important leader of Baghdad disguised himself and went on a journey to see how his subjects lived. Close to the town of Bassora he saw a crippled beggar traveling the same road. In mercy, he offered to give him a ride into town on his fine horse. When they rode into town together the beggar told the leader to dismount! He said that no one there would know who really owned the horse. Shocked, the leader refused, and when the beggar insisted, the leader decided to take him before a judge.

The judge asked, "Who are you and what is the problem?" First, the leader told of the beggar's ingratitude and of his attempt to steal his horse. Then the beggar cried and threw a fit while telling his side of the story. The judge listened thoughtfully, then said, "Leave the horse in my stable overnight and pick him up in the morning." Though he thought it odd, the leader did as the judge had asked. Both men returned the next morning. Immediately, without a word, the judge gave the horse to the proper owner. Amazed, the leader asked, "How did you know?" "Simple," said the judge. "I watched when the beggar passed by the stable. The horse did nothing. But when you passed, he snorted and whinnied in recognition." Because of the judge's great wisdom, the leader made him grand judge over Baghdad.

1. What <u>one word</u> from the legend describes the leader's motive in picking up the beggar?

   mercy

2. Describe the character of the beggar in the legend.

   Answers will vary.

3. Do you think the leader in this legend is a wise man? Tell why or why not.

   Answers will vary.

Reading 3B: "The Legend of William Tell," pp. 83-89, Lesson 97
Comprehension: recognizing motive of character; analyzing character actions
Literature: recognizing legends as part of the genre folk literature

159

The Courageous Hero

▶Read and Mark

Mark the sentence that describes William Tell more clearly.

_____ The archer, William Tell, became a hero.

___✗___ The skillful archer, William Tell, became a courageous hero.

▶Read and Answer

Read the sentences. Answer the questions using the correct descriptive words.

1. In big black letters was written, "Whosoever shall not bow to this hat shall thereby take his life into his hands."
   What two words describe the kind of letters on Gessler's sign?

   _____
   big, black

2. "What man would not love his son?" he replied quietly. "Peter is a good, obedient boy."
   What two words describe the kind of boy that Peter is?

   _____
   good, obedient

3. "I'm sure of that." Gessler's lips curled in a thin smile.
   What word describes Gessler's smile?

   _____
   thin

4. "You are a wicked man, Gessler," Tell said quietly.
   What word describes the kind of man that Gessler is?

   _____
   wicked

5. As the skillful archer lifted the bow, a voice rang out, "I trust you, Father!"
   What word describes the kind of archer William Tell is?

   _____
   skillful

6. William Tell took careful aim with a steady hand. He let the arrow fly.
   What word describes the kind of aim William Tell takes?

   _____
   careful

   What word describes the kind of hand William Tell has?

   _____
   steady

Reading 3B: "The Legend of William Tell," pp. 83-89, Lesson 97
Literature: noting the author's use of adjectives

Invisible Pictures

▶Choose and Mark

Put an *X* by the sentence that gives the reader the more complete mental picture.

_____ My puppy's tongue is rough.
__X__ My puppy's tongue feels like sandpaper.

__X__ The gentle rain kissed my cheek.
_____ My face got wet from the rain.

_____ The waves hit the deck of the ship.
__X__ Giant waves spanked the deck of the ship.

_____ The flag blew in the wind.
__X__ The flag snapped in the brisk breeze.

__X__ Yellow dandelions dot the lawn.
_____ There are dandelions on the lawn.

_____ The horse ran fast down the track.
__X__ The horse thundered toward the finish line.

There—
green as the meadow
and shivery as the wet pond—
stood the little rubber tree,
shining.

__X__ The sparkling waterfall reflected the sunlight.
_____ The sun shone on the waterfall.

__X__ The icy wind chilled our very bones.
_____ The wind made us cold.

Reading 3B: "Something Special and Shiny," pp. 90-96, Lesson 98
Literature: developing awareness of imagery that uses the senses to communicate meaning

161

Right As Rain

▶Read and Mark

Put a check in the raindrop beside the correct definition
for the colored word in each of the sentences.

1. He took Momma to the side and
   said something in a deep,
   gravelly voice.

   ✓ hoarse or scratchy
   □ full of stones

2. He crept back to his room,
   making not a speck of noise.

   □ a dark spot
   ✓ a little bit

3. A breeze stirred the rubber
   tree's leaves.

   □ mixed together
   ✓ moved

4. She saw the rubber tree in
   its little red tub.

   ✓ bowl-like container
   □ where you take a bath

5. The tingly air would waken her
   and put pink rounds to her
   cheeks.

   □ a cut of beef
   ✓ circles

6. Whispering breezes might even
   put a dance in her feet.

   ✓ quiet or soft
   □ talking quietly

7. Three big drops, big as tree
   leaves, slapped his face.

   ✓ fell onto
   □ hit with the hand

Reading 3B: "Something Special and Shiny," pp. 90-96, Lesson 98
Vocabulary: using context clues to determine word meaning

Chart Challenger

▶Choose One

Read the sentences in the boxes. Choose a speaker from the list and put his or her name in the box.

| Marcia | Poppa | Momma |
| Marcos | Grandmomma | |

"True. But we're so far from the beach and the water." (page 98)

"Why, where did the beautiful plant come from?" (page 93)

_____
Momma
_____

_____
Poppa
_____

_____
Marcia
_____

Marcos's Family

"All Marcia needs now is plenty of fresh air." (page 98)

"Silly! You can't bring an ocean into a house!" (page 99)

_____
Grandmomma
_____

_____
Marcos
_____

"Shhh! You must be quiet. Marcia is very sick. We have to walk softly and whisper so she can rest." (page 91)

"It's a sunshiny rubber tree. It came from the hot country. It's growing like a giant." (page 96)

Reading 3B: "Something Special and Shiny," pp. 97-102, Lesson 99
Comprehension: matching character and dialogue

Sweet Potato Party

▶Mark It

1. Draw a sweet potato around the syllable that has *age*.
2. Put a caterpillar through the silent *e* in that syllable.

cab•bage   vil•lage   car•riage

lug•gage   pas•sage   cot•tage

▶Write It

Choose the correct word from above and write it in the blank.

1. On our vacation we visited a quiet little _____*village*_____ in Pennsylvania.

2. We drove through a tunnel with only a narrow _____*passage*_____ .

3. The driver stopped in front of a cute _____*cottage*_____ , and we unloaded our _____*luggage*_____ .

4. We enjoyed _____*cabbage*_____ soup for supper before falling sound asleep in the cozy loft.

Reading 3B: "Something Special and Shiny," pp. 97-102, Lesson 99
Phonics: reading words with *age* as /ĭj/ in *leakage*

Making Tracks

▶Read and Choose

Read the sentences and write the name of the forest animal each one describes.

rabbit	porcupine	deer	bear
raccoon	beaver	squirrel	

1. This black-masked bandit stopped at a rushing stream to wash his food. What is he?

raccoon

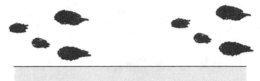

2. Fast, bounding leaps on the snow left these tracks of a small, long-eared animal with a powder-puff tail. What is he?

rabbit

3. Do you hear that chattering up in the swaying treetops? What scolding animal is frisking there, half-hidden by a curling tail?

squirrel

4. Across the creek a majestic animal tosses his head and turns to race away, leaping logs in a single bound. What is he?

deer

5. Slap! goes a broad, flat tail against the water as this animal pads his river home with mud. What is he?

beaver

6. A low growl warns the forest animals that this big, hulking beast is on the prowl. What is he?

bear

7. This small, bristly animal need not fear other forest creatures. Who wants to end up looking like a pincushion? What is he?

porcupine

Reading 3B: "The Diary of George Shannon," pp. 104-8, Lesson 100
Comprehension: drawing conclusions

Incredible Opposites

See teacher's edition to introduce the activity.

correct   *in*correct

proper   *im*proper

in = not

im = not

▸Think and Draw

Finish the puzzle by drawing a picture in the empty box.
Then fill in the blank by writing either *im* or *in*.

edible   inedible

1.    *in* = not   *Answers will vary.*

possible   impossible

2. *Answers will vary.*   *im* = not

perfect   imperfect

3. *Answers will vary.*   *im* = not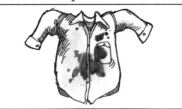

flexible   inflexible

4.    *in* = not   *Answers will vary.*

Reading 3B: "The Diary of George Shannon," pp. 104-8, Lesson 100
Word work: using prefix *im-*, *in-* to determine word meaning

History in the Making

▶Put in Order

Number Mr. Shannon's journal entries in the correct sequence.

__3__ I usually spend most of the day out on hunting expeditions looking for deer and buffalo.

__1__ Now that we've finished building Fort Mandan and settled in for the winter, my days have fallen into a routine.

__5__ In the evenings, the Mandans often visit us. We clean and repair our weapons together, tell stories, and sing.

__4__ When we come home from hunting, there is usually smoked buffalo meat to eat.

__2__ As soon as I wake up, I fold up my buffalo robe and have some breakfast.

Number these journal entries in the correct sequence.

__5__ When the bulls saw that I wouldn't run, they lost interest and turned in another direction.

__3__ Thinking to catch the bear by surprise, I turned around, stopped, raised my spittoon, and said firmly, "Go home!" Amazingly enough, the bear obeyed.

__1__ What a day! In twenty-four hours, I have had three close encounters with wild creatures.

__4__ About an hour after the bear had disappeared, I came upon a herd of buffalo. Three bulls left the herd and charged me. I kept walking toward them, staring them right in the eyes.

__6__ To top off the day, I killed a rattlesnake. He had a beautiful diamondback skin. I'll save that as a souvenir of my adventures.

__2__ First, a bear rushed out of the woods and chased me.

Reading 3B: "The Diary of George Shannon," pp. 109-13, Lesson 101
Comprehension: ordering sequence of events

Encyclopedia Exploration

▸Find and Write

Use an encyclopedia to locate the key word your teacher has assigned to you. Fill in the page using the information in the encyclopedia.

This is a practice page and is not intended to be graded.

Key Word: _____

Vol. #: _____

Guide Word: _____

Three interesting things I learned:

1. _____

2. _____

3. _____

Two related articles (if given):

1. _____

2. _____

Reading 3B: "The Diary of George Shannon," pp. 109-13, Lesson 101
Study skills: locating information in an encyclopedia

Picture a Prairie Dog

An author chooses words carefully to appeal to your senses. He must help you see the prairie dog as well as feel it and hear its bark.

▶Circle the Best
Circle three phrases in each group.

1. Which phrases help you **see** things clearly in the setting?
   a. the western plains
   b. a prairie dog burrow
   c. barks ring out often
   d. a furry brown head pops up

2. Which phrases help you **see** the prairie dog's enemies moving carefully?
   a. hawks circle and swoop
   b. sound of the warning bark
   c. creep through tall grasses
   d. slither without a sound

3. Which phrases help you **hear** the prairie dog's bark?
   a. spring into action
   b. rings out often
   c. special, high-pitched warning
   d. sounds the "all-clear"

4. Which phrases help you **feel** the prairie dog?
   a. a furry brown head
   b. weighs up to three pounds
   c. long, hard claws for digging
   d. fighting over their food

5. Which phrases help you **see** the prairie dog?
   a. favorite food is grass
   b. brown with white bellies
   c. as long as fifteen inches
   d. have stubby legs

6. Which phrases help you **see** the prairie dogs defending themselves?
   a. dart into their burrows
   b. make barking sounds
   c. flatten themselves against the ground
   d. wait and listen for danger to pass

Reading 3B: "Friends of the Prairie," pp. 114-19, Lesson 102
Literature: developing awareness of the author's use of imagery

Prairie Pals

▶Listen and Write

Read the words in the list and listen to the vowel sound of the colored vowels. Write each word by the prairie dog whose burrow contains the same vowel sound as the colored vowels.

anoint

proud

annoy

autumn

about

amount

awful

auto

powder

defrost

shower

oyster

softly

enjoy

author

boyhood

destroy

tower

joy /oi/

anoint

annoy

oyster

enjoy

boyhood

destroy

house /ou/

proud

about

amount

powder

shower

tower

call /ô/

autumn

awful

auto

defrost

softly

author

Reading 3B: "Friends of the Prairie," pp. 114-19, Lesson 102
Phonics: applying letter-sound association: /ô/, /oi/, /ou/

Name

▶Read and Mark

Read each phrase. Put an *X* under each toy that the phrase at the left describes.

	flutter mill	bull-roarer	hard berries	beanshooter	burr furniture	corncob house
1. toys for girls					×	×
2. toys for boys	×	×	×	×		
3. toys to improve your aim			×	×		
4. a noisemaker		×				
5. something used in place of marbles			×			
6. a water toy	×					
7. toys you have to make	×	×		×	×	×
8. toys that come from nature	×	×	×	×	×	×
9. a toy that is hollow				×		

Reading 3B: "Toys from Nature," pp. 120-25, Lesson 104
Comprehension: classifying information

Pioneer Playthings

▶Choose and Write

Write the compound word from the dart that matches the clues.

playthings   dugout
outdoors   cornstalk
necklace   corncob

1. _**cornstalk**_ —— the long, slender stem of a plant that boys used as a toy spear

2. _**playthings**_ —— another name for toys and games

3. _**necklace**_ —— a chain of daisies or seeds to decorate a doll's outfit

4. _**outdoors**_ —— where pioneer children liked to be on a warm, breezy day

5. _**dugout**_ —— a dollhouse made by clearing dirt away from tree roots

6. _**corncob**_ —— the dry, scraped ear of corn used to make darts and dolls

▶Match Them

Look at each word. Choose a synonym from the acorn and write it in the blank.

/chər/
nature
creature
fracture
picture
puncture
capture

wildlife _**nature**_   photograph _**picture**_

arrest _**capture**_   hole _**puncture**_

animal _**creature**_   crack _**fracture**_

Reading 3B: "Toys From Nature," pp. 120-25, Lesson 104
Vocabulary: matching compound words and definitions; matching synonyms
Phonics: reading words with the schwa syllable /chər/ as *ture* in *nature*

Learn to Do Good

> **JAMES 4:17**
> *Therefore to him that
> knoweth to do good,
> and doeth it not,
> to him it is sin.*

▶Choose and Circle
Answer the questions by circling *Yes* or *No*.

Yes   (No)   1. When Jacob said, "Won't everyone be
             surprised when I come home leading a pony!"
             was he planning to tell his family about the pony?

(Yes)   No   2. When Jacob was glad that Abigail could not go to the
             pasture, was it because he did not want her to see the pony?

Yes   (No)   3. Did Jacob do the right thing when he grumbled about watching
             the cows?

(Yes)   No   4. When Jacob settled the cows in the pasture, was he doing his job?

▶Think and Write   *Answers will vary.*

1. Why did Jacob get up early in the morning after
   he saw the horse?

   _____

   _____

2. Why did Jacob offer his apple to the horse?

   _____

   _____

3. What was Jacob planning to do with the rope?

   _____

   _____

   _____

   _____

Reading 3B: "The Secret Pony," pp. 126-31, Lesson 105
Comprehension: inferring the motives of characters

The Branding Iron

▶Brand and Color

Brand each horse with an ŏ if it has a word with a short *o* sound in it. Then color each branded horse brown. The first horse is branded for you.

ŏ swan   *color*

colt

go

ŏ swat   *color*

hoof

ŏ swap   *color*

ŏ shop   *color*

ŏ watch   *color*

ŏ swallow   *color*

clover

pony

ŏ trot   *color*

Reading 3B: "The Secret Pony," pp. 126-31, Lesson 105
Phonics: using letter-sound association: /ŏ/ as *o* in a closed syllable (*hot*) and as *a* after *w* (*watch*);
recognizing and using the diacritical mark for short vowels: *breve* (˘)

The Tail End

▶Finish It

Read the three possible endings to the story, "The Secret Pony."
Choose the phrase from the box that completes each one.

1. Jacob became more unhappy as the days passed. He began to think of Molasses instead of himself. Molasses knew Jacob wasn't her owner. Jacob wondered if the cave got cold or damp at night. One morning Jacob came to the cave. He didn't bring Molasses breakfast. He didn't pat her or comb her or play with her like before. He just said, "It's what I have to do. I can't keep you. Go on now, your owner misses you." He waved her away, pointing toward the fields. Jacob

_____

_____*set her free*_____

_____ .

2. The next morning Jacob took the cows to pasture and played with Molasses in the warm sunshine. Abigail, who had permission to come to the pasture, saw Molasses. They played together for the rest of the morning. When Frau Stahl came to the pasture to bring Abigail home for lunch, she saw Molasses. She asked Jacob all about her. That night, Jacob's father had a talk with Jacob and

_____

told him to find the pony's owner

_____ .

3. Jacob awoke early. What a nightmare! He had dreamed that he had forgotten to tie Molasses up and that when he came to the cave, she was gone. He was glad to find it was a dream, but still he really couldn't remember tying Molasses up and covering the cave. As he thought about it, he became sure that he hadn't tied her up. After breakfast he hurried to the cave. Sure enough, Molasses had not been tied up, and she

_____

_____*had run away*_____

_____ .

set her free
told his father
decided to keep the secret
had run away
told him to find the pony's owner
tried to feed Molasses better

How Puzzling!

▶Match and Complete

Match the definitions with the
words from the list to complete the puzzle.

pasture
whinny
molasses
gallop
mustache
brand
peering

ACROSS

2. a sweet, thick, dark
   syrup made from
   sugar

3. wide, open grazing land

6. looking closely at someone or
   something

DOWN

1. the fastest movement of a horse

2. hair that grows on a man's upper lip

4. to neigh in a soft tone

5. a mark burned into an animal to
   show ownership

▶Think and Write

Write two sentences using at least one word from the list above in
each sentence.   *Answers will vary.*

1. _____

2. _____

Reading 3B: "The Secret Pony," pp. 132-35, Lesson 106
Vocabulary: matching words and definitions

Name

> ## II CORINTHIANS 13:7
> *Now I pray to God that ye . . . should do*
> *that which is honest.*

▶Read and Draw

Read the sentences. Draw a ☺ if Jacob is deciding to do right in the sentence. Draw a ☹ if Jacob is doing wrong.

☹ "Well, I'll find out who you belong to later," Jacob decided.

☹ That night Jacob still didn't tell his family about the pony.

☹ "Maybe I wouldn't have to give you up right away. This is the perfect hiding place."

☺ "I can't keep Molasses hidden forever," Jacob thought. "Soon I'll have to tell my father."

☹ Jacob thought of a plan to keep the pony.

☺ "I'm sorry, Father. I wanted her so badly. I want to return her myself, Father."

☺ "I'm sorry, sir. I hid your son's pony because I wanted to keep her. I don't deserve a reward."

▶Think and Write

Write your conclusion.

Do you think William Franklin convinced Jacob to take the reward and ride Molasses when he came on market days? Why or why not?

Answers will vary.

_____

_____

_____

_____

Reading 3B: "The Secret Pony," pp. 136-41, Lesson 107
Comprehension: inferring the motives of characters; drawing conclusions

Similar but Different

▶Read and Think
Read the following articles.

Benjamin Franklin

Even when Benjamin Franklin was a boy, he had a strong sense of humor. He started doing important things when he was young, and he never stopped.

Franklin was born in America, but he traveled to several other countries in his lifetime. He was a great statesman and an ambassador to other countries. He played an important part in the shaping of our nation before and after the War for Independence.

Unfortunately, as far as we know, Benjamin Franklin never became a Christian. He lived a life of service for his fellow men, but he did not serve the Lord.

George Whitefield

George Whitefield was a great evangelist before the War for Independence. He was born in England but traveled to America more than once to tell people about the saving grace of Jesus.

Whitefield took sermon examples from things around him. He seemed to understand what the common people needed. Benjamin Franklin thought Whitefield's preaching was so good that once he gave Whitefield all the money he had in his pockets. (Whitefield witnessed to Franklin many times, but Franklin never really responded.) This mighty preacher's work was done for the Lord rather than for man, but many men benefited by receiving eternal life.

▶Describe Him
Read the phrases below. Put an X in the box under the man or men that the phrase describes.

	Franklin	Whitefield
1. born in America	✕	
2. born in England		✕
3. lived a life of service	✕	✕
4. became a Christian		✕
5. lived before the War for Independence	✕	✕

Reading 3B: "The Secret Pony," pp. 136-41, Lesson 107
Study skills: identifying comparisons and contrasts

Have You Heard the News?

▶Match Them

You're the new mail carrier and in order for the newspapers to get to the right homes, you have to get the papers in the right bags. Match each newspaper clue to the correct sack(s).

classified ads

much color

no color

few pictures

Old Time Newspapers

Modern Newspapers

many photographs

many columns

▶Choose and Write

Choose the correct word from the box to complete each sentence.

dictionary
price
words
classified
index
sentences

1. A _____classified_____ ad advertises goods to be bought or sold by individuals.

2. You could locate a certain article in the newspaper quickly by looking in the _____index_____ .

3. The cost of the ad is based on how many _____words_____ it has.

4. The three main parts of a classified ad are a description of the item, the _____price_____ , and a phone number.

Reading 3B: "News About Ads," pp. 142-44, Lesson 108
Comprehension: comparing old and new newspapers; recalling facts and details

Hot off the Press!

▶Read Them
Read these classified ads carefully.

blue Fine oak barrels, made by an expert in the craft. The buyer can be sure that he will find no warps or cracks in the wood; otherwise his money will be refunded in full. The cooper may be found on sunny days <u>at the edge of the King's Woods.</u>

Willing, industrious, young Christian man needed to sweep floors. Call at <u>Everhard's Blacksmith Shop</u> on the edge of town, just beyond Peyton Street. *yellow*

One fine, strong, black Morgan horse, only two years old. Whoever finds her is asked to return her to the subscriber at the Arm's Inn. A substantial reward is offered for his trouble. <u>Samuel Phyfe</u>   *green*

orange

One plow, <u>made of sturdy oak with a strong blade</u> for hard, rocky ground. The subscriber will sell it for a reasonable price. Ask for the subscriber at the woodmaker's shop. John Drury.

Candles and tapers of standard weight, all made from the very finest whale oil available. They will light easily, providing many hours of unwavering illumination and giving off no foul odor. They will not melt in the heat of summer. These fine candles can be found in the home of <u>Mistress Wythe on Hopkins Street.</u> *red*

▶Find and Color
Use your crayons to follow the directions.

1. Underline with blue the place where you could see the barrel maker.

2. Underline in yellow the place where you could interview for a job as a floor sweeper.

3. Draw a red line under the name and address of the candlemaker.

4. Draw an orange line under the phrase that describes John Drury's plow.

5. Underline in green the name of the lost horse's owner.

▶Write About It
Answer the following questions.

1. After reading John Drury's ad, do you think someone would want to buy his plow? Why or why not?

_____

Answers will vary.

_____

2. List some words and phrases Mistress Wythe uses to show the quality of her candles.

_____

finest whale oil, will light easily, hours of unwavering

_____

illumination, no foul odor, will not melt

Reading 3B: "News About Ads," pp. 142-44, Lesson 108
Study skills: reading classified ads to gain information; identifying advertising strategies

X Marks the Spot

▶Read and Mark

Read the question and mark an *X* over the letter with the correct answer.

1. When did Phillis have her first critical illness?
    - X̶. when she was a child
    - B. when she began writing poems
    - C. after the British fired their smoky muskets

2. How did Mrs. Wheatley discover that Phillis wanted to learn to write?
    - A. She found Phillis crying about it one night.
    - B̶. She found Phillis trying to write on the wall.
    - C. She heard Phillis whispering about it.

3. Phillis's poem to King George was in celebration of what event?
    - A. Independence Day
    - B̶. the repeal of the Stamp Act
    - C. freedom from slavery

4. What did Phillis first learn to read?
    - A. classics
    - B. poetry
    - C̶. the Bible

5. Where did Phillis learn about an accident at sea?
    - X̶. at the Wheatleys' home while serving their guests
    - B. at Boston Common while watching the fireworks
    - C. in her room while reading a newspaper

6. Why was Phillis so concerned about the men's escape at sea?
    - A. They were friends of hers from America.
    - B. She thought they were relatives.
    - C̶. She was concerned about whether they would go to heaven or hell.

7. Which of Phillis's poems was published first?
    - A. a poem about the repeal of the Stamp Act
    - B̶. a poem about heaven and hell
    - C. a poem about reading the Bible

8. As a slave how was Phillis treated?
    - A. The family resented her illness.
    - B̶. The family loved and cared for her.
    - C. The family mistreated her.

Reading 3B: "Phillis Wheatley," pp. 145-50, Lesson 109
Comprehension: identifying time and place relationships; recalling facts and details

Catch the Poetry Bug!

/ē/

▸Choose and Write

The mystery mosquito has been "buzzzzy" making lists of words for you.

1. In each box, color the words yellow that have the long *e* sound spelled with an *i* or a *y*.
2. Choose a colored word from the first box and a rhyming colored word from the second box to answer each riddle.

List 1

happy
repeal
spaghetti
sloppy
crazy

List 2

confetti
daisy
pappy
reveal
copy

1. A cheerful grandpa is a

   **happy pappy** .

2. A second page that is messy is a

   **sloppy copy** .

3. Tiny decorations for an Italian pasta party are

   **spaghetti confetti** .

4. A silly flower is a

   **crazy daisy** .

▸Circle It

Circle the vowel that makes the long *e* sound in each word.

d i a r ⓨ

l i b r a r ⓨ

s k ⓘ

i n j u r ⓨ

182

Reading 3B: "Phillis Wheatley," pp. 145-50, Lesson 109
Phonics: using letter-sound association: /ē/ as *i* in *ski* and as *y* in *merry*; choosing rhyming words

Guess Who

▶Choose and Write

As you read the story, you learned about its characters. The statements below are not found in the story, but they might have been. Write the name of the character from the box who might have said each statement.

Mary	Mrs. Wheatley	ship's captain
Phillis	Mr. Wheatley	printer

1. "Most of the slaves will make it, but I wonder about this little one. She looks too sick to live until we reach the shore."

   ship's captain

2. "This little girl you brought home has become quite a student. She's a credit to your judgment, dear wife."

   Mr. Wheatley

3. "Oh, Mother, she's such a pretty little girl! May I help you care for her?"

   Mary

4. "I wish my mother could be here to watch my baptism and learn about God."

   Phillis

5. "Writing poetry in London is not as important as going to see Mrs. Wheatley."

   Phillis

6. "These poems are very good. I'd like to print them in a book."

   printer

7. "Thank you for staying here with me even though you are free."

   Mrs. Wheatley

Reading 3B: "Phillis Wheatley," pp. 151-55, Lesson 110
Comprehension: predicting character dialogue

The Angles of Analogies

▶Draw It

Read the sentence. Choose one of the pictures to complete the sentence and draw it in the space provided.

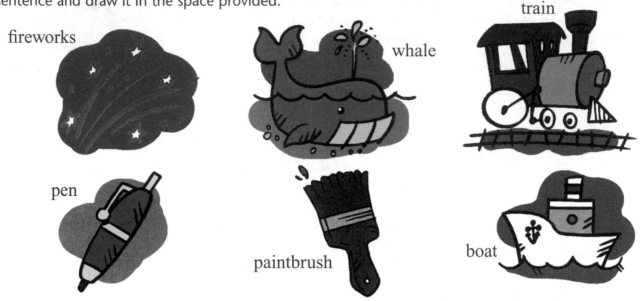

fireworks

whale

train

pen

paintbrush

boat

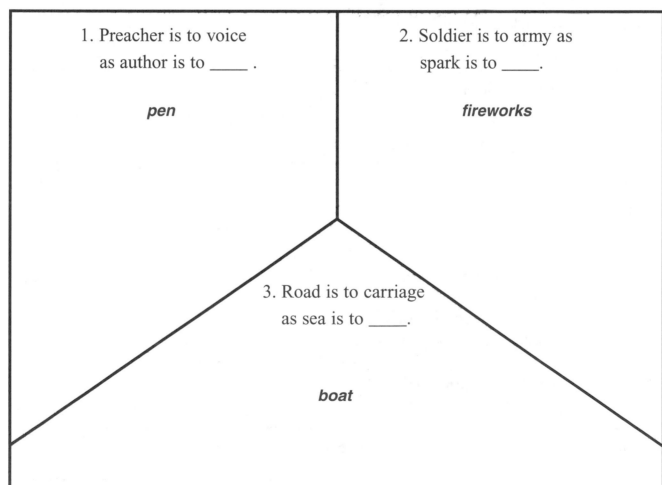

1. Preacher is to voice
   as author is to _____ .

   pen

2. Soldier is to army as
   spark is to _____.

   fireworks

3. Road is to carriage
   as sea is to _____.

   boat

Reading 3B: "Phillis Wheatley," pp. 151-55, Lesson 110
Comprehension: finding relationships between pairs of words

The play takes place at night. The weather is cold.

Secrets in the Shadows

▶Think and Answer

Use your book to answer the questions below. Use complete sentences.

1. During what time of day does the play take place?

   The play takes place at night.

2. What is the weather like as the play begins?

   The weather is cold.

3. Through what town are Billy Dawes and his friend hurrying?

   They are hurrying through Boston.

4. Do they sneak to the doctor's house in the shadows or walk straight down the street?

   They sneak along in the shadows.

5. Why are they frightened?

   Possible answer: They were afraid of getting caught by British soldiers.

6. What does Dr. Warren want the men to do?

   He wants them to warn others that the British are coming.

7. How would you feel if you lived in Boston at this time? Why?

   Answers will vary.

Reading 3B: "A Dark Night," pp. 156-60, Lesson 111
Comprehension: recalling facts and details; making inferences; relating story content to personal life

185

"Redcoats?"

▶Read and Label

1. Read the paragraph.
2. Label the diagram using the colored words from the paragraph.

The bright British uniform had many useful parts. A **cockade**, or badge, on the hat told the soldier's position. Officers had a fancy **lapel** along the front of their coat. Underneath the showy red coat, the soldier wore a plain vest or **waistcoat**. For pants he wore **breeches** which went only to the knee. Stockings covered the middle of his leg and **spatterdashes** protected his lower leg. A bayonet hung by his side from a **crossbelt** strapped across his chest. A **cartridge box** hung from another belt across his chest. This box held the ammunition for the soldier's musket. Distinctive and useful, the British uniform stands out in history.

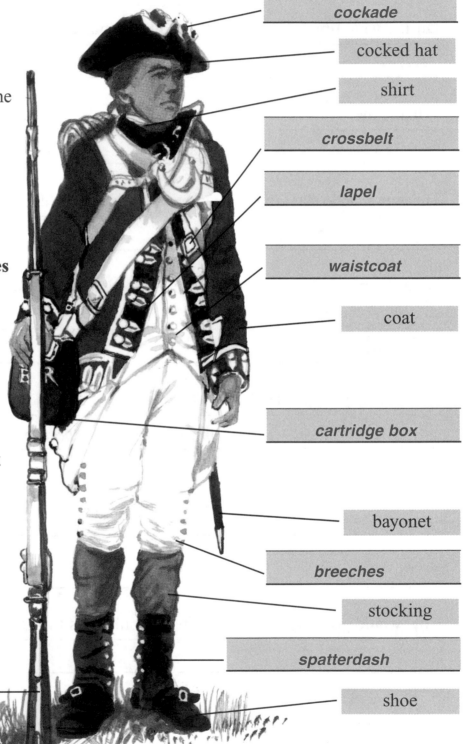

cockade

cocked hat

shirt

crossbelt

lapel

waistcoat

coat

cartridge box

bayonet

breeches

stocking

spatterdash

shoe

musket

Reading 3B: "A Dark Night," pp. 156-60, Lesson 111
Vocabulary: expanding vocabulary
Study skills: labeling a diagram
Comprehension: making inferences

Name

▶Match Them

Match each character to the correct action by writing the letter in the circle.

A. lit two lanterns in North Church

B. rowed the boat with Paul Revere past the Somerset

C. provided the best horse in Charleston

D. warned the villages of the British attack

E. rode his horse into a pond

F. prayed for her husband's safety

C	A	D	E	F	B
Colonel Conant	Robert Newman	Paul Revere	British soldier	Rachel Revere	Tom Richardson

▶Choose and Write

Put the names of the characters above in the blank beside what they said.

"May America be blessed by your courage."   *Rachel Revere*

"You can depend on me. Two if by sea—right?"   *Robert Newman*

"Be careful! Watch for the patrols!"   *Colonel Conant*

"Halt, I say, in the name of the king!"   *British soldier*

"And God bless our land."   *Paul Revere*

Reading 3B: "A Dark Night," pp. 161-67, Lesson 112
Comprehension: matching characters and actions; matching characters and dialogue

Charting Progress

▸Choose and Write

Choose the correct words from the box to fill in the blanks.

ammunition	pealed	minutemen
England	Redcoats	neck

musket balls

ammunition

narrow strip of land

neck

British soldiers

Redcoats

War for Independence

country that the British soldiers came from

England

soldiers who were ready in a flash

minutemen

what the church bells did

pealed

Reading 3B: "A Dark Night," pp. 161-67, Lesson 112
Vocabulary: matching words and definitions

▶Read and Think

Think about the main idea of each paragraph as you read.

1. Paul Revere's ride was not an uncommon danger. The king of England had sent his soldiers to many American towns to control the citizens. But the patriots desired the freedom to make a country of their own. They often attempted many actions just as dangerous as Paul Revere's ride.

2. The moon hadn't risen yet on April 18, 1775. Patriot spies were quietly slipping and darting along dark alleys and sneaking from house to house sharing the news they had overheard. It seemed that the British were up to something!

3. That night the British patrols planned to attack. They expected to march to the town of Concord and seize the weapons and gunpowder hidden there. They would attempt to find and arrest Samuel Adams and John Hancock.

4. When the alert patriots became aware of those plans, they lit their lantern signal. Paul Revere rowed a boat across the river. His horse awaited him on the other shore. He galloped through the night to all the little farmhouses and villages between Boston and Lexington. He awakened the townspeople and alerted them to prepare to defend themselves.

5. Paul Revere arrived safely at Lexington around 1:00 A.M. He had ridden to protect the citizens, and he believed that God had protected him.

▶Choose and Write

Write the number of each paragraph beside the correct main idea.

__2__ Patriot spies shared the news that they had.

__3__ The British planned to attack.

__5__ Paul Revere trusted in God.

__1__ The patriots often faced danger.

__4__ Paul Revere warned the citizens.

Good or Superb?

▶Choose and Mark

Mark an *X* by the sentence that makes you hear the church bells more clearly.

_____ The church bells rang.

__X__ Church bells pealed out the message.

▶Choose and Write

Write the best words for the sentences.

1. Paul Revere said good-bye and _____**slipped**_____ into the night.

   (went out, slipped)

2. Paul Revere _____**raced**_____ toward Lexington.

   (went, rode, raced)

3. His horse's hooves _____**clattered**_____ on the cobblestones.

   (clattered, were heard)

4. A British soldier _____**spurred**_____ his horse after Paul Revere.

   (spurred, hurried)

5. Paul Revere _____**startled**_____ the sleeping townfolk.

   (awoke, startled)

6. Windows _____**flew open**_____ and nightcapped heads popped out.

   (were opened, flew open)

7. Men dressed in a flash and _____**snatched**_____ their guns.

   (got, snatched)

Reading 3B: "A Dark Night," pp. 156-67, Lesson 113
Literature: noting the author's use of verbs to clarify meaning
Vocabulary: choosing vocabulary to create imagery

190

How Do You Feel?

▶Read Them

In the poem "Lullaby," Robert Hillyer writes of quiet sounds that make the reader feel sleepy. Other sounds in the night can make one feel scared or excited. Listed below are more phrases that describe sounds you might hear at night.

raindrops tapping on the window   popcorn popping   a purring kitten

a wailing siren   marching music   a creaking door

▶Choose and Write

Read each phrase above. Write the phrase under the description of how it might make you feel. In the last blank in each group, write one idea of your own.
Accept reasonable answers.
Answers may vary from those listed.

Sounds that might make you feel sleepy or contented

1. *raindrops tapping on the window*

2. *a purring kitten*

3. *Answers will vary.*

Sounds that might make you feel happy or excited

1. *popcorn popping*

2. *marching music*

3. *Answers will vary.*

Sounds that might make you feel scared or worried

1. *a wailing siren*

2. *a creaking door*

3. *Answers will vary.*

Reading 3B: "Lullaby," pp. 168-69, Lesson 115
Literature: developing awareness of the author's use of imagery

A Miracle at Sea

▸Read the Story

A Storm at Sea

After the five thousand were fed, Jesus sent His disciples to the ship. He remained on shore to send the multitudes of people away. When they were gone, Jesus went up on a mountain to pray. When darkness came, He was there alone.

The wind began to blow, and storm clouds hid the stars. The little ship, now in the middle of the sea, tossed back and forth in the rough waves. The wind blew harder, and the waves rose higher around the ship. The disciples were afraid.

Late in the night, Jesus went out to the ship. When the disciples saw Him walking on the water, they were even more afraid. They thought that He was a spirit. Then Jesus spoke, telling them who He was. Peter called out, "Lord, if it be thou, bid me come unto thee on the water."

Jesus answered, "Come."

And when Peter climbed over the side of the ship, he went to Jesus, walking on the water.

▸Choose and Write

Choose from the story the colored word that is a synonym for each word below. Write the answer in the space given.

1. small _____little_____

2. night _____darkness_____

3. land _____shore_____

4. followers _____disciples_____

5. crowds _____multitudes_____

6. talked _____spoke_____

7. boat _____ship_____

8. started _____began_____

9. frightened _____afraid_____

10. sea _____water_____

11. covered _____hid_____

12. crawled _____climbed_____

Reading 3B: "Lullaby," pp. 168-69, Lesson 115
Vocabulary: recognizing synonyms

Reading the Signs Carefully

Name

▶Read and Think

Pioneer girls were often trained to leave signs to help aid in their rescue if they were ever captured by Indians. Bits of torn cloth, heelmarks, or broken twigs were messages to the careful, alert rescuers.

Sometimes, in reading, there are words you may have trouble understanding. Other words in a sentence can give you clues. These clues may help you find the meaning of the "trouble word." All you have to do is be a careful, alert reader.

▶Choose and Color

Read the message. Choose the correct meaning of each word in dark print. Color the correct meaning yellow.

Daniel,

I was **stalking** (following, a vegetable stem) a deer in the forest when I heard someone coming. I **concealed** (laid, hid) myself behind a tree. Soon a group of Indians came into sight. They had three girls with them. One of the girls was your daughter, Jemima.

The girls looked as if they had **roved** (eaten, traveled) all night. The Indians had cut off the girls' skirts to the knee. Their legs were **swathed** (wrapped, soaked) with rags to protect them from scratches.

The girls were walking straight and tall. Jemima was leaving signs as you had taught her to do. The **traces** (signs, stars) should be easy to follow.

As the Indians passed out of sight, I could hear the girls singing a **canticle** (hymn, canteen). I will **pursue** (follow, pattern) them through the forest. When you get this message, hurry! We can rescue the girls in the night while the Indians **slumber** (flee, sleep).

The Deerhunter

Symbols of Friendship

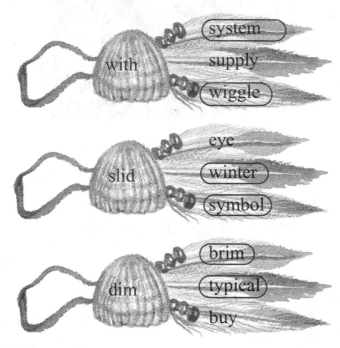

▶Choose Two

Circle the two words on the feathers that have the vowel sound of the word on the shell.

ĭ
- gymnast
- hymn

with
- (system)
- supply
- (wiggle)

myth
- (riddle)
- (symptom)
- dye

slid
- eye
- (winter)
- (symbol)

twist
- rely
- (Scripture)
- (syllable)

dim
- (brim)
- (typical)
- buy

gym
- (little)
- (crystal)
- try

▶Write Them

Use words you circled to fill in the blanks.

1. A heart is a ___**symbol**___ of true love.

2. God is pleased when we memorize ___**Scripture**___ .

3. A bad cough is one ___**symptom**___ of a cold.

4. In science we are learning about our solar ___**system**___ .

5. Do you know the answer to this funny ___**riddle**___ ?

6. My cup of hot chocolate is full to the ___**brim**___ .

7. This glass is so clear it sparkles like ___**crystal**___ .

8. It is very cold in the ___**winter**___ .

Reading 3B: "Captured!" pp. 170-76, Lesson 116
Phonics: using letter-sound association: /ĭ/ as *i* in *sin* and as *y* in *hymn*

Where and When?

Setting:
Putting the story in a place and time.

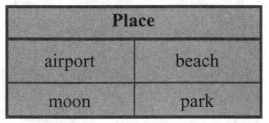

▶Read and Decide
Read the paragraphs. Choose the place and time from the boxes. Write them on the blanks. Draw a picture for each one.

Place	
airport	beach
moon	park

Time	
1942	2192
1492	1992

1. Whitecaps raced the seagulls to land. The setting sun shone on the white sails of the three ships. The warm water swirled around the feet of the men as they landed boats on the sand. Their leader, a man named Christopher Columbus, walked toward the people on land. He believed he was on an island near India, so he called the people Indians.

   Place ___**beach**___   Time ___**1492**___

2. Owen bounced up and down as he waited for the school rover. He did not feel nearly as heavy as on Earth. He gazed across the dark gray plains marked with small craters. He had become used to seeing animals only in special areas of the underground city, but he still missed trees and flowers.

   Place ___**moon**___   Time ___**2192**___

The Warriors' Path

▶Read and Answer

Read the paragraph and use the map to answer the questions.

Daniel Boone had heard about a mysterious Indian path leading through Ohio. Cherokee warriors had made the trail while searching for their northern Shawnee enemies. Now Daniel Boone followed the Warriors' Path from Martin's Settlement to a long valley. There he discovered the Cumberland Gap. This became the one and only way for settlers to go from Kentucky to lands farther west.

Key

– –	state lines
★	Cumberland Gap
▲	Indian towns
••••	Warriors' Path
〰	rivers
■	settlements

1. Near what lake does the Warriors' Path end?

   Lake Erie

2. What is the name of the French fort in what is now the state of Michigan?

   Fort Detroit

3. Name one Indian town from the map.

   Little Chillicothe or Rocky Point

4. Name two settlements in what is now the state of Kentucky.

   Boonesborough

   Harrodsburg

5. The settlement closest to the Cumberland Gap is

   Martin's Settlement

6. What is the name of the river near the Cumberland Gap?

   Cumberland River

7. What is the name of the other river?

   Ohio River

Reading 3B: "Captured!" pp. 177-80, Lesson 117
Study skills: using a map key; locating places on a map

On a Definition Mission

Name

> **sign** | sīgn | — *noun* 1. A mark or symbol that stands for a word. *The subtraction sign let James know what to do on his math paper.* 2. Evidence or proof. *There was no sign that anybody had been there.*

A sample sentence helps you better understand the meaning of a word.

▸Read and Circle

Read each sentence and the definitions below.
Circle the footprint beside the correct meaning.

1. Betsey tore the *lace* from her handkerchief and dropped it on the trail.

    lace | lās | A delicate fabric of fine threads woven in an open pattern.

    lace | lās | A cord or string drawn through holes or around hooks to pull or tie opposite edges together|.

2. Jemima brushed away cobwebs as her captor led her through the *cane*.

    cane | kān | A stick used for help in walking.

    cane | kān | A hollow, woody plant stem.

3. Daniel Boone followed the *tracks* in the snow.

    track | trăk | A mark left behind by something moving.

    track | trăk | The rail or rails on which a train or trolley moves.

4. Far behind them the girls could hear a faint *bark*.

    bark | bärk | The outer covering of the trunks, branches, and roots of trees.

    bark | bärk | The short, gruff sound made by certain animals.

5. "I'll always *mind* Father from now on," Jemima thought.

    mind | mīnd | To obey.

    mind | mīnd | The part of a human being that thinks.

6. The girls pushed with their paddles, making the boat *rock*.

    rock | rŏck | A hard material that is formed naturally and is of mineral origin.

    rock | rŏck | To move back and forth or from side to side.

Reading 3B: "Captured!" pp. 181-84, Lesson 118
Vocabulary: recognizing word meaning from context; using a dictionary entry

197

Graphic Information

▶Look and Compare

The following pictograph shows the number of different animals available for the Shawnee Indians to hunt in their territory. Each arrowhead stands for one hundred.

▶Think and Write

Read the pictograph carefully and answer the questions below.

Animals									
buffalo	⬆								
deer	⬆	⬆							
beaver	⬆	⬆	⬆	⬆	⬆	⬆	⬆		
turkey	⬆	⬆	⬆	⬆	⬆				
rabbit	⬆	⬆	⬆	⬆					
squirrel	⬆	⬆	⬆	⬆	⬆	⬆	⬆	⬆	⬆

key: ⬆ = 100

1. Which animal is most plentiful in this area?

   squirrel

2. Are there more rabbits or more beavers in the area?

   beavers

3. Which animal is hardest to find in the area?

   buffalo

4. How many deer live in the area?

   200

5. Do you think there is enough water available? Why or why not?

   Yes; there are many beavers (or many animals).

6. Does this area have mostly large animals or mostly small animals?

   small animals

7. Do you think the Indians should remain in this area or move to another? Why?

   Answers will vary.

Reading 3B: "Captured!" pp. 181-84, Lesson 118
Study skills: reading a pictograph

A Telling Title

Name

▶Choose One

Each paragraph below tells something that happened in
the story "Captured!" Read each paragraph. Then select a possible
title for the chapter in which each paragraph might belong.

One Sunday afternoon, Jemima Boone and
Betsey and Fanny Calloway went canoeing. Their
canoe struck a sandbar. Five Indians jumped
out of their hiding place and captured the girls.

_____ Ferocious Animals
_____ An Official Welcome
_____ Special Friends
__X__ Indian Captives

The Indians led the girls north toward a
Shawnee village. Jemima used the sun, moss,
and vines to help her tell what direction they
were walking.

_____ Preparing for Travel
_____ Toward the Ocean
__X__ Signs from Nature
_____ Climbing the Mountain

The next morning the girls washed at the
stream. Jemima told them how to mark the
trail. The girls broke twigs, dug heel prints into
the mud, and left scraps of cloth behind them.

__X__ Sharing a Secret Plan
_____ Spring Water
_____ Fishing at the Stream
_____ Looking for Seashells

All day long the Indians covered up the
girls' tracks. So Jemima acted like her foot
hurt too badly to walk without falling over.
The Indians put her on a pony. But she kept
falling off it to break more twigs.

_____ A Gracious Indian
_____ Healing Jemima's Foot
__X__ A Pony for Jemima
_____ Sudden Surprises

Reading 3B: "Captured!" pp. 185-88, Lesson 119
Comprehension: relating a possible chapter title to story facts and details

199

Puz•zle Jug•gle

▶Decide and Write

Write the words on the blanks in the correct list.

1. pickle
2. bugle
3. rifle
4. kettle
5. cackle
6. tackle
7. purple
8. candle
9. crinkle
10. bramble
11. sparkle
12. knuckle
13. trickle
14. freckle
15. twinkle
16. prickle
17. speckle
18. chuckle

> A word ending with a consonant plus *le* is usually divided before the consonant.

> A word ending with *ck* plus *le* is divided after the *ck.*

a n	k l e
b u	g l e
r i	f l e
k e t	t l e
p u r	p l e
c a n	d l e
c r i n	k l e
b r a m	b l e
s p a r	k l e
t w i n	k l e

b u c k	l e
p i c k	l e
c a c k	l e
t a c k	l e
k n u c k	l e
t r i c k	l e
f r e c k	l e
p r i c k	l e
s p e c k	l e
c h u c k	l e

Reading 3B: "Captured!" pp. 185-88, Lesson 119
Structural analysis: applying syllable rule 3: words ending with a consonant + *le* are divided into syllables before the consonant (exception: words ending with *ckle* divide after the *ck*)

The Boonesborough Bulletin

▶Read and Write

Read a paragraph of this newspaper from Boonesborough.
Finish writing the news as you think it happened.

The Boonesborough Bulletin

While Mr. Boone Was Gone

Last week three young ladies of our town, the Calloway girls and Jemima Boone, were kidnapped by Indians. As soon as they discovered that the girls were missing, Samuel Henderson and Mr. Boone started tracking them. Because an Indian attack was feared, extra guards were posted around the settlement. Two days after the men left . . .

Answers will vary.

Reading 3B: "Captured!" pp. 189-93, Lesson 120
Comprehension: predicting outcomes
Composition: writing a news article

Daniel Boone

▶Write a Rhyme

Write on the lines the ending that matches the story and completes the rhyme.

To splash in the sea and to play in the foam.	My daughter and friends from the Indian brave.	My wife and my son from a bear in a cave.
I followed the girls who left clue after clue.	I followed a bear who attacked my canoe.	I wanted to find a new land for a home.

Daniel Boone,
Daniel Boone,
Why did you roam?

_____

I wanted to find a new land for a home.

_____

_____

Daniel Boone,
Daniel Boone,
What did you do?

_____

I followed the girls who left clue after clue.

_____

_____

Daniel Boone,
Daniel Boone,
Whom did you save?

_____

My daughter and friends from the Indian brave.

_____

_____

Reading 3B: "Captured!" pp. 189-93, Lesson 120
Word work: discriminating rhyming words
Comprehension: recalling story details

▶Circle One

Circle the letter of the phrase that best completes the sentence.

1. Matthew thought Old Blue was acting funny because he smelled
   A. a mountain lion.
   B. the soup.
   C. Indians.

2. Pa kept Sooner as a puppy because he thought that
   A. Sooner would be a lot like Blue.
   B. the girls would enjoy a new dog.
   C. Blue needed a companion dog.

3. Pa was disgusted with Sooner because Sooner
   A. wouldn't grow up.
   B. loved Samantha too much.
   C. was too much like Old Blue.

4. Ma thought the Indians were restless because
   A. spring was coming soon.
   B. autumn had come late.
   C. it had been a hard winter.

5. When Pa left with Matthew, he said to Ma,
   A. "Wish us luck."
   B. "Pray for us."
   C. "We might never come back."

6. Ma told the girls that they would pray and
   A. huddle quietly together.
   B. cry.
   C. quote Bible promises.

▶Match Them

Match the verses and references. You may need to use your Bible.

__C__ I Peter 5:7

__B__ Psalm 56:3

__A__ Psalm 4:8

A. I will both lay me down in peace, and sleep: for thou, Lord, only makest me dwell in safety.

B. What time I am afraid, I will trust in thee.

C. Casting all your care upon him; for he careth for you.

▶Write One

Choose one verse from above that you could remember in a frightening time and write it in the space below.

_____
_____ Answers will vary. _____
_____
_____

Reading 3B: "Sooner or Later," pp. 194-98, Lesson 121
Comprehension: recalling facts and details; relating story content to personal experience

203

Who's in the Doghouse?

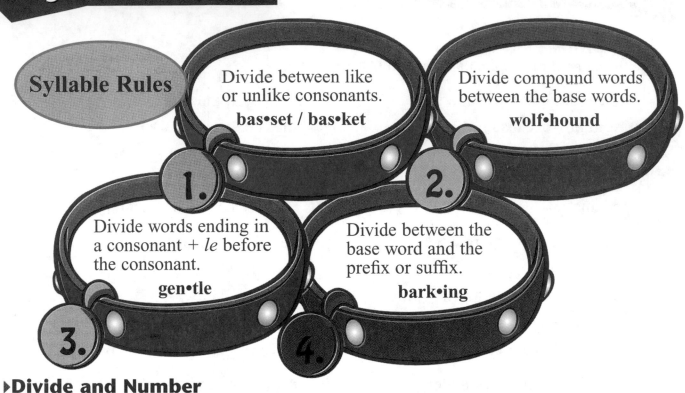

Syllable Rules

1. Divide between like or unlike consonants.
   bas•set / bas•ket

2. Divide compound words between the base words.
   wolf•hound

3. Divide words ending in a consonant + *le* before the consonant.
   gen•tle

4. Divide between the base word and the prefix or suffix.
   bark•ing

▶ Divide and Number

1. Write each word on a doghouse and divide it into syllables with a dot.
2. Write the rule number for each word on the doghouse doorway.

3	tur•tle
4	clean•est
1	scam•per
4	en•joy

turtle

sudden

cleanest

dustmop

scamper

rushes

enjoy

cradle

1	sud•den
2	dust•mop
4	rush•es
3	cra•dle

Reading 3B: "Sooner or Later," pp. 194-98, Lesson 121
Structural analysis: demonstrating mastery of the four syllable rules by dividing words into syllables and identifying the rules used

204

Mountain Lions vs. Coonhounds

Name _____

▶Choose and Write

Choose the correct answer from the box and write it in the blank.

1. *Coonhound* is to *protect*
   as *mountain lion* is to ____**attack**____.

2. *Coonhound* is to *bark*
   as *mountain lion* is to ____**howl**____.

3. *Coonhound* is to *friend*
   as *mountain lion* is to ____**enemy**____.

> enemy
>
> attack
>
> howl

▶Choose and Mark

Check every sentence that tells something that the story taught about the <u>mountain lion.</u>

_____ 1. It is a gentle animal.

✓ 2. It can live in cold regions.

✓ 3. It has sharp claws and teeth.

_____ 4. It is about the size of a mouse.

_____ 5. It is a friend to man.

✓ 6. It attacks other animals.

Check every sentence that tells something that the story taught about the <u>coonhound</u>.

✓ 1. It whines and scratches to let its master
     know it wants to come indoors.

✓ 2. It has a strong sense of smell.

_____ 3. It likes to eat fish.

✓ 4. It can be watchful even while lying down.

✓ 5. It can fight fiercely and bravely.

_____ 6. It is friendly to cows.

Reading 3B: "Sooner or Later," pp. 199-204, Lesson 122
Comprehension: finding relationships between pairs of words; drawing inferences

205

A Picture Mixture

picture
future
posture

/chər/

▶Circle and Write

1. Circle the syllable in each word that sounds like *ture* in *adventure*.
2. Write the correct word under each picture.

_____
Scripture

furni(ture)

pic(ture)

_____
vulture

_____
signature

Scrip(ture)

tempera(ture)

_____
furniture

_____
temperature

vul(ture)

signa(ture)

_____
picture

pun(ture)

_____
puncture

▶Read and Circle

Circle the words that have the /chər/ sound in the sentences below.

1. The boys had (ventured) across the (pasture) when they heard the horrible scream of the (creature.)

2. The girls dreaded (capture) by the Indians and quoted (Scripture) verses to calm their fears.

Reading 3B: "Sooner or Later," pp. 199-204, Lesson 122
Phonics: decoding words with the schwa syllable *ture* as /chər/ in *nature*

How's Your Memoreeeee?

Name _____

▶Decide and Circle

If the statement is true, circle the frog.

1. Oliver and Charles were on a mission for the queen.

2. It was Oliver's idea to build the balloon.

3. The Island creatures liked working together.

4. The sea dogs followed the Island Rule carefully.

5. Boofo was slow to agree to help build the balloon.

6. The *Westing Wind* was a pirate ship.

▶Choose and Circle

Circle the letter of the best answer.

1. When Oliver said, "Sorry to burst your balloon, Charles," he meant,
   - a. "I'm sorry I popped your balloon."
   - b. "I'm sorry your idea won't work."
   - c. "Your balloon idea was very silly."

2. When Boofo croaked, "Juicy flies. Thanks!" he was referring to
   - a. berries the mice had thrown to him.
   - b. his breakfast of large flies.
   - c. a gift of fruit flies from the mice.

3. Why was the cave especially good for the mice?
   - a. It was dark so they slept well.
   - b. There were no tree frogs in it.
   - c. There were no bugs in it.

Reading 3B: "Mice of the Westing Wind," pp. 206-12, Lesson 124
Comprehension: recalling facts and details; drawing conclusions

207

Be a "Cheese Wiz"

e x c **e** l l e n t
c y l i n d e r
i m a **g** i n e
g e n e r a l
c i d e r
g e o l o **g** y

▶Circle and Draw

Circle each word below that has a soft *g* or *c*. Color a yellow cheese wedge on each *e*, *i*, or *y* that signals the soft *g* or *c* sound.

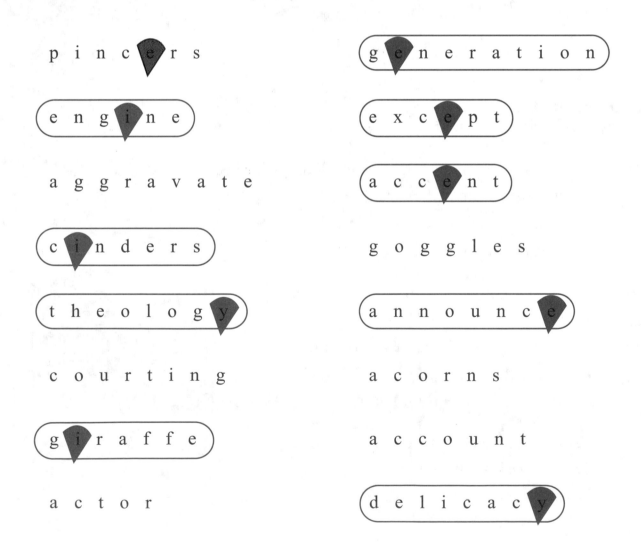

p i n c **e** r s

(e n g **i** n e)

a g g r a v a t e

(c **i** n d e r s)

(t h e o l o g **y**)

c o u r t i n g

(g **i** r a f f e)

a c t o r

(**g** e n e r a t i o n)

(e x c **e** p t)

(a c c **e** n t)

g o g g l e s

(a n n o u n c **e**)

a c o r n s

a c c o u n t

(d e l i c a c **y**)

Reading 3B: **"Mice of the Westing Wind,"** pp. 206-12, Lesson 124
Phonics: applying soft *c* and *g* generalization to multisyllable words: *c* as /s/ and *g* as /j/ when followed by *e, i,* or *y*

Create a Creature

▶Think and Write

It's your turn to be a creative writer! Take some time to think of another creature who could help build the balloon. Then describe him and his special job on the lines below.

Answers will vary.

_____

_____

_____

_____

_____

_____

_____

_____

_____

_____

_____

_____

▶Draw It

Draw your creature as he helps build the balloon.

Reading 3B: "Mice of the Westing Wind," pp. 213-17, Lesson 125
Comprehension: thinking creatively
Composition: writing creatively

209

Really Fanciful Balloons

▶Read It

ballast

basket

Ballooning is an exciting sport in which the competitors race to see who can fly the farthest and stay in the air the longest. The pilot mans his balloon from the **basket.** He must know how to control his balloon using several different techniques. For instance, he can raise the balloon one of two ways.

He can drop a sand- or water-filled bag called a **ballast** to make the balloon lighter or he can fill the **gas bag** with more hot air by using his **propane burner.** To lower his balloon he opens a valve which releases the hot air from the bag. The pilot can only hope to land in a specific place. The landing of a balloon is as unpredictable as the wind that drives it!

gas bag

propane burner

▶Label It

Draw lines from each label below to the correct part of the fanciful balloon.

basket

ballast

gas bag

Reading 3B: "Mice of the Westing Wind," pp. 213-17, Lesson 125
Study skills: reading and labeling diagrams

Name

▶ Choose and Write

Choose the correct word for each clue and write it in the puzzle.

balloon
Westing Wind
Emilio
Boofo
Charles
Oliver
hummingbirds
leaves
gondola
gecko
slime

ACROSS

4. He designed the balloon.
6. They stitched the leaves together for the balloon.
8. The mice flew off the Island in this "basket."
10. He brought bark for the gondola.
11. He thought it would take too long to make a balloon.

DOWN

1. He played his shell drums during the meal.
2. This was the name of the pirate ship.
3. The crabs cut these to the right size.
5. He was the lead bat.
7. This lifted the mice over the mountain.
9. Frogs used this to waterproof the gondola.

Reading 3B: "Mice of the Westing Wind," pp. 218-22, Lesson 126
Comprehension: recalling facts and details

The Island Rule

▶Read the Poem

Read the following poem from the book, *Mice of the Westing Wind.*

"The Island Rule"

Bat in thee cave, an' fish in thee school
   Nobody break-a thee Island rule!
Frogs hopping 'round on mo-skee-to fuel
   Nobody break-a thee Island rule!

Hummin'bird here an' crab een thee bay
   Nobody break-a thee Island rule!
Want to be wise, then hear what it say
   Nobody break-a thee Island rule!

"First you can give, and then you can take."
   Nobody break-a thee Island rule!
Sea dogs come, make a beeg mistake!
   Nobody break-a thee Island rule!
   Nobody break-a thee Island rule!

▶Think and Write

Think about how the "Island Rule" would work in your home or classroom. Write a paragraph telling why you think it would or would not work.

Answers will vary.

Reading 3B: "Mice of the Westing Wind," pp. 218-22, Lesson 126
Comprehension: predicting outcomes
Composition: writing a paragraph explaining predicted outcomes

Comparing Kids

Name _____

▸Compare and Decide

Teacher direction recommended for this page.

Read the storyteller's words in the clouds. In the chart below write
the storyteller's words next to Nora's sentence about the same topic.

Storyteller's Words

> I heard only the tall silence of the pines.

> air so cold it made my teeth ache

> I did not know of any bird with such sharp white feathers.

Nora	Storyteller
1. She said, "Look! Clouds!" and blew into the air—	*air so cold it made my teeth ache*
2. She said, "Look! Feathers!" She pointed out white, angled frost on windows.	*I did not know of any bird with such sharp* *white feathers.*
3. "Listen," she said, at the beady repeats of the chickadee.	*I heard only the tall silence of the pines.*

▸Think About It

Which character has the brightest outlook on life ?

_____ *Nora* _____

▸Write About It

On your own paper, write how you would feel if you had to move
to a strange new home right before Christmas.

Reading 3: "Chickadee Winter," pp. 223-25, Lesson 127
Comprehension: comparing dialogue to evaluate character attitude

Getting Down to "Bird" Business

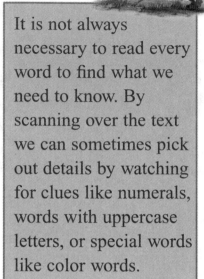

▶Scan and Find

Scan over the paragraphs below to find the answers to the questions. Write the answers in the blanks.

1. How big does a black-capped chickadee usually get? (Scan the paragraph about chickadees for sentences with numerals.)

   4 ¾ to 5 ¾ **inches long**

2. What are the two colors on a roadrunner? (Scan the roadrunner paragraph for color words.)

   **brown and white**

3. Name one place where you could find a chickadee. (Scan the chickadee paragraph for words with uppercase letters.)

   **Alaska, Canada, or the United States**

It is not always necessary to read every word to find what we need to know. By scanning over the text we can sometimes pick out details by watching for clues like numerals, words with uppercase letters, or special words like color words.

The **black-capped chickadee** usually grows from 4¾ to 5¾ inches long. It has a noticeable black cap and bib and white cheeks. It sings *chick-a-dee-dee-dee* or *dee-dee-dee* and often whistles *fee-bee-ee*. It is found in Alaska, Canada, and the northern half of the United States, where it nests in shade trees and thickets. An unusually friendly bird, the chickadee is often found visiting feeders and suet bags.

The **roadrunner** is actually a kind of cuckoo bird that runs on the ground. It is usually 20-24 inches long and is streaked brown and white with a long, white-tipped tail. At the end of its long legs are feet with four toes—two forward and two backward. It sings a song like a dove with 6-8 low *coo*s. It can be found from the southwestern United States to central Mexico. This bird feeds on snakes, insects, and small animals.

Reading 3B: "Chickadee Winter," pp. 223-25, Lesson 127
Study skills: using textual clues to scan for specific details

See It, Hear It

▸Find and Write

Look at each page given to find what the author says that helps you see or hear something in the story. Write it in the blank.

(p. 223) The narrator remembers that in New Mexico when the sun went down the

whole world was bronze .

(p. 225) When Nora ran to the feeder to make the chickadees fly, they flew in

a thrum of wings .

(p. 228) When Grandpa fed the chickadees, they

flicked around him

.

(p. 227) When the narrator followed Grandpa to the barn, the snow went

scruncha-grunch .

(p. 227) When Grandpa milked the cows, the narrator could hear them

snuffling

through their hay-dinners.

As Cheery As a Chickadee

▶Read and Choose

Read the phrases below. Find a simile in the story that uses each phrase. Write the phrases in the correct blanks.

like a dust storm

as dry as the desert

like the pines in the snow

like a Christmas sky

like a drift

1. **(p. 226)** The dumplings were

   _____

   as dry as the desert

   _____.

2. **(p. 227)** Grandfather was always quiet,

   _____

   like the pines in the snow

   _____.

3. **(p. 225)** The birds swirled toward him

   _____

   like a dust storm

   _____.

4. **(p. 227)** Grandfather's eyes were ice blue

   _____

   like a Christmas sky

   _____.

5. **(p. 227)** Grandfather's hair was white and smooth

   _____

   like a drift

   _____.

Reading 3: "Chickadee Winter," pp. 226-29, Lesson 128
Literature: understanding the meanings of similes

O Christmas Tree, O Christmas Tree

Name _____

▶Decorate the Tree

Match the clue in each box with the answer on the tree. Write the letter from the clue in the correct ball on the tree.

called Nora a "chickadee"
E

icy branches clicking on the window pane
A

live tree decorations that moved and sang
F

decorated the tree one time in his whole life
B

Jack — E

said nothing about her concern for the furniture
G

H — Nora

G — Grandmother

F — chickadees

Jack's first home
C

B — Grandfather

C — New Mexico

clear Popsicles
A

blue spruce — D

the kind of tree Grandfather cut out of the woods
D

was eager to decorate the tree
H

▶Think and Write

At the end of the story when Jack said, "No, but we'll get used to it," was he just talking about getting used to the Christmas tree? What else could he have been talking about? Write your ideas on your own paper. **Answers will vary.**

Reading 3: "Chickadee Winter," pp. 230-36, Lesson 129
Comprehension: recalling facts and details; inferring information from character dialogue

217

Personification Identification

▶Choose and Answer

1. Put an X beside the sentence in each pair that uses **personification**.
2. Answer the questions.

> *I never knew that cold could paint on glass.*

1. _X_ I felt only keen-eyed stars watching down and down.

   ____ The stars shone brightly in the night sky.

   What was personified? _____ *stars* _____

   What were they doing that a person can do? _____ *watching* _____

2. ____ Everywhere I looked it was white.

   _X_ I saw only whiteness stretching out forever.

   What was personified? _____ *whiteness* _____

   What was it doing that a person can do? _____ *stretching out* _____

3. _X_ The lights from inside pushed the dark a little way out from the house.

   ____ The lights made the dark house brighter.

   What was personified? _____ *lights* _____

   What did they do that a person can do? _____ *pushed* _____

Reading 3: "Chickadee Winter," pp. 230-36, Lesson 129
Literature: recognizing personification in realistic prose

The Real Reason

Name

▶Circle One

Circle the letter of the choice that answers the question.

1. The princes knew a person who would always pray even if they made a law against prayer. Who was it?

   a. King Darius
   b. Daniel
   c. Jerusalem

2. Why did the princes plan to cast anyone who broke the law into the lions' den?

   a. They wanted someone to show his bravery.
   b. They wanted someone to tame the lions.
   c. They wanted someone to be eaten by the lions.

3. Why did the princes ask the king to make the law?

   a. They were jealous of Daniel.
   b. The people wanted them to make the new law.
   c. They were honest men who loved their king.

4. Why were the princes watching for Daniel to begin praying?

   a. They wanted to learn to pray.
   b. They wanted to catch him breaking their law.
   c. They wanted to see if he prayed on his knees.

5. When the king found out that Daniel had been praying, why did he spend the whole day talking with his counselors and wise men?

   a. He wanted to save Daniel from the lions' den.
   b. He wanted to forget about what he had done to Daniel.
   c. He wanted to visit with those friends.

6. Why did the king run to the den as soon as the morning dawned?

   a. He hated Daniel.
   b. He wanted to be sure his word had been obeyed.
   c. He cared about Daniel.

7. Why did the king order the princes to be thrown into the lions' den?

   a. They deserved to be punished.
   b. They lied about the king.
   c. The lions needed to be fed.

Reading 3: "Den of Lions," pp. 237-43, Lesson 131
Comprehension: inferring the motives of characters

Delivered from Lions

> **PSALM 37:40**
> *And the Lord shall help them,*
> *and deliver them.*

▶Find and Write

Locate the following verses in the Bible.
Write the correct word or words on each line.

Daniel 6:27   . . . who hath delivered Daniel from the

_____

_____ *power of the lions* _____ .

_____

Psalm 107:6   He delivered them out of their _____ *distress(es)* _____ .

_____

Psalm 116:8   For thou hast delivered my soul from _____ *death* _____ , . . .

Psalm 34:4   He heard me, and delivered me from

_____

_____ *all my fears* _____ .

_____

Proverbs 11:8   The righteous is delivered out of _____ *trouble* _____ . . . .

▶Think and Write

What "lions" can the Lord deliver you from?

_____

_____ *Answers will vary.* _____

_____

_____

Reading 3B: "Den of Lions," pp. 237-43, Lesson 131
Study skills: locating verses in the Bible

A Particular Pet

▸Write About It

Choose one of the following.

1. Write about your pet. Tell how you got it, how you care for it, and what makes it special to you.

2. Write about an unusual kind of pet that you would like to have. Think of a name for it and tell why you would give it that name.

3. Write about an animal at the zoo or a fun time you have had playing with a pet.

Answers will vary.

_____

_____

_____

_____

_____

_____

_____

_____

_____

_____

_____

_____

_____

_____

Reading 3B: "A Lamb's Tale," pp. 244-52, Lesson 132

Composition: writing a description

221

A Very Colorful Continent

►Read About It
Read the paragraph.

The continent of South America is full of colors! The people themselves wear bright-colored clothing. Tropical birds show off the brilliant colors the Lord has given them. The red deserts, blue oceans, and green tropical forests demonstrate our Creator's great love of beauty.

►Use the Map
Use the map and compass rose to follow the directions below.

1. Color the country directly west of Suriname orange.

2. Circle the number that tells how many countries the Andes Mountains pass through.

   1   ④   10

3. Color Rico's country yellow.

4. Color the desert region of Argentina red.

5. Draw the symbol for a country capital next to Brasilia.

   _____

6. Brasilia is the capital of what country? _____ *Brazil* ___

7. What body of water is north of South America?

   _____
   Caribbean Sea
   _____

Caribbean Sea

Guyana   **Guyana = orange**
Venezuela   Suriname
   French Guiana
Colombia
Ecuador
yellow
Peru
Brazil
Andes Mountains
Brasilia •★
Bolivia
Paraguay
Chile
Andes Mountains
Argentina
Uruguay
red
Atlantic Ocean
N
W   E
S

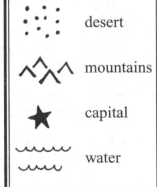

⋮⋮⋮   desert

⋀⋀⋀   mountains

★   capital

〰〰   water

222

Rico Had a Little Lamb

Name

▶Circle the Letter

Circle the letter of the phrase that best completes the sentence.

1. Rico prayed for
   a. many shoes to shine.
   b. the lamb to get well.
   c. a good potato crop.

2. Rico believed the Lord would
   a. help the lamb get well.
   b. provide medicine.
   c. give him a different lamb that wasn't sick.

3. Rico and his mother
   a. didn't want the lamb.
   b. decided to give the lamb away.
   c. trusted God and tried their best to help the lamb.

4. Rico thought the lamb would
   a. help grind the corn.
   b. give him a new blanket.
   c. give his mother a new skirt.

5. Rico was
   a. thoughtful.
   b. selfish.
   c. lazy.

6. Mercy was very unhappy because
   a. Rico went away every day.
   b. she had to be penned up.
   c. she missed her mother.

7. Rico's shoeshine business was good because
   a. many people came by.
   b. there were many colors of shoes.
   c. his muscles began to ache.

8. Business was good at the vegetable stand because
   a. Rico's mother liked vegetables.
   b. many tourists traveled the road.
   c. there were many vegetable stands in town.

9. When Mercy was dying, Rico's father said that
   a. God could not heal Mercy.
   b. God did not care about Mercy.
   c. God chose not to heal Mercy.

10. The vet offered the lamb to Rico because
    a. he was tired of caring for it.
    b. it was sick.
    c. its mother had died.

Reading 3B: "A Lamb's Tale," pp. 253-60, Lesson 133
Comprehension: relating one story detail to another; recalling facts and details

223

Catching the Clues

Were you surprised when Mercy died at the end of the story? Did you expect that to happen? Often an author will give you clues throughout a story to prepare you for what will happen at the end. Let's see if you caught the clues.

▶Read and Circle

Read the question on the baseball. Circle the glove with the best clue to what will happen to Mercy.

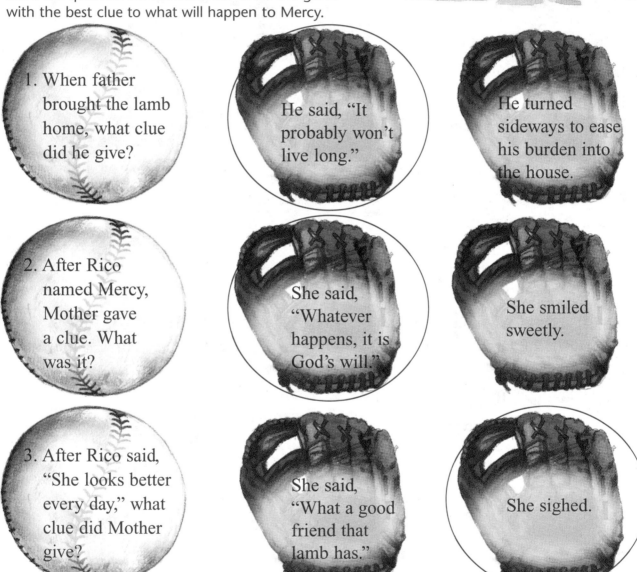

1. When father brought the lamb home, what clue did he give?

He said, "It probably won't live long."

He turned sideways to ease his burden into the house.

2. After Rico named Mercy, Mother gave a clue. What was it?

She said, "Whatever happens, it is God's will."

She smiled sweetly.

3. After Rico said, "She looks better every day," what clue did Mother give?

She said, "What a good friend that lamb has."

She sighed.

▶Think and Write

Throughout the story, one character was always very positive.

Who was he, and why do you think he wouldn't give up on Mercy? *Rico; He loved Mercy.*

Write about it on your own paper.

Reading 3B: "A Lamb's Tale," pp. 253-60, Lesson 133
Comprehension: identifying the author's use of foreshadowing to make the outcome believable

Writing Sounds

Some words sound just like the action they describe.

▶Read, Circle, and Color

1. Read the poem. Circle the rhyming words at the end of each pair of sentences.
2. Read the poem again and color yellow the words that you think sound like an action.

Answers may vary.

This page is not intended for grading.

Chasing the Fly
by Eileen Berry

There's a fly in the house—whiz, buzz!
But now that you're looking, he's not where he was.

There he goes past the lamp with a whoosh!
Get him with this newspaper, please—swoosh!

Missed him again. There he is on the clock!
He's at half past three—see him there? Tick, tock!

You've almost got him; I'm sure I'm not wrong.
He's still on the clock, but—oh, dear—BONG!

The chime scared him off. He's headed this way.
I'll try to swat him if he'll only stay.

He's still in the air. If only he'd stop!
Look, he's down on the table—snap, pop!

He's too quick for me. Oh, wait, take a look!
There he is, crawling up the page of your book.

This shouldn't be hard; you've got him, don't jerk!
Just close up the book—slam, squash! Good work.

Word Pictures

▶Read and List

List the words chosen by the poet/artist to create the "poem picture."

_____

wooly

_____

floppy (ears)

_____

white   _stubby (tail)_

_____

▶Choose and Circle

Choose and circle three more words that could have been used in this "poem picture."

(chattery)

slow

(furry)

scary

(frisky)

slimy

▶Choose and Create

Now it is time for you to become the poet/artist. Use List A to create an old, tired dog or use List B to create a frisky puppy.

List A
brown
lazy
whimpering
scratching
hairy

List B
brown
bouncy
yipping
tumbling

226

Name _____

▸**Read and Answer**

Read the question and answer it using
a complete sentence.

1. How do you think the people felt about having to meet in secret?

   _____
   Answers will vary.
   _____
   _____

2. How would you feel if your father had been arrested and might
   be put to death for his faith in Christ?

   _____
   Answers will vary.
   _____
   _____

3. According to the description of the messenger boy on pages 262
   and 263, how did he feel while delivering his message?

   He was afraid. His eyes showed fear. His red cheeks, his gasping breath,

   and his hurting side show that he ran very fast.

4. How would you feel if you were Mr. Havers, watching the spider
   from your hiding place?

   _____
   Answers will vary.
   _____
   _____

5. How do you think Mr. Havers felt right after the men left?

   _____
   Answers will vary.
   _____
   _____

Reading 3B: "A Curtain of Spun Silver," pp. 262-65, Lesson 135
Comprehension: thinking critically and appreciatively about character feelings and actions

Saved by a Spider

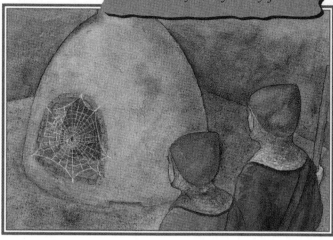

▶Read and Circle

Read each sentence. Circle the word in each sentence that answers each question.

1. The congregation rose to leave as Mr. Havers hummed the closing hymn (thoughtfully.)
   - What word describes how Mr. Havers hummed?

2. (Silently) the congregation hurried to their cottages in the nearby villages.
   - What word describes how the people hurried home?

3. Mr. Havers grabbed his Bible, shut the door (softly,) and dashed into the woods.
   - What word describes how Mr. Havers closed the door?

4. Mr. Havers slipped into an empty malt house and (quickly) crawled into an old kiln.
   - What word describes how Mr. Havers crawled into the kiln?

5. Soon a spider began (carefully) spinning a web across the doorway of the kiln.
   - What word describes how the spider spun its web?

6. (Suddenly) the door burst open, and heavy boots tramped across the floor of the malt house.
   - What word describes how the door burst open?

7. After the men left, Mr. Havers (gratefully) thanked the Lord for His protection.
   - What word describes how Mr. Havers thanked the Lord?

▶Think and Write

Why were the men searching for Mr. Havers? Write your answer on the lines below.

Archbishop Sheldon wanted to arrest him for holding church services.

Reading 3B: "A Curtain of Spun Silver," pp. 262-65, Lesson 135
Literature: focusing on the author's use of adverbs
Comprehension: recalling facts and details

Name

▶**Order Them**

Read the four steps a spider follows when making a web. Study the pictures.
Write the number of the step under the picture that matches it.

4

2

1

3

1. The spider anchors the web in place between branches or another surface.

2. The spider uses non-sticky thread to connect the long cables and the lines of the web.

3. The spider spins non-sticky thread in spirals around the cables, starting at the middle of the web.

4. The spider spins sticky thread from the outside in to the middle.

▶**Circle It**

Circle the correct answer.

1. All spiders make silk.
   a. True
   b. False

2. Each spinneret makes a different kind of thread.
   a. True
   b. False

3. A spider won't get stuck on his web because
   a. he doesn't step on the sticky threads.
   b. his feet have a special protection.

4. How long does it take to weave the average web?
   a. less than an hour
   b. at least one day

Reading 3B: "The Web Weavers," pp. 266-69, Lesson 136
Comprehension: interpreting pictures literally for sequence of events; recalling facts and details

229

A Closer Look

▸Read and Write

Read the paragraph. Use the words in bold print to label the diagram.

God designed the spider for hunting by giving him special features that aid him in capturing his prey. At the end of his body are small **spinnerets** for making threads. These are located on the rear part, or **abdomen.** His eight feet are specially designed to walk on the sticky web. He is usually equipped with four pairs of **eyes** that enable him to see in many different directions. Two **pincers** help him handle his prey once caught. At the tips of the pincers are little **fangs** that inject poison into the victim for the final kill. Though small, the spider has all the necessary equipment to survive.

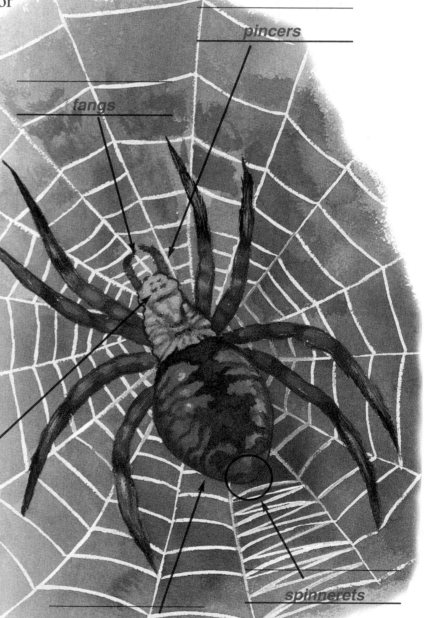

pincers

fangs

eyes

spinnerets

abdomen

Reading 3B: "The Web Weavers," pp. 266-69, Lesson 136
Study skills: demonstrating understanding of written information by labeling a diagram

Picture Windows

▶Draw It

In each window, draw a picture of the sky described in the line of poetry below the window.

> Imagery is words used to create pictures in your mind.

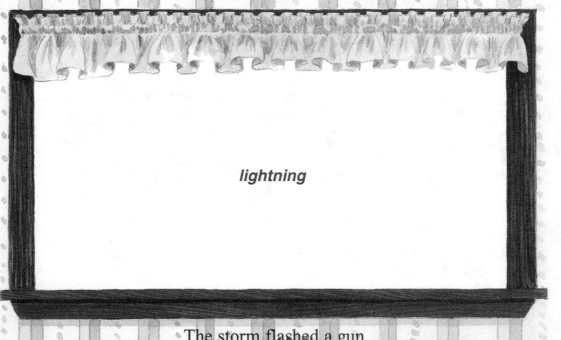

lightning

The storm flashed a gun.

animal-shaped clouds

The animal-clouds marched one by one under the tent of the sky.

Reading 3B: "Under the Tent of the Sky," pp. 270-71, Lesson 137
Comprehension: interpreting imagery in poetry

231

Circus in the Sky

▶Circle and Draw

1. Read each word in the clouds and circle the base word.
2. Draw a flash of lightning (like an accent mark) above every base word.

cloud•y

catch•es

re•fill•ing

word•less

un•break•able

care•ful

droop•y

dis•like

mis•lead•ing

quick•ly

kind•ness

strong•er

un•fold•ed

tall•est

a•sleep

im•prove•ment

Reading 3B: "Under the Tent of the Sky," pp. 270-71, Lesson 137
Structural analysis: applying the accent generalization: in words with affixes, the accent falls in the base word (un•lock´•ing)

Is That a Fact?

Name

▶Read and Write

Read the following sentences. If the sentence is a fact about a
dolphin, write *fact* below the sentence. If the sentence is an opinion
about a dolphin, write *opinion* below the sentence.

1. A dolphin is a mammal and breathes air.

   fact

2. Dolphins and eels both live in the water.

   fact

3. The dolphin's "nose" is on top of its head like a whale's.

   fact

4. Dolphins jump and play because they are happy.

   opinion

5. Dolphins are friendly and have been trained by man.

   fact

6. Even though dolphins can kill a shark, they rarely attack people.

   fact

7. Dolphins are the most unusual pets in the world.

   opinion

8. A dolphin is a prettier animal than a lamb.

   opinion

9. Dolphins are fun to watch.

   opinion

10. The sonar system in a dolphin is better than the sonar in our ships.

    fact

11. The dolphin's tricks are better than any other animal's tricks.

    opinion

▶Write and Draw

Pretend you have taken pictures of different animals in action.

1. Think of a better word to replace the word given.
2. Draw a picture of your animal doing the action.   *Answers will vary.*

1. The dolphin (swam) _____
   through the pool, chasing the ball.

2. The cat (walked) _____
   up to the mouse and pounced on it!

4. The monkey

   _____

3. The elephant (took) _____
   the tree out of the ground with its trunk.

   (went) _____

   from tree to tree playfully.

234

Reading 3B: "What About Dolphins?" pp. 272-78, Lesson 138
Word work: choosing verbs that describe actions

Ads and Ideas

Name _____

While Monty is looking at ads in the paper about frogs, he finds several other interesting things. Here are some things he clips out and the ideas that cause him to clip them.

▶Read and Match

Read the clippings and Monty's ideas. Match the information in the newspaper with Monty's ideas.

Clippings

1. __B__ For all farmers! Don't miss this bargain! Orbit's animal feed on sale—half price! Squirrels, turkeys, and turtles all love these delicious kernels of special corn mixed with other starchy vegetables. Run to the market for Orbit's brand today!

2. __D__ Are you dirty, hot, and thirsty from all that yard work in this burning heat? Do you feel like you could melt an iceberg? Don't worry. We have a cold, refreshing cola that you are certain to enjoy! New Purple Perky will perk up any hot, thirsty person.

3. __C__ The answers to Friday's puzzle are *curtain, island, carpet, fiction, reverse, explore.*

4. __A__ If you have hornets on your porch, Barber's Bug Spray will take care of them.

Monty's Ideas

A. I wonder if frogs eat hornets.

B. If turtles like it, maybe frogs do too.

C. Mom wanted these answers.

D. Maybe I could sell this drink instead of lemonade.

Reading 3B: "Fremont's Frog Farm," pp. 279-87, Lesson 140
Comprehension: recalling facts and details; matching related ideas; drawing inferences

235

Leapin' Lily Pads!

In compound words, the accent falls on the first syllable.

frog´man

▶Draw and Mark

1. Draw the frog's tongue to the word that is divided correctly.
2. Draw an accent mark over the correct syllable.

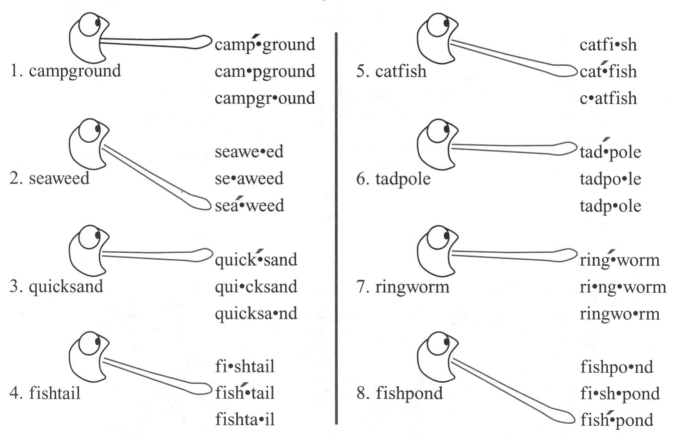

1. campground

   camp•ground
   cam•pground
   campgr•ound

2. seaweed

   seawe•ed
   se•aweed
   sea•weed

3. quicksand

   quick•sand
   qui•cksand
   quicksa•nd

4. fishtail

   fi•shtail
   fish•tail
   fishta•il

5. catfish

   catfi•sh
   cat•fish
   c•atfish

6. tadpole

   tad•pole
   tadpo•le
   tadp•ole

7. ringworm

   ring•worm
   ri•ng•worm
   ringwo•rm

8. fishpond

   fishpo•nd
   fi•sh•pond
   fish•pond

▶Look It Up

Just what exactly is a "frogman"?

Reading 3B: "Fremont's Frog Farm," pp. 279-87, Lesson 140
Structural analysis: applying the accent generalization: in compound words, the primary accent
falls on the first syllable

"Frogword" Puzzle

Name _____

▶Complete the Puzzle

Use the words and clues to fill in the puzzle.

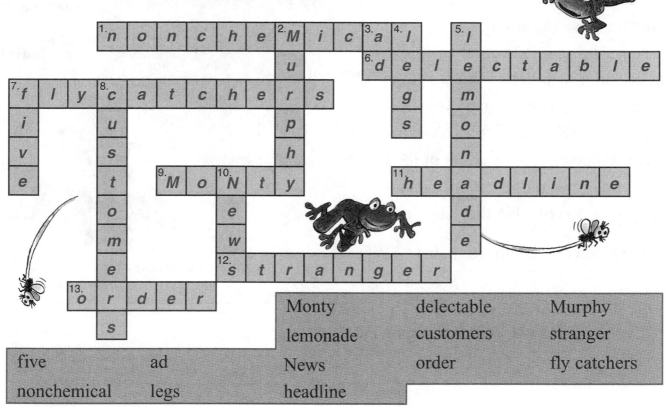

Words:

Monty	delectable	Murphy
lemonade	customers	stranger
five	ad	order	fly catchers
nonchemical	legs	News headline	

ACROSS

1. Scientists looked for a _____ way to kill flies.
6. Monty described the frog legs as _____.
7. Monty decided to sell the frogs as _____.
9. Patti Ann did not want _____ to raise frogs.
11. Monty got the idea about flies from a newspaper _____.
12. A _____ asked to see the frogs.
13. Not one _____ came from Monty's ad.

DOWN

2. Monty tried to sell his frogs to Mr. _____.
3. Monty put an _____ in the newspaper.
4. Mrs. Murphy did not want to cook frog _____.
5. Monty sold _____ before he tried selling frogs.
7. Monty caught twenty-_____ frogs at the pond.
8. The frog upset Mr. Murphy's _____.
10. Monty put his ad in the _Shelbyville_ _____.

Creative Kids

▶**Compare and Answer**

Like Monty, many children find creative ways to earn money.

A graph is a good way to compare information without writing a paragraph. In a circle graph the complete circle stands for the total. Each wedge represents a part of the whole.

Pretend you are the one earning money as described in this circle graph.

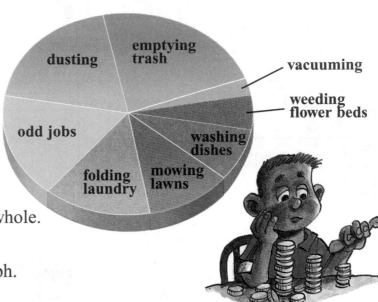

1. What job do you do that helps you earn the most money?

   emptying trash

2. Do you earn more from dusting or from weeding flower beds?

   dusting

3. What three jobs give you less income than mowing lawns?

   vacuuming, weeding flower beds, washing dishes

4. What job could you do to earn about the same amount as doing odd jobs?

   folding laundry

5. What job would you enjoy doing the most?

   Answers will vary.

▶**Think About It**

Which of the two ways, circle graph or paragraph, do you prefer for getting information?

Reading 3B: "Fremont's Frog Farm," pp. 288-92, Lesson 141
Comprehension: relating lesson content to personal experience
Study skills: reading and interpreting information on a circle graph

Name _____

▶True or False?

Write *T* if the sentence is true and agrees with the story.
Write *F* if the sentence includes details that are not in the story.

1. __*T*__ Monty wanted to earn money for a new baseball mitt.

2. __*T*__ He tried to sell lemonade to raise money.

3. __*T*__ Monty read in the newspaper about a restaurant that served frog legs.

4. __*F*__ In the morning he took a fishing pole and bait and walked barefoot down to the pond.

5. __*F*__ Monty kept the frogs in the garage.

6. __*F*__ Monty advertised his frogs on the radio.

7. __*T*__ Monty took his frogs to the Country Kitchen.

8. __*T*__ By accident, the frogs escaped from Monty's box.

9. __*T*__ Monty decided to sell his frogs as fly catchers.

10. __*F*__ After selling frogs to all the neighbors, Monty had enough money for the mitt.

11. __*F*__ Monty had never before seen the man who came to the house for dinner.

12. __*T*__ Before leaving Monty's house, Mr. Bailey gave Monty money to pay for the frogs.

13. __*F*__ Mr. Bailey planned to use the frogs to kill flies.

14. __*F*__ Patti Ann wanted to help Monty begin a frog farm.

15. __*T*__ Monty dreamed of earning a lot of money selling frogs.

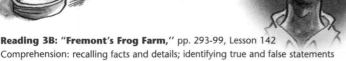

Reading 3B: "Fremont's Frog Farm," pp. 293-99, Lesson 142
Comprehension: recalling facts and details; identifying true and false statements

What'll You Have?

Scanning is looking over information to locate facts quickly. One way to scan is to read only the facts under the topic heading that you are interested in.

Country Kitchen Menu

Main Dishes		*Sandwiches*	
Country Fried Steak	$3.95	Country Ham on a	$1.75
served with:		Hot Biscuit	
Fluffy Mashed Potatoes			
Tender Pole Beans		Roast Beef on	$1.95
		Fresh White Bread	
Crispy Chicken	$2.95		
served with:		*Specialties*	
Golden French Fries		Fried Frog Legs	$4.25
Fresh Coleslaw			
		Desserts	
Beverages		Apple Pie	$0.75
Iced Tea	$0.40	with cheese	$0.95
Fresh Milk	$0.50	Pecan Pie	$0.85
Creamy Buttermilk	$0.60		

▸Scan and Choose

It is time for you to order at the Country Kitchen.
Answer each question using the menu above.

1. What main dish would you like to eat? __*varied*__ Price? __*varied*__

2. What would you like to drink? __*varied*__ Price? __*varied*__

3. What would you like for dessert? __*varied*__ Price? __*varied*__

4. What is the most expensive item on the menu? __*Fried Frog Legs*__

5. What is the least expensive drink available? __*Iced Tea*__

6. Does it cost less to buy apple pie with or without the cheese? __*without*__

7. What kinds of pies are available? __*Apple and Pecan*__

8. Can you get a hamburger at the Country Kitchen? __*no*__

Reading 3B: "Fremont's Frog Farm," pp. 293-99, Lesson 142
Study skills: scanning to find information quickly; reading a menu

Name

▶Read and Answer

Read the story. Answer the questions.

The Farmer's Net and the Stork

One day cranes landed in a field and pecked out many of the kernels of corn that had been planted. The next morning the farmer stretched a net across the ground to catch the robbers as they landed. Each day the net trapped many cranes.

One day a tired stork, who was flying near the cranes, followed them down into the field to rest his weary wings. No sooner had the birds' claws struck the earth than they tangled up in the farmer's net. The birds tried to flap their wings and pull themselves free. But try as they might, none of them escaped. There they stood—trapped—the small flock of cranes and the one stork.

Realizing all too late that he had gotten into the wrong crowd, the stork began to cry, "I flew with the cranes; now I'm caught in their net."

1. Is this story long or short?

   short

2. Name the characters.

   cranes

   farmer

   stork

3. Select a moral that would fit this fable:

   Pride comes before a fall.

   Liars often get caught in their lies.

   Misery loves company.

   You are judged by the company you keep.

   You are judged by the company you keep.

Bony Business

unclean

cleaning

clean

> In words with prefixes and suffixes, the accent is usually in the base word.

▶Color and Mark
1. Color the base word yellow.
2. Draw an accent mark over the correct part of the word.

1. asleep

2. painter

3. actor

4. recall

5. enclose

6. joyful

7. fixable

8. disarm

9. bimonthly

10. fruity

11. boxes

12. misuse

13. unsafe

14. teacher

15. freshest

Reading 3B: "The Greedy Dog," pp. 300-301, Lesson 143
Structural analysis: applying the accent generalization: in words with prefixes and suffixes, the accent usually falls in the base word

Name _____

▶Read and Answer

Read the following directions and write your answers on the lines.

Write four places found outside that a beetle   *Answers will vary.*

might choose for a beetle home.

_____

_____

_____

_____

_____

_____

_____

_____

Write three things that you might use as a
beetle house if you kept a beetle as a pet.

_____

_____

_____

_____

_____

Pretend that you have a pet beetle. How can you
make sure that you will recognize him if he gets out?

_____

_____

_____

_____

_____

Reading 3B: "Forgiven," pp. 302-4, Lesson 144

Comprehension: solving problem situations; relating poetry content to personal experience

What's So Funny?

▶Read the Poem

Read the poem and find out what's so funny.

My Dad's a Secret Agent

My dad's a secret agent.
He's an undercover spy.
He's the world's best detective.
He's the perfect private eye.

He's a Pinkerton, a gumshoe,
He's a snoop and he's a sleuth.
He's unrivaled at detecting
and uncovering the truth.

He's got eyesight like an eagle.
He's got hearing like a bat.
He can out-smell any bloodhound.
He's as stealthy as a cat.

He can locate nearly anything
with elementary ease.
But no matter how he looks and looks
my dad can't find his keys!

Kenn Nesbitt

Now that you've read the poem, did you find out what's so funny?

▶Think and Circle

Read the lines below taken from the poem. Look at the colored
word or words. Circle the correct meaning of the words as they are
used in the poem.

1. He's a Pinkerton, a gumshoe / He's a snoop and he's a sleuth.

   (a.) a detective   b. a sticky shoe   c. a dog catcher

2. He's unrivaled at detecting / and uncovering the truth.

   a. terrible   (b.) the best   c. forgetful

3. He can locate nearly anything / with elementary ease.

   (a.) simple   b. confusing   c. difficult

Reading 3B: "Forgiven," pp. 302-4, Lesson 144
Literature: identifying elements of humor in poetry
Vocabulary: determining the meaning of words through context clues

Name

The Lord Jesus has told us in His Word that we who are saved will be His witnesses to those who are lost. Many people do not even know that they are lost. We must tell them that the Lord Jesus Christ will forgive their sin and save them.

MATTHEW 4:19
*Follow me,
and I will make you
fishers of men.*

▶Draw and Write

1. Draw a fish on every hook that would draw men to the Lord Jesus.
2. At the bottom of the sea, write the words from the hooks that would not help a lost person get saved.

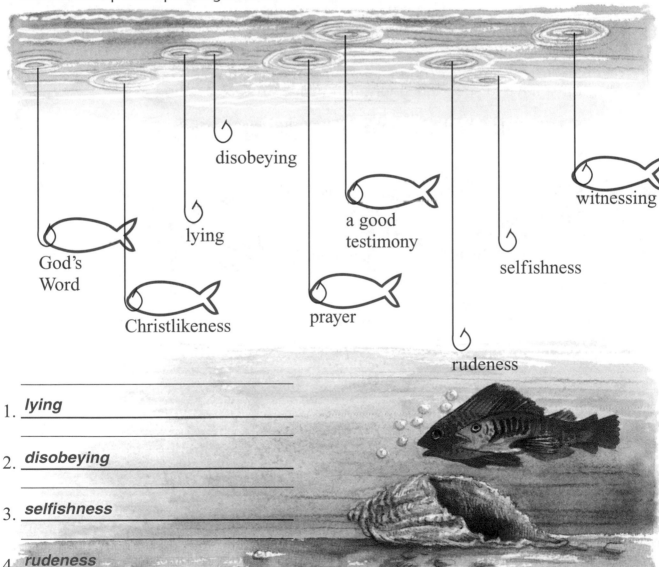

disobeying

lying

a good
testimony

witnessing

God's
Word

selfishness

Christlikeness

prayer

rudeness

1. *lying*

2. *disobeying*

3. *selfishness*

4. *rudeness*

Reading 3B: "A Gift for Uncle Tom," pp. 305-11, Lesson 146
Comprehension: drawing conclusions

Fishing for Opposites

▶Choose and Draw

Draw a fish around the word in the sentence that is
an antonym of the word at the right.

1. Up into the air flew blankets, sheets, and pillows.　down

2. Toby could hear Mother's long skirts swishing angrily.　happily

3. He lifted one corner of the blue blanket.　dropped

4. "Get out from under those blankets," Mother ordered.　over

5. "There's too much to do before your Uncle Tom arrives this afternoon."　after

6. "You'll just have to spend the morning outside."　evening

7. Sighing, he wandered around to the back of the large brick house.　tiny

8. "Ouch!" he exclaimed, hastily pulling his hand out of his pocket.　slowly

9. "Uncle Tom loves fresh fish. I'll catch him the biggest and best one he ever ate!"　spoiled

10. Toby stuffed a fresh hot cross bun with white icing into his jacket pocket.　stale

11. For a while nothing happened. Toby jiggled his fishing line. He pulled a little on the line.　pushed

12. Suddenly, something pulled back.　nothing

13. Toby gave the string a hard yank.　gentle

14. Triumphantly Toby headed home, the fish in his arms and a grin on his face.　frown

246

Fishing for Causes

▶ Think and Write

Answer the questions in complete sentences.

Name _____

1. Why did Toby throw a rag at the chandelier?

   He was trying to help dust.
   _____
   _____

2. What gave Toby the idea of catching a fish for Uncle Tom?

   He found a fishhook in his pocket and remembered that Uncle Tom loved fish.
   _____
   _____

3. What made the cats follow Toby?

   They were hungry and could smell the fish.
   _____
   _____

4. What made Toby suddenly hurry into town with the fish in his jacket?

   He heard the church bells ringing.
   _____
   _____

5. Why did the people begin to sniff the air?

   They could smell the fish.
   _____
   _____

6. Why did the fish begin to smell bad?

   The fish began to smell bad because of the hot weather.
   _____
   _____

Reading 3B: "A Gift for Uncle Tom," pp. 312-17, Lesson 147
Comprehension: identifying cause-and-effect relationships; recalling facts and details

Fishy Business

▶Color and Mark

1. Color the salmon with two-syllable words pink.
2. Divide the two-syllable words with a dot.
3. Place an accent mark over the correct syllable.

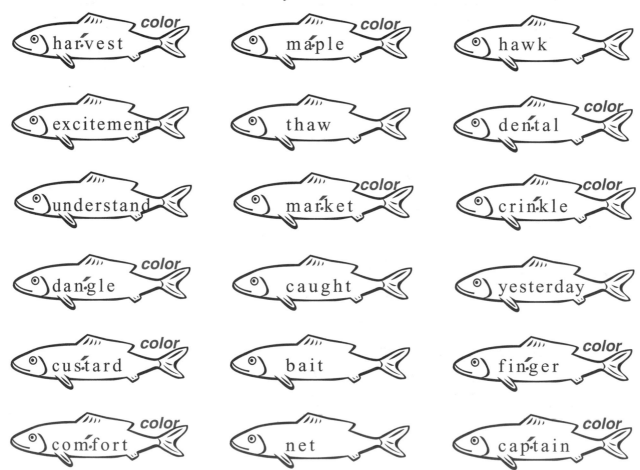

har·vest color

ma·ple color

hawk

ex·cite·ment

thaw

den·tal color

un·der·stand

mar·ket color

crin·kle color

dan·gle color

caught

yesterday

cus·tard color

bait

fin·ger color

com·fort color

net

cap·tain color

Reading 3B: "A Gift for Uncle Tom," pp. 312-17, Lesson 147
Structural analysis: dividing two-syllable words into syllables; applying the accent generalization:
in a two syllable word, the accent usually falls on the first syllable

About the Skill Station Lessons

This section of the worktext presents teaching and practice of each of the major reading subskills.

The pages provide follow-up for the special skill lessons in the Reading 3 teacher's edition.

The first Skill Station lesson (Lesson 3) comes after the first story in the reader.

The pages are not here in the back of the book for you to do at the end of the school year, but rather they are here so that you can find them easily and return to them for reference again and again. As reference material, the pages are not intended to be torn out.

The Shorts Sitting in Closed Syllables

▶**Think About It**

How are these words alike?

just	band	clash	top
get	wink	plug	bell

Each one has a vowel.
Each one ends with a consonant. Some end with two.

Mrs. Short is the vowel found in short vowel words.
Write the five short vowels.

___ ___ ___ ___ ___
_a_ _e_ _i_ _o_ _u_

Look for the Shorts in words.

b u s

h a n d

Mr. Short is the consonant that stands beside her.
Uncle Short is the other consonant that sometimes follows too.
Many letters are consonants. Which consonants would fit here?

h u __

b i __

Answers will vary.

l a __

Short vowels are usually found in closed syllables.

▶Sort Them Out
Write each word in the correct column.

lamp
self
in
pond
chin
glum
trot
pack

_in_

chin

glum

trot

lamp

self

pond

pack

▶Add a Bit
Add more words to these word families.

possible answers: *pest, rest, vest;*
slip, lip, trip;
jump, hump, clump

best
jest

dip
hip

bump
dump

Two Make One

▶Working Together

When some consonants come together they make only one sound.
These pairs can be at the end of a word . . .

ring   cla**ng**   swi**ng**

gong

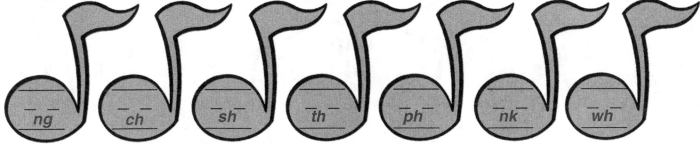

or at the beginning or in the middle.

chant   kit**ch**en   ri**ch**

chink

In the words below are more pairs of consonants that make one sound.
Circle the pairs.

di(sh)   ga(th)er   dol(ph)in   bli(nk)   (w)here

Write all the consonant pairs on the notes.

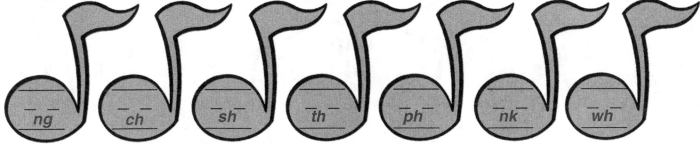

_ng_   _ch_   _sh_   _th_   _ph_   _nk_   _wh_

Some pairs of consonants make only one sound.

252

▶Circle One

Circle the best word to complete each sentence.

1. Sandy knows how to play the ___ .
   checks
   (chimes)
   child

2. At the beach we made instruments out of sea ___ .
   should
   ships
   (shells)

3. I once heard a song played by pushing buttons on the ___ .
   (phone)
   phony
   phrase

4. Music in the sky is called ___ .
   thistle
   they
   (thunder)

5. The baby makes music when she ___ pot lids together.
   wheels
   (bangs)
   drinks

6. The white bird ___ in the tree is singing.
   fresh
   graphed
   (perched)

Reading 3A: Skill Station Day, Lesson 3
Phonics: reading and using words with consonant digraphs (ch, sh, ph, th, ng) in sentences

253

Finding Miss Long

▶Seeing Her

These words have long vowels. Miss Long is pointing to herself. Who is she in each word?

I
me
my

That's me.

When a vowel is at the end of a syllable, it is Miss Long. The vowel makes its long sound.

Remember us?

men
got
in

Here I am again.

me
go
I

Syllables that end with a consonant are closed syllables. Syllables that end with a vowel are open syllables.

See if you can find me in these words.

▶Finding Her

Circle Miss Long in each open syllable.

ⓔ•ven   tⓘ•tle   ⓞ•val
ⓤ•nit   chⓞ•sen   nⓐ•tion

The vowel at the end of an open syllable is long.

254

▶Play the Game

Help Miss Long and the Shorts play ticktacktoe on the grid below.
If the word has Miss Long, mark an *X* above the word.
If the word has the Shorts, mark an *O* above the word.
Write the winner's name at the right above the trophy.

O dent•ed	X cry	O back•stop
X sta•ble	X ri•fle	X ta•ble
X go	O can•dle	O sim•ple

_ _ _ _ _ _ _ _
Miss Long

▶Write the Words

Use the words from the game above to complete the sentences.

1. When the lights went out, Miss Long lit a ____ *candle* ____ .

2. Her dog began to whimper and ____ *cry* ____ in fear.

3. Miss Long set the candle on a ____ *table* ____ .

4. She said to her dog, "I'll ____ *go* ____ see what's wrong with the lights."

5. "Don't worry, fellow, the lights are ____ *simple* ____ to fix."

Reading 3A: Skill Station Day, Lesson 6
Phonics: recognizing the long vowel, open syllable pattern *V*; reading and using
long vowel words in sentences

Friendly Signals

▶Deciding Together

Marker *e* signals that Miss Long is near.
Where is Marker *e* in these words?

brave   choke

grace   tune

drive   strike

t r a d e

Miss Silent also signals that Miss Long is near.
Can you tell which letter Miss Silent is?

brain   screech

frail   coast

eagle   value

t r e a t

These two signals tell you that the other vowel makes its long sound.
Look for the signal; then read the word.

▶Add the Signal

Add Marker *e*.

mad_*e*_   rob_*e*_

rip_*e*_   wok_*e*_

bit_*e*_   slid_*e*_

Add Miss Silent.

ra_*i*_n   co_*a*_t

ma_*i*_n   bo_*a*_t

pa_*i*_n   flo_*a*_t

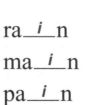

Marker *e* and Miss Silent signal that
the vowel before them is long.

▶Sort Them Out
Write each word from the box in the correct column below.

fruit	he	dive	I
name	dream	throat	slide
go	rule	sail	spy

go	name	fruit
he	rule	dream
I	dive	throat
spy	slide	sail

▶Use a Few
Write three sentences. Use at least one word from each column above. *Answers will vary.*

1.

2.

3.

Reading 3A: Skill Station Day, Lesson 6
Phonics: recognizing the long vowel patterns V, VCe, and VV; writing sentences with long vowel words

257

Bossy R in Charge

▶Choosing Together

barn   horse   herd

stirrup

spur

c a r t

When *r* follows a vowel, it usually influences the vowel's sound. _____

Shade in any spaces that have a Bossy *R* word.   _ _ _ _ _ _ _ _ _

What instrument does Bossy *R* play?   _____ **harmonica** _____

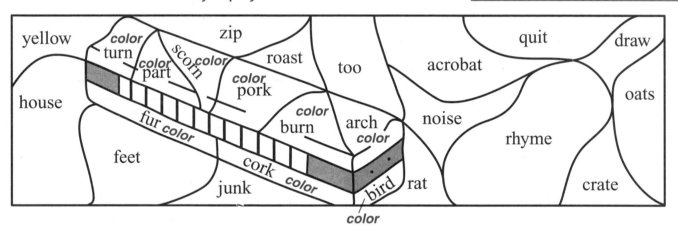

yellow · turn · *color* · *color* · part · scorn · *color* · zip · roast · too · acrobat · quit · draw

house · *color* · pork · color · fur · *color* · burn · arch · *color* · noise · rhyme · oats

feet · cork · *color* · junk · bird · rat · crate

color

Read about the cowboy's actions in the yellow box below. Write one of the following words in the green box to show what each action tells us about the cowboy.

harsh	alert
nerve	normal

If a cowboy does this . . .   We might say . . .

If a cowboy does this . . .	We might say . . .
1. stands up to a bully	He has _ _ _ _ _ _ _ _ _ _ _ **nerve** .
2. sees danger before it happens	He is _ _ _ _ _ _ **alert** .
3. does very odd things	He is not **normal** .
4. gives orders gruffly	He is **harsh** .

▶Think It Through

Read each yellow box.
Write one of the following words in each green space to tell about someone.

darling	hardy	nurse	tardy	smart

If someone . . .   **We say he is . . .**

If someone . . .	We say he is . . .
answers a hard question	_smart_
is late to class	_tardy_
is strong and healthy	_hardy_
is well-loved	_darling_
takes care of sick people	_nurse_

▶Write It Out

Write a sentence using one of the words in the green box above.

Answers will vary.

When *r* follows a vowel, it usually influences the vowel's sound.

© 2000 BJU Press. Reproduction prohibited.

Reading 3A: Skill Station Day, Lesson 9
Phonics: reading words with *r*-influenced vowels: /är/ as in *shark,* /or/ as in *stork,* /ûr/ as in *nurse, sir,* and *her*
Comprehension: describing character traits

259

A Rare Steer

▶Listen and Think

Bossy *R* shows his bossiness in several ways.
Look what he does with these letter combinations.
When *r* follows two vowels it usually influences the sound.

Use the words to complete the sentences about a pet Bossy *R* owns.

deer
peer
cheer
steer

Bossy *R*'s pet is a _____ *steer* _____.

ear
dear
tearful
fear

Once the steer ran away. Bossy *R* was _____ *tearful* _____ until it came back home.

rare
care
share
stare

The steer is in good shape because

Bossy *R* takes _____ *care* _____ of it.

air
chair
fair
hair
stair

The steer once won a blue ribbon at the county _____ *fair* _____.

The judge hung the ribbon in the steer's _____ *hair* _____.

▶Choose a Word

Read each sentence and write the word that best completes it.

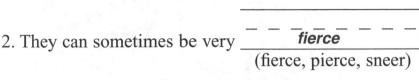

1. Coyotes and men should _____ **beware** _____ of mule deer.
   (tear, beware, here)

2. They can sometimes be very _____ **fierce** _____
   (fierce, pierce, sneer)

3. An angry mule deer will not be _____ **scared** _____ of a coyote.
   (rare, repair, scared)

4. The deer will charge and try to stomp a _____ **careless** _____ coyote that has gotten too close.
   (careless, barely, pear)

5. Men have also been cut by an angry mule deer's hooves or

   _____ **speared** _____ by its antlers.
   (cared, cheered, speared)

6. Mule deer got their name from their big _____ **ears** _____ that look like those of a mule.
   (tears, ears, peers)

7. Explorers who named the deer said that they found the deer

   on the _____ **prairie** _____ .
   (prairie, nearly, airport)

8. The explorers said that the mule deer like _____ **clear** _____ land with few trees.
   (tear, clear, gear)

Cook's Broom and Tool Band

▶Working Together

Read the sentence below. Circle the words that have *oo* in them.

Before Mr.(Cook)got home,
they blew up(balloons.)

What two special sounds can *oo* make?
The o͝o in *Cook* is the short sound of *oo*.
The o͞o in *balloons* is the long sound of *oo*.

Read the names of the items used to make
the instruments. Circle the names of the
items with o͝o. Underline the names with o͞o.

spools	hoop
broom	(wooden) spoons
stool	spoons

▶Finding the Items

Which one of these instruments . . .

can be sat on after it is played?   *stool*

can remove leaves from the sidewalk?   *broom*

can be used to hold thread?   *spools*

can be used to eat ice cream?   *spoons*

can be used to stir oatmeal?   *wooden spoons*

could be the rim from a barrel?   *hoop*

There are two different
sounds for *oo*.

▶ Long or Short?

1. Circle the words that have the ŏŏ sound as in *cook*.
2. Underline the words that have the ōō sound as in *moon*.

(soot)	food	(shook)
(cookies)	(stood)	proof
snoop	(nook)	shoo

▶ Which One?

Use the words above to complete the sentences below.

1. Mr. Cook ___ before his group of musicians.

___ ___ ___ **stood** ___ ___ ___

2. Something smelled good, so Mr. Cook began to ___ around.

___ ___ ___ **snoop** ___ ___ ___

3. Someone must be eating ___, but he didn't know who it was.

___ ___ ___ **food/cookies** ___ ___ ___

4. He thought it was the boy with the broom, but he needed ___.

___ ___ ___ **proof** ___ ___ ___

5. The boy had a black smudge on his face, but it wasn't food. It was ___.

___ ___ **soot** ___ ___

6. Mr. Cook checked every ___ and cranny.

___ ___ ___ **nook** ___ ___

7. At last he found the tray of chocolate chip ___ that Mrs. Cook had made.

___ ___ ___ **cookies** ___ ___ ___

8. The band gathered around the tray. Mr. Cook began to ___ them away.

___ ___ ___ **shoo** ___ ___ ___

9. He ___ his head at them. "Let's play first. Then we'll eat."

___ ___ ___ **shook** ___ ___ ___

Caught Talking!

▸Finding the Connection

How do Katrina's words sound alike?
Circle the different spellings
of the /ô/ sound.

s(a)l t

l(a)u n c h

c(o)s t

c(a)l l

s t r(a)w

▸What Did She Say?

Write some things that Katrina might have said. Use her words from above.

Answers will vary.

One sound sometimes has
several different spellings.

264

▶Choose an Answer

1. Read the following questions.
2. Circle the word that answers the question.

1. What is a sunrise? (dawn) gnaw daunt	2. Where do your teeth rest? jaunt (jaw) floss
3. What is a lobster's arm? caught crawl (claw)	4. What is the opposite of short? talk (tall) salt
5. What is a stretch that your mouth makes? naught brawn (yawn)	6. What is something to drink through? (straw) stalk squaw
7. What is ice on the window? flaw fawn (frost)	8. What is a place to walk between rooms? gloss (hall) halt
9. What is the green carpet in the front yard? (lawn) law halt	10. What keeps something from being perfect? bawl (flaw) saw

Joyful Sound

▸Read and Find

Read the sentence and think about the words.

<u>Troy</u> (bowed) as the people clapped
(loudly) and <u>pointed</u> at him.

Circle two words in the sentence above that contain the /ou/ sound.

Notice the two spellings.

What letter combinations make the /ou/ sound?

_____ow_____ and _____ou_____

Underline two words in the same sentence that contain the /oi/ sound.

Notice the two spellings.

What letter combinations make the /oi/ sound?

_____oy_____ and _____oi_____

▸Read and Write

1. What is something you might *enjoy* doing but *doubt* you will ever be able to do?

   Answers will vary.

2. When we focus on *our disappointment* can we be *joyful?*

   _no_

3. Look *around* for what God has for you and believe,

   "*Thou* wilt shew me the path of life: in thy presence

   is fulness of *joy;* at thy right hand there are pleasures for evermore."

> Some pairs of vowels make special sounds.

▶Add Two

1. Add *ou* to the first word in each phrase. Add *ow* to the second word.
2. Read each pair of words.
3. Choose a pair of words and draw a picture using both words.

1. tr _**ou**_ t   t _**ow**_ el

2. cl _**ou**_ d   cr _**ow**_ n

3. m _**ou**_ se   t _**ow**_ er

4. pr _**ou**_ d   c _**ow**_

Answers will vary.

▶Add Two More

1. Add *oy* to the first word in each phrase. Add *oi* to the second word.
2. Read each pair of words.
3. Choose a pair of words and draw a picture using both words.

1. t _**oy**_   p _**oi**_ nting

2. j _**oy**_ ful   n _**oi**_ se

3. l _**oy**_ al   c _**oi**_ l

4. cowb _**oy**_   c _**oi**_ n

Answers will vary.

Reading 3A: Skill Station Day, Lesson 15
Phonics: reading and using words with *ou, ow* as /ou/ in *hound* and *owl* and *oi, oy* as /oy/ in *coin* and *toy*

267

It's Just a Bump

▶Listen and Think
Listen to the words.
Notice the sound of the light blue syllable.

ba • ton′   no′ • ble

po • lite′   pen′ • cil

a • like′   doc′ • tor

op • pose′   cir′ • cus

Note: As you read the words aloud, be careful not to give unnatural emphasis to the light blue syllable.

This little "bump" sound is like the sound you hear when you bump a balloon in the air. It is called a schwa and looks like this in a dictionary. The schwa syllables are printed in light blue.

ə

▶Find It
Write the vowel letter that is used to spell schwa in these words.

___*o*___ po • lite′   ___*e*___ no′ • ble

___*i*___ pen′ • cil   ___*a*___ ba • ton′

___*u*___ cir′ • cus

▶Color It Blue
Color the schwa syllable in each of these respellings light blue.
Color each syllable with an accent mark dark blue.

offend

/ ə ∘ fend′ /
light blue   **dark blue**

about

/ ə ∘ bout′ /
light blue   **dark blue**

The small vowel sound called *schwa* is heard in many syllables. Schwa never appears in the syllable with the accent mark.

▶Pick One

Use the words in the box to complete the sentences about the picture.

snuggle	towels	breakfast	bacon
awake	around	corners	open

1. Robert and José are camping in a tent with trees all _____*around*_____ .

2. They make their tent by hanging an old blanket over a clothesline

    and holding down the _____*corners*_____ with rocks.

3. They drape big beach _____*towels*_____ over the ends of the tent to make doors.

4. It is fun to _____*snuggle*_____ all night in their sleeping bags.

5. Max, their big dog, stays _____*awake*_____ to protect them.

6. As the sun comes up, José throws _____*open*_____ the tent door.

7. The wonderful smell of _____*bacon*_____ invades the tent.

8. Dad is cooking a special _____*breakfast*_____ for them.

Why Did You Say That?

▶Figure It Out

The consonant letter *c* can stand for /k/ or /s/.
Why does it do that?
Is there a cause?

	Hard				Soft	
cream	closed	cut		Cindy	cereal	cellar
company	can	came		century	cement	cymbals

C usually makes its soft sound
when followed by __*e*__, __*i*__, or __*y*__.

The consonant letter *g* can
stand for /g/ or /j/.
What causes it to change?
Is it the same cause as the *c*?

	Hard				Soft	
going	God	grandma		Gigi	strange	gem
grabbed	gave	game		fudge	giant	gym

G usually makes its soft sound
when followed by __*e*__, __*i*__, or __*y*__.

C and *g* usually represent soft sounds
when followed by *e, i,* or *y.*

▶Choose and Color

Color the word bubbles that have soft *c* or soft *g*.

color cymbals

color mice

color city

cream

cat

color damage

color gentle

gobbled

color gigantic

game

▶Read and Write

Use some of the words above to compose a story.

Answers will vary.

Reading 3A: Skill Station Day, Lesson 22
Phonics: identifying *ce, ci,* and *cy* as patterns signaling soft *c* and *ge, gi,* and *gy* as patterns signaling soft *g*
Composition: writing a story using soft *c* and *g* words

271

Seen but Not Heard

▶Which Ones?

Read the song titles from this song book.
Notice the colored letter combinations.
Which consonant letters are seen but not heard?

Table of Contents

Write the combinations to watch for: | **lk** | **igh** | **kn** | **wr** | **mb** | **lm** |

▶Make an X

Cross out the silent consonant letters in the following words.

c l i m b̸   a̸ l m o n d   w̸ r o n g

c h a l̸ k   k̸ n o c k i n g   k̸ n i f e

l i m b̸   w̸ r a p p e r   s i g̸ h̸

t a l̸ k   c a l̸ m   b r i g̸ h̸ t

Sometimes consonant letters are silent
if grouped with certain other letters.

272

▶Mark the Ones
Color the songbooks that have words with silent consonants on them.

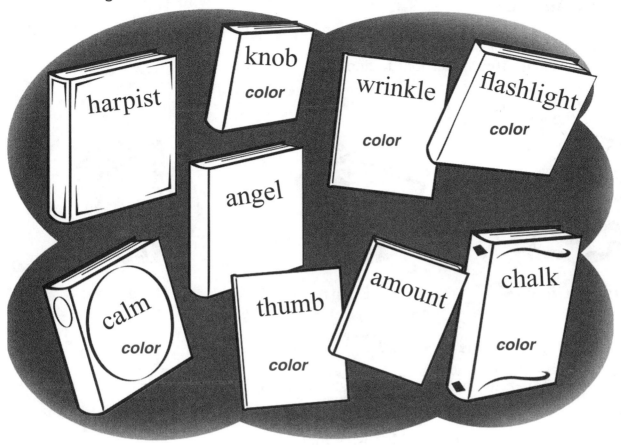

harpist

knob
color

wrinkle
color

flashlight
color

angel

calm
color

thumb
color

amount

chalk
color

▶Finish It Up
Write one word to complete these phrases and titles from hymns.

Knew	_ _ _ _ _ _ _	
1. Kneel	**Kneel**	at the Cross
Knee		

Wren	_ _ _ _ _	
2. Wrist	**Write**	thy new name upon my heart.
Write		

Mighty	_ _ _ _ _ _	
3. Sight	A **Mighty**	Fortress Is Our God
Fight		

walks	_ _ _ _ _ _	
4. talks	He walks with me and **talks**	with me.
calms		

Reading 3A: Skill Station Day, Lesson 22
Phonics: identifying silent consonant patterns: *lk* as /k/, *lm* as /m/, *kn* as /n/, *mb* as /m/, *wr* as /r/, *igh* as /ī/

273

What's the Big Idea?

▶**Thinking About It**

Think about the story "Mr. Deeds's Deed."
What is the main idea of the story?
Circle the answers for these questions to find out.

1. Whom is the story about?

Mrs. McGinty   (Mr. Deeds)   Mr. Henderson

2. What is special about the character?

She is a bad driver and hits the produce stand.

(He goes out of his way to help Mrs. McGinty.)

He owns the produce stand that Mrs. McGinty hit.

3. Put the two answers together.

What is the main idea of "Mr. Deeds's Deed"?

_____

Mr. Deeds goes out of his way to help Mrs. McGinty.

_____

_____

_____

To find the main idea, find whom or what the story is about and what is special about that person or thing.

274

▸Choose and Write

1. Read the story.
2. Circle the answers to the two questions.
3. Write the main idea of the story.

Jesus and the Girl

All the people crowded around Jesus. Everyone wanted to see Him. Jairus, a ruler, wondered how he could ever get through the crowd to Jesus. He pressed and pushed and nudged. Finally he reached Jesus and fell down at His feet. "My daughter is only twelve years old, but she is dying," he said. "Please come to my house and heal her."

When they went to Jairus's house, they found that the ruler's daughter had already died. Jesus went into the room and took the little girl by the hand. "Maid, arise," He said. Immediately the little girl sat up. Her parents and the disciples stared as she stood up and walked.

"She is alive!" they exclaimed.

1. Whom is the story about?

(Jesus)   Jairus   the girl

2. What is special about the character?

He had something important to tell Jesus.

(He raised Jairus's daughter from the dead.)

She was dead.

3. What is the main idea of this story?

Jesus raised Jairus's daughter from the dead.

Patterns to Follow

▶Let's Divide

How are these words alike?
They all have double consonants.
Words with double consonants are
divided between those consonants.
Place a dot to divide each word into syllables.

cab•bage apple let•tuce carrot cherries

▶Divide Again

How are the words on the basket alike?
They all have two unlike consonants in the middle.
Words with two unlike consonants are divided
between the unlike consonants.
Write the words on the basket again and
divide them into syllables.

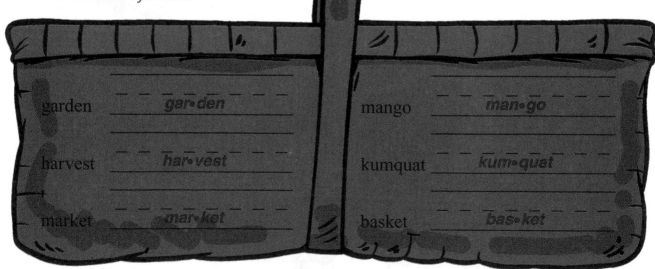

garden	*gar•den*	mango	*man•go*
harvest	*har•vest*	kumquat	*kum•quat*
market	*mar•ket*	basket	*bas•ket*

Divide words into syllables between
like or unlike consonants.

▶Mark the Spot

Draw a line under the two middle consonants.
Put a dot between the syllables.

t i m·b e r

b e t·t e r

l i s·t e n

f i n·g e r

b a s·k e t

s w a l·l o w

s u m·m e r

c o f·f e e

p o w·d e r

▶Think and Write

Use a word from above to help you think of a good deed
you could do to help someone. Then write a sentence
about it, using the word from above.

Answers will vary.

Reading 3A: Skill Station Day, Lesson 28
Structural analysis: dividing words into syllables between like and unlike consonants in *VC/CV* pattern

277

Realistic or Fanciful

▶Deciding Together

Think about each of these stories from your reading book.
Circle the correct word to tell what type of story it is.

Story Title	Type of Story	
"The Singing Knight"	realistic	(fanciful)
"Music in Your Heart"	(realistic)	fanciful
"Trumpets and Pitchers"	(realistic)	fanciful
"An Instrument for God"	(realistic)	fanciful
"Song Signals"	(realistic)	fanciful
"The Coyote's Song"	realistic	(fanciful)
"The Amazing Mozart"	(realistic)	fanciful

▶Add Some

Add two realistic elements and two fanciful elements to the picture.

Stories that could happen are called *realistic*.
Stories that could not happen are called *fanciful*.

▶Finish the Tales

Read and finish each story. Remember if the story is realistic to include only realistic characters and events. If the story is fanciful, include something fanciful.

Yesterday all the birds in the forest heard about a music contest. They all wanted the honor of winning. Dove had a beautiful voice and the other birds expected her to win the contest. But Dove was a humble and kind bird. Dove knew that Blue Jay was very sad because he could not sing well.

_____

_ _

_____*Answers will vary but should include fanciful elements.*_____

_ _

_____

_ _

_____

_ _

_____

Mr. Hamil, the handyman, knew it was almost time to go home. He hammered the last nail into the new steps he had built for Mrs. McDonald and gathered his tools. As he stood up to leave, he saw Mrs. McDonald wandering around her yard. Mrs. McDonald was holding a new bird feeder and was looking for a place to hang it up.

_____

_ _

_____*Answers will vary but should include only realistic elements.*_____

_ _

_____

_ _

_____

_ _

_____

Two Words in One

▶Find and Mark

What is a *compound word*?
Circle the compound words in these sentences.

1. Dad has special plans for the (weekend.)

2. We are going to a (baseball) game!

3. My little brother is talking about (popcorn) and (peanuts.)

4. I am thinking about (fastballs) and (strikeouts.)

> Compound words are two words in one.

▶Listen Together

Read this list of baseball compound words.
Divide the words into syllables by placing a dot between the base words.

base•ball   dug•out   grand•stand

short•stop   bull•pen   out•field

Clap the syllables as you read the words aloud.
Notice that one syllable gets a stronger beat (or accent) than the other.
Which syllable is accented in all these baseball compound words?
Put an accent mark above the last letter in the first syllable.

▶Think and Write

Use the words above to answer the questions.

1. What do we call the part of the *field* that is *out* beyond the bases?

    _ _ _ _ _ _ _ _
    outfield

2. What do we call the *stand* where spectators sit to cheer for the teams?

    _ _ _ _ _ _ _ _ _ _
    grandstand

3. What do we call the area (or *pen*) set aside for the relief pitchers to wait and warm up?

    _ _ _ _ _ _ _
    bullpen

Two-syllable compound words are divided between their two base words. In a compound word the accent is on the first base word.

▸Find and Divide

1. Read the story.
2. Find and circle seven compound words.
3. Color yellow each accented syllable in the compound words.

grape•vines

The Promised Land

Moses gathered twelve men. "Go to the mountains. Travel around and find out about the people, the cities and the land."

As the men traveled, they were amazed at the riches they saw. From a lookout they watched tall men farm the land. They saw huge walled cities, and on the way home they stopped to cut huge bunches of grapes from grapevines.

When the men returned to camp, all were eager to hear of the new land. Joshua and Caleb told of farmlands rich with milk, honey, and fruit. But ten of the men were afraid. "The people are strong," they said. "We are like grasshoppers to these people. No one in our camp is as tall as these men."

When the people heard the report, they were afraid too. A loud outcry went up from the camp.

All during the nighttime, weeping could be heard from the tents. The people were homesick for the land they had left. "We will go back to Egypt," they decided.

God was angry with their lack of faith. He told Moses that now the people of Israel would wander in the wilderness for forty years. Of the men who listened that day, only Joshua and Caleb would ever enter the Promised Land.

▸Think and Write

Use a compound word to answer each question.

1. With what did the ten men compare themselves when they talked about the giants in the land?

   _ _ _ _ _ _ _ _ _ _ _
   grasshoppers

2. How did the people feel about the land they had left?

   _ _ _ _ _ _ _ _ _
   homesick

Reading 3A: Skill Station Day, Lesson 34
Structural analysis: dividing two-syllable compound words into syllables between the two base words;
identifying the accented syllable of the first base word of compound words

281

Same Sounds

▶**Remember the Phrases**
Using the same sound in more than one word is called *alliteration.*
Underline the words that begin with the same sounds.

a <u>horrible</u>, <u>hollow</u>, <u>howling</u> sound

something <u>huge</u> and <u>hairy</u>

a <u>wet</u> <u>whale</u> of a dog <u>wallowing</u>
on top of him

▶**Brainstorm and Write**
Practice being an author who uses alliteration.

1. Write a complete sentence using at least three words beginning with the same sound.

Answers will vary.

2. Write another complete sentence using words that begin with a different sound.

Answers will vary.

Alliteration is using two or more words that contain the same sound. Authors use alliteration to make text more enjoyable.

▶On Your Own

Add words beginning with the same sound as the main word in these phrases to form alliteration. You may add more than one word.

Read	Write
a _____ skateboard	*Answers will vary.* *Note: Beginning letters do not have to be the same; only the sounds have to match.*
a _____ tangle	
a _____ ring	
a _____ letter	
a _____ storm	
a _____ game	

Midnight Riddle

▶**Remember and Show**
Where should these words be divided?

d i n•n e r   n a p•k i n   u n•d e r

Where should compound words be divided?

r a c e•t r a c k   d r u m•s t i c k

▶**Something New**
Where should these words be divided?
How do these words end? Look at the last three letters.
Draw candle flames to divide the words before the
consonant + *le*.

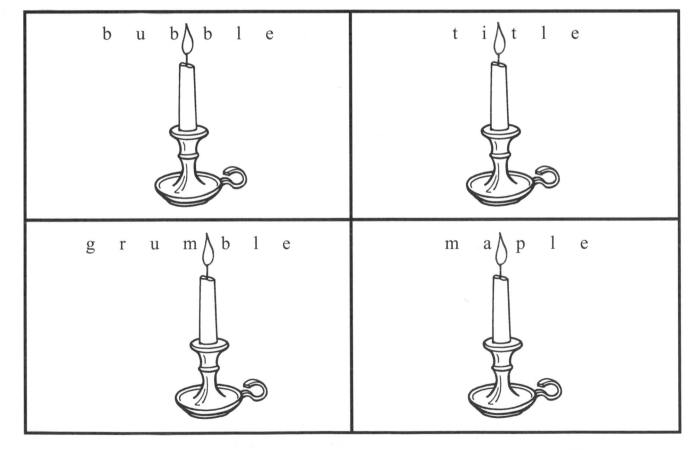

b u b b l e

t i t l e

g r u m b l e

m a p l e

Divide words ending with a consonant + *le*
before the consonant + *le*.

▶Light the Candles

Draw lighted candles to show where these words
should be divided. Place the flame between the correct letters.

p e o|p l e	u n|c l e	l a|d l e
f i d|d l e	j u n|g l e	s e t|t l e
s n i f|f l e	m u z|z l e	f u m|b l e

▶Mark the Spot

Draw dots to show where to divide these words.

s i d e•w a l k	c r u m•p l e	d o l•l a r
t r a c•t o r	g o g•g l e	p o p•c o r n

Reading 3A: Skill Station Day, Lesson 38
Structural analysis: dividing words ending with a consonant + *le* into syllables before the consonant;
applying the syllable rules 1 (*VC/CV* pattern), 2 (compound words), 3 (words ending with consonant + *le*)

Does It Belong?

▶ Mark It Together

Relevant information has some connection with the rest of the information.
Irrelevant information has no connection.
Cross out the *irrelevant* word in each box.

steeple ~~mallet~~ church	swings ~~ink~~ playground	~~books~~ needle thread
car tire ~~duck~~	pencil ~~pond~~ paper	bat ~~library~~ ball

▶ Underline It

Read the following paragraphs. Underline the irrelevant sentence in each one.

Sandy and Bob love visiting their grandfather's farm and doing chores for him. Sandy grooms the horses and helps Grandfather shoe them. Bob feeds the chickens and helps Grandfather milk the cows. <u>I like to feed my cat.</u> Bob and Sandy also like working the butter churn.

Marguerite was given a cute little puppy named Tricks for her birthday. The puppy has thick, golden brown fur. His legs are short and his fat tummy almost drags on the ground when he walks. <u>Their house has six rooms.</u> Tricks has a little pointed nose and big black eyes that always look happy.

Relevant information is related to the rest of the given information. *Irrelevant* information is not related.

286

▶Find Five

Read the story. Underline the one sentence in each paragraph that does not belong in the story.

Plenty for Everyone

My family and I were glad when we arrived at Yellowstone National Park. "Here's a picnic spot just past the woods," Dad said to us as he parked the car. ~~Mark eats cereal for breakfast.~~ "Everyone carry something for Mother."

"Bears are found all through the park," Dad said. "After lunch we'll drive around and look for them." ~~Riding a bicycle is fun.~~

Mother began preparing lunch. Dad, Mark, and I hiked to the lake. Suddenly we spotted three bears. Mark went running back to Mom. "Mom! Come here! We've found some bears!" ~~I played the flute.~~

Mark led Mother back to where Dad and I were standing. ~~Dad likes to play tennis.~~ Mark pointed to two bears, but then he looked disappointed. "There were three bears before, Mom," he said sadly. "One cub is missing."

The cub still hadn't returned by the time we started back. When we got to our picnic spot, I yelled, "Look! There's the missing cub eating our lunch!" ~~My favorite game is baseball.~~ Food lay everywhere. When he heard me yell, the frightened cub ran back to the woods. Our picnic plans had come to an unexpected ending!

Added On

▶Circle and Count

Circle the base word.
Think about the last sound of the base word.
Then circle the number of syllables in the whole word.

(ad d)e d	1	(2)
(c r u s h)e d	(1)	2
(t a l k)e d	(1)	2
(w a n t)e d	1	(2)
(l a u g h)e d	(1)	2
(h o p p)e d	(1)	2
(c a l l)e d	(1)	2
(b l i n d)e d	1	(2)
(g l o a t)e d	1	(2)

▶Talk It Over

Look at each word. Find the base word and the prefix or suffix.
In each row, circle the word that is divided correctly.

1. (re•place)   jud•gment   unp•ack

2. pav•ement   (care•less)   rus•hes

3. fearl•ess   chu•rches   (box•es)

4. sinles•s   fe•arful   (load•ing)

5. ba•tting   (rest•ed)   plan•ted

Divide words into syllables between the base word and the prefix or suffix.

If a base word ends with a /d/ or /t/, the suffix *-ed* will be a separate syllable.

288

▶Circle and Write

1. Circle the base words in the list below.
2. Write the base words on the boxes.

(load)ing

(care)less

(quiet)ly

(fool)ish

(sin)less

(hope)ful

(big)gest

re(place)

un(happy)

(sad)ly

▶Find Them

In each row, circle the word that is divided correctly.

1. (church•es)	hi•ghest	unhapp•y
2. bri•ghtness	(un•tie)	kin•dness
3. (treat•ment)	rep•ay	unp•ack
4. fea•rful	cle•anest	(box•es)
5. unl•oad	(near•ly)	caref•ul
6. (un•lock)	disa•ppear	trus•ting
7. (want•ed)	ag•o	redo•ne
8. tigh•tly	darknes•s	(un•fair)

Reading 3A: Skill Station Day, Lesson 45
Structural analysis: dividing words between the affix and the base word (un•lock•ing);
recognizing that -ed is a separate syllable after /d/ or /t/ (land•ed, lift•ed)

Parts of a Tale

▶**Finding the Problem**

Read the story. Underline two sentences that tell what the problem is.

A Fishy Adventure

"Come on, Wally!" Ferdie called. "If we don't hurry, we'll be late for school!"

The two little fish swam for all they were worth. Then, suddenly, they came face to face with two huge eyes. It was an octopus!

"Look out!" yelled Wally. But it was too late. Two of the octopus's eight long legs curled around the two little fish.

"Wally," Ferdie said, trembling, "we're done for unless we think fast. He's strong, but at least he's not very smart. Try to swim in crazy circles."

With all the strength they had, Ferdie and Wally swam in and out, under and over, behind and in front of the confused octopus. They got those two legs tangled up with his other legs, and before long all eight legs were tied up in knots. The octopus reeled back in a dizzy daze, and he let go of the two little fish.

"Swim for it, Wally," Ferdie yelled, "before he starts chasing us again!"

And they swam as hard as they could, all the way to the schoolhouse. The octopus was too dizzy to chase them until they were far away.

"Boys, it's good to see you here at school so early," the teacher greeted them. "You must have been very diligent in getting started this morning—or else someone encouraged you to move quickly."

"Yes, ma'am," the two fish panted. "Someone encouraged us to move quickly. But we'd rather never get that kind of encouragement again!"

Every story has three parts: a beginning, a middle, and an end. The middle part of the story begins when we learn the big problem.

▶Put in Order

Read the story, "A Fishy Adventure," again. Then
number the events of the story in the correct order.

___3___ Ferdie has an idea to get Wally and himself
loose from the octopus.

___6___ Ferdie and Wally get to school early.

___2___ An octopus appears and nabs them with
two of his arms.

___4___ Ferdie and Wally start swimming in circles.

___1___ Ferdie and Wally start off to school.

___5___ The octopus has to let them go.

▶Draw It Out

Illustrate one event from each section of the
story to match the label for each box.

Beginning	Middle	End

Reading 3A: Skill Station Day, Lesson 53
Literature: recognizing the beginning, middle, and end of a story plot; identifying the inciting moment of the plot
Comprehension: sequencing story events

291

What Did You Say?

▶Hearing It
Read the lists.
How are the words alike?

ant-aunt	berry-bury	peace-piece
cellar-seller	morn-mourn	pray-prey
him-hymn	hall-haul	close-clothes

These pairs are called *homonyms.*

▶Finding More
Write *a, e, i, o,* or *u* in each crossword
puzzle to form a new pair of homonyms.

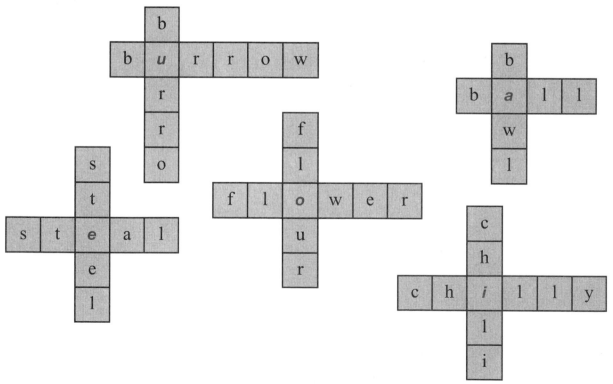

Words that sound alike but have different
meanings and often different spellings are
homonyms.

292

▶Circle Two
Circle the words in each sentence that are homonyms.

1. I (knew) that my brother was buying a (new) bike.

2. My soccer team (won) six games and lost only (one.)

3. Tie a (knot) in your shoestring or you will (not) be able to run well.

4. I paid two dollars for a box of (tacks) and paid ten cents in (tax.)

5. We (ate) our dinner at (eight) o'clock last night.

▶Choose One
1. Read the sentences and the homonyms.
2. Circle the letter for the homonym that belongs in the sentence.

1. Dad made _____ for our dinner last night.
   a. chilly—cool   (b.) chili—a spicy food

2. The teacher asked us to line up in _____ .
   (a.) rows—objects in straight lines   b. rose—a type of flower

3. A scarecrow will help _____ birds out of the garden.
   (a.) shoo—scare away   b. shoe—something worn on the foot

4. The stairs in the old house _____ when someone walks on them.
   a. creek—a stream   (b.) creak—make a squeaky sound

5. The _____ led her fawn deep into the forest.
   (a.) doe—a female deer   b. dough—unbaked bread

6. I was surprised when I _____ the right answer.
   a. guest—a visitor   (b.) guessed—predicted

A Time and a Place for Everything

▶Deciding Together

Listen to the selection that is read. Choose the picture that best fits the description. Describe the setting by answering the questions *where* and *when* about each picture.

Blue Bowl of Sky

Where: _ _ _ _ _ _ _ _ _ _ _ _
on a wagon train

When: _ _ _ _ _ _ _ _ _ _ _ _
spring

White Paint

Where: _ _ _ _ _ _ _ _ _ _
Indian camp

When: _ _ _ _ _ _ _
winter

A Place at the Rail

Where: _ _ _ _ _ _ _ _
riverboat

When: _ _ _ _ _ _
summer

The setting tells us where and when a story takes place.

▶Show the Setting

Read the paragraph. Draw your own picture to show
the setting that is described. Below your picture tell about
the setting by writing where and when the story takes place.

She threw back the furs and tiptoed to the flap. She
pulled the flap back and looked out into a white world.
Snow covered the bare trees in a blanket softer than the
white fox skin Swift Arrow had brought home last week.
It mounded over the rocks and drifted in banks next to the
tree trunks.

Where: _____ *an Indian tepee* _____

When: _____ *winter* _____

go′·ing

a·long′

▶Accent It

Place an accent mark over each accented syllable.

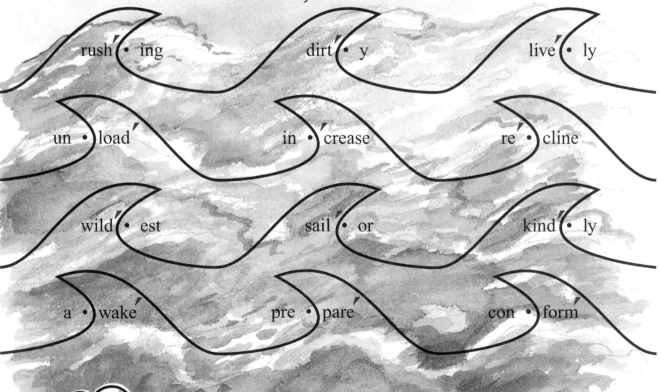

rush′·ing   dirt′·y   live′·ly

un·load′   in·crease′   re′·cline

wild′·est   sail′·or   kind′·ly

a·wake′   pre·pare′   con·form′

In words with prefixes and suffixes,
the base word is accented.

winding	rounded	unloading	cheerful	ahead	headed

▶Fill It In

Use words from the top of the page to complete the sentences.
Divide each word and mark the accented syllable.

1. The *River Queen* sailed down the _____ **wind • ing** _____ river.

2. Then as it _____ **round • ed** _____ the bend, St. Joseph came into sight.

3. Many _____ **cheer • ful** _____ shouts went up from the people.

4. "St. Joe just _____ **a • head** _____," they called.

5. Soon they were _____ **un • load • ing** _____ boxes and bags.

6. They were _____ **head • ed** _____ for the Wild West.

Reading 3A: Skill Station Day, Lesson 60
Structural analysis: applying the accent generalization: in words with prefixes and suffixes the
accent usually falls in the base word

297

Can You Prove It?

▶Let's Talk About It

A *fact* is something that is true.

An *opinion* is what a person thinks about something.

Example: Words in a dictionary are in alphabetical order.

Example: A newspaper is the best source of information.

▶Choose and Circle

Read each sentence. Circle *F* if it is a fact and *O* if it is an opinion.

1. Mr. Winthrop was preparing to print the first copy of the *Cheyenne Weekly*.　　(F)　　O

2. The townspeople were the best writers.　　F　　(O)

3. The desert is the worst part of the country.　　F　　(O)

4. The Candy Cactus requires little water.　　(F)　　O

5. Cactus candy is the most wonderful-tasting candy!　　F　　(O)

6. The Candy Cactus grows in the desert.　　(F)　　O

sense of sight	sense of taste	sense of smell
encyclopedia	sense of touch	sense of hearing
	dictionary	

▶Choose and Write

1. Read each sentence. Circle *F* if it is a fact and *O* if it is an opinion.
2. If it is a fact, choose a source from above that would help to determine that it is true. Write it in the space provided.
3. If it is an opinion, leave the space blank.

1. Ripe strawberries are red.　　(F)　O　　*sense of sight / taste*

2. Asparagus is a delicious vegetable.　　F　(O)

3. A circle is round.　　(F)　O　　*sense of sight / touch*

4. Washington, D.C., is the capital of the United States.　　(F)　O　　*encyclopedia*

5. The smell of baking bread is pleasant.　　F　(O)

6. Dogs are the best pets.　　F　(O)

7. A week has seven days.　　(F)　O　　*dictionary*

8. An ice cube is cold.　　(F)　O　　*sense of touch*

A Spark of Imagination

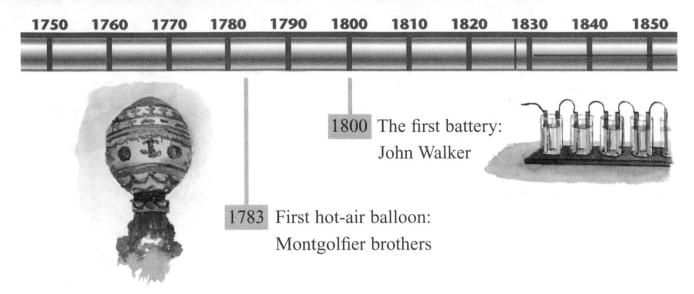

1750 1760 1770 1780 1790 1800 1810 1820 1830 1840 1850

1800 The first battery: John Walker

1783 First hot-air balloon: Montgolfier brothers

▶**Read About It**
Read the story.

Match Maker

John Walker, a British chemist, created the first modern matches in 1827. He took a small splinter of wood and dipped the tip into an inflammable mixture. Once it dried, he scratched the tip over a piece of sandpaper. The heat from the friction created a spark which made a flame. The flame used almost the whole splinter, giving the user plenty of time to light a fire or candle without getting burned. These first matches, called "Lucifers," could be struck on anything rough. This turned out to be a little dangerous, so they are not as common today. The matches that we usually use are made to strike only on the side of the box in order to prevent accidents.

▶**Look and Answer**
Look at the time line at the top of pages 300-301.

1. Place a line on the time line where you think the "Lucifers" belong.
   The date is in the story.

2. Which forty-year part of the time line shows no inventions?
   Circle the correct answer.

   (1830-1870)   1750-1790   1910-1950

1880 Ballpoint pen: John Loud

1903 First airplane flight: Wright brothers

| 1860 | 1870 | 1880 | 1890 | 1900 | 1910 | 1920 | 1930 | 1940 | 1950 | 1960 |

1891 Zipper:
Whitcomb Judson

1926 Television:
John Baird

1876 Telephone:
Alexander Bell

▶Find and Write

Look at the time line at the top of pages 300-301 to find the answers.
Write the answer in a complete sentence.

1. Which flying invention came first?

The hot-air balloon came first.

2. Abraham Lincoln lived from 1809 to 1865. Could he have
zipped up his coat to keep warm in the winter?

Abraham Lincoln could not have zipped his coat.

3. What means of communication was invented 50 years
after the telephone?

The television was invented fifty years after the telephone.

4. How many years after the battery were matches invented?

Matches were invented twenty-seven years after the battery.

Reading 3A: Skill Station Day, Lesson 67
Study skills: sequencing events on a time line; getting information from a time line

301

Rosie to the Rescue

▶Fill It In

Use information from the story to fill in the blanks.

Setting:

_____

___Dust River Gulch___

_____

_____

Main Characters:

_____

a. _____ J.D. _____

_____

b. _____ Rosie _____

_____

c. _____ Billy the Kid _____

Problem:

_____

___J. D. cannot catch Billy___

_____

___the Kid.___

_____

_____

Character who thought of the answer or solution: _____ Rosie _____

Solution: ___J.D. wears a skillet in his hat so that Billy gets knocked out___

___when he runs into J.D.___

Stories begin with a problem and end with a solution.

▶Rosie Again?

Read the story.

Rosie was in a panic! Gruffle O'Buffalo had challenged J.D. to a roping contest in the Okey-Dokey Corral. The crowd gathered as Gruff stated the plan for the competition. First, J.D. would rope Gruff, then Gruff would rope J.D. The one finished in the least amount of time would win. Well, Gruff's gang fixed it so that Gruff got a big head start; and when J.D. finally roped him, his rope snapped! (Now how do you suppose that happened?) When it was Gruff's turn to rope, he came chargin' out of the gate early and roped J.D.'s neck in a flash. Before J.D. knew what was happening, Gruff was stringin' him up in a tree! The townsfolk were horrified!

Just then Gruff gasped as an arrow split through the rope, dropping J.D. back to the ground! Quicker than lightnin', J.D. tied up Gruff with the rope and then turned to wink a "thank you" to the secret archer (guess who!).

▶Be Creative

Think of another way to solve J.D.'s problem. On your own paper, write a new ending paragraph, solving the problem in another way.

Reading 3B: Skill Station Day, Lesson 79
Comprehension: identifying problems and solutions in a story; finding solutions to problems

303

The World of Words

▶Use Your Glossary

1. Find the colored word in your glossary and write the guide words in the boxes.
2. Write the part of speech on the blank beside the word.
3. Find and read the word as it is used in the story in Reader 3B.
4. Write a sentence using the word as the correct part of speech.

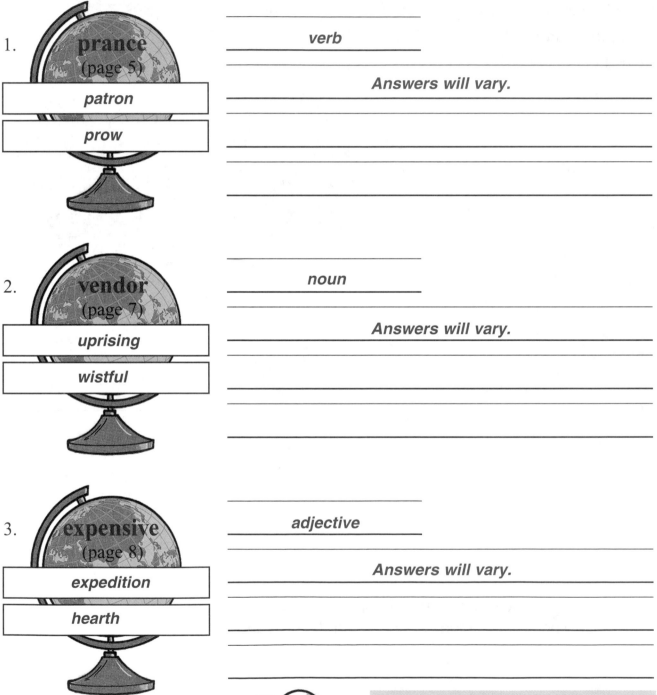

1. **prance**
   (page 5)

   | patron |
   | prow |

   _____ verb _____

   _____
   _____ Answers will vary. _____
   _____
   _____
   _____
   _____

2. **vendor**
   (page 7)

   | uprising |
   | wistful |

   _____ noun _____

   _____
   _____ Answers will vary. _____
   _____
   _____
   _____
   _____

3. **expensive**
   (page 8)

   | expedition |
   | hearth |

   _____ adjective _____

   _____
   _____ Answers will vary. _____
   _____
   _____
   _____

A glossary helps us pronounce and use words correctly.

▶Check It Out

1. Read each sentence and find the colored word in your glossary.
2. Place a check in the box by the correct guide words, the correct pronunciation, and then the correct part of speech.

1. The birds built a nest in the old belfry.

Guide Words	Pronunciation	Part of Speech
☑ bay, celebrate	☐ | bēl´ frī |	☑ noun
☐ acknowledge, barricade	☑ | bĕl´ frē |	☐ adjective

2. Missionaries often travel to **outlying** parts of the country.

Guide Words	Pronunciation	Part of Speech
☐ hesitate, luxury	☑ | out´ lī ing |	☑ adjective
☑ mandolin, parchment	☐ | out´ ling |	☐ adverb

3. Anna watched the doctor **cradle** her brother in his arms.

Guide Words	Pronunciation	Part of Speech
☑ company, dependent	☐ | crāt´ l |	☐ noun
☐ chandelier, communicate	☑ | krād´ l |	☑ verb

4. Father paid the porter for his services.

Guide Words	Pronunciation	Part of Speech
☑ patron, prow	☐ | pō´ trə |	☐ adjective
☐ mandolin, parchment	☑ | pôr´ tər |	☑ noun

Reading 3B: Skill Station Day, Lesson 79
Study skills: identifying parts of a glossary; getting information from a glossary

305

Whom Do You Know?

▶Tell What You Know

Identify the person in the picture. List several facts about that person.

FACTS

_____

Answers will vary.

_____
_____
_____
_____
_____
_____
_____
_____
_____
_____
_____

▶Find Out

If you wanted to write a biography about George Washington,
which of the following would you do? Circle the correct answers.

1. Talk to George Washington himself.   Yes   (No)

2. Talk to members of George Washington's family.   Yes   (No)

3. Read something George Washington wrote about himself.   (Yes)   No

4. Read what others have said about George Washington.   (Yes)   No

A biography gives details about a person's life.

▶Read and Reap

Read the following paragraphs and answer the questions below.

Jonathan Goforth and his wife, Rosalind, went to China as missionaries in 1888. Mr. Goforth was 29 years old. For the next 47 years, Mr. Goforth would preach God's Word to the people of China and tell them about Christ.

The Goforths had been in China only a few weeks when a fire burned their house. Almost all the things they had brought from home were lost in the fire. Only Mr. Goforth's Bible and their money were saved. This loss was very hard for his wife, but Mr. Goforth told her that God would take care of them, even in China.

1. When did Jonathan and his wife Rosalind become missionaries to China? _____*1888*_____

2. How old was Mr. Goforth when he went to China? _____*29 years old*_____

3. How many years did the Goforths spend in China? _____*47 years*_____

4. What happened to the Goforths' house? _____*It burned.*_____

5. What was saved from the house? _____*Bible and money*_____

▶Write It

Write a few sentences telling what you think Mr. and Mrs. Goforth might have said to each other after the house burned down.

_____

_____*Answers will vary.*_____

_____

_____

_____

_____

_____

How to Know

▶Read It
Compare the following biographical entries.

Wheat•ley (hwēt´lē, wēt´-), **Phillis.** 1753?-84. African-born Amer. poet whose works include *Poems on Various Subjects* (1773).

[Copyright © 1997 by Houghton Mifflin Company. Text reproduced by permission from *The American Heritage Dictionary, Third Edition.*]

Wheat•ley \\'hwēt-lē, 'wēt-\\, Phillis. 1753?-1784. American poet, b. probably Senegal. Kidnaped and taken as slave to Boston (1761); maid-servant to wife of John Wheatley, Boston; m. John Peters, a free Negro (1778). At age of 13 began writing poetry in English; regarded as a prodigy in Boston; to England (1773), where she achieved great popularity; published *Poems on Various Subjects, Religious and Moral* (1773).

[By permission. From *Merriam-Webster's New Biographical Dictionary* ©1995 by Merriam-Webster, Incorporated.]

▶Compare It
Put an *X* on the line by each fact that is found in both entries.

 ___X___ 1. where Phillis Wheatley was born

 ___X___ 2. a book of poetry Phillis Wheatley wrote

 _____ 3. the man Phillis Wheatley married

 ___X___ 4. how the name *Wheatley* is pronounced

 ___X___ 5. Phillis Wheatley's year of birth

 ___X___ 6. the year Phillis Wheatley's book of poetry was published

The dictionary contains very short biographies of famous people.

▶Read and Record

Read the biographical entries and answer the questions below.

Louisa May Alcott

Johann Gutenberg

Al•cott, Louisa May. 1832-88. Amer. writer and reformer best known for her novel *Little Women* (1868-69).

Bar•nard (bär´nərd, bär-närd´), **Christiaan Neething.** b. 1923. South African surgeon who performed the first human heart transplant (1967).

Car•ver (kär´vər), **George Washington.** 1864?-1943. Amer. botanist, agricultural chemist, and educator who developed hundreds of uses for the peanut, soybean, and sweet potato.

Gu•ten•berg (gōōt´n-bûrg´), **Johann** or **Johannes.** 1400?-68? German printer who is considered the inventor of movable type, using it to print the *Mazarin Bible* (c. 1455).

[Copyright © 1997 by Houghton Mifflin Company. Text reproduced by permission from *The American Heritage Dictionary, Third Edition.*]

1. When was the writer of *Little Women* born? _____**1832**_____

2. What is the middle name of the man who did the first open

   heart surgery? _____**Neething**_____

3. In what year did the man who found many uses for the peanut die?

   _____**1943**_____

4. In what year do we think Gutenberg was born? _____**1400**_____

5. What country was Christiaan Barnard from? _____**South Africa**_____

6. Which two of these people did not live in the 1800s? **Barnard and Gutenberg**

Reading 3B: Skill Station Day, Lesson 87
Study skills: using a biographical dictionary entry to find out details about a person

309

The World's Most Unusual Pyramids

▶Under Construction

Use the information from the article your teacher reads to "build" this pyramid. Use only as many words as there are spaces.

Labs on Top in Training School

train	dogs	to	help	owners

Why?

Paradine	Park	Banter	County

Where?

June	5-9

When?

canine	school

What?

owners

Who?

The first paragraph in a newspaper article gives the most important facts.

▶Read and Build

Read the article below and use the information to "build" the pyramid.
Remember, use only as many words as there are blanks.

Hero Receives Award

_____   _____   _____
pulling   comrade   from

_____   _____
burning   building
Why?

_____ _____ _____ _____
Memorial   Hall   Jackson   County
Where?

_____ _____ _____
Saturday   July   4th
When?

_____ _____
Bravery   Pin
What?

_____ _____
Mr.   Yaplee
Who?

Hero Receives Award

Mr. Yaplee received the Bravery Pin on Saturday, July 4th. The ceremony was held at Memorial Hall in Jackson County. He was awarded the pin for pulling his comrade from a burning building during World War II.

When asked how he felt about receiving the award, he stated, "I was just protecting my friend. Any other man would have done the same." The rescue story can be found in the *Memorial Records Book* under "Heroic Accounts."

Reading 3B: Skill Station Day, Lesson 91
Study skill: reading a newspaper article; identifying the information in the first paragraph of a newspaper article

311

Let's Try Paraphrasing

▶Read and Record

Read the newspaper article below
and record the important details.

Smithville Weekly

| Volume 222, No. 587 | Smithville, Michigan | Monday, March 12, 2001 |

County Science Fair Draws Dozens of Young Scientists

On Thursday, March 8, local winners from all over the county participated in the 15th annual county-wide Science Fair. The competition this year focused on things that grow. The Walker High School gymnasium displayed the 60 top projects from Bruce County. Participants attended several science seminars and an honors banquet as part of the all-day event. One scientist, serving as a judge for the event, said the purpose of the competition was to give the students a chance to use their science skills of predicting, observing, researching, and reporting rather than just to make a good display.

William Trapik from the Buncomb Public Schools and Caleb Reed, a home schooler from Smithville led the elementary school division. Sherril Hanson from Pike Street School and Mia Chai from TriCity Christian took the honors in the middle school division. Caleb Reed's observation project on how seeds are dispersed won honors for the best display of information.

Caleb Reed won in the elementary school division

Use brief phrases to give the following main ideas.

Who? *possible answers: local winners, students, young scientists*

What? *participated in a science fair*

When? *Thursday, March 8*

Where? *Walker High School gymnasium*

Interesting detail? *Answers will vary.*

When paraphrasing, the writer finds the most important ideas and tells them in his own words.

312

▶Pretend and Paraphrase

Pretend that you are Caleb Reed. How would you feel about winning the highest award? Would you be happy to represent your hometown at the contest? Do you think you might have talked to the judges?

Write a letter as though you are Caleb Reed. Combine the information you learned from the newspaper article and your personal experience. Tell your grandmother all about the science fair. Complete your letter on your own paper if needed.

Answers will vary.

The Keys of Knowledge

▶Match Them

Choose the volume number that matches the key word and write it in the blank.

Vol. 1	Vol. 2	Vol. 3	Vol. 4	Vol. 5	Vol. 6	Vol. 7	Vol. 8	Vol. 9	Vol. 10	Vol. 11	Vol. 12
A	B-Ch	Ci-D	E-F G-H	I-J K-L	M	N-O	P-Q	R-Se	Sh-Sz	T-U V	W-X Y-Z

Key Words

__6__ 1. Morocco

__10__ 2. skydiving

__4__ 3. France

__12__ 4. whippoorwill

__5__ 5. jaguar

__4__ 6. Geronimo

__3__ 7. crater

__1__ 8. Alaska

▶Choose and Underline

Read the questions and underline the key word or words.

1. When was <u>skiing</u> first included in the <u>Olympics</u>?

2. What is the <u>pupa</u> of a <u>butterfly</u>?

3. What kind of <u>airplanes</u> were used in <u>World War II</u>?

4. How large is an <u>ostrich</u>?

5. Did the <u>dinosaur</u> actually exist?

> Use key words to locate information in an encyclopedia.

▶ Choose and Write

Choose a key word and volume number for each topic.

Vol. 1	Vol. 2	Vol. 3	Vol. 4	Vol. 5	Vol. 6	Vol. 7	Vol. 8	Vol. 9	Vol. 10	Vol. 11	Vol. 12	Vol. 13	Vol. 14	Vol. 15	Vol. 16	Vol. 17	Vol. 18	Vol. 19	Vol. 20	Vol. 21	Vol. 22	Vol. 23	Vol. 24
A	B	Ca-Ch	Ci-Cz	D	E	F	G	H	I-J	K	L	M	N	O	P	Q	R	S	T	U	V	W	X-Z

Topic	Key Word	Volume
the food a walrus eats	*walrus*	*23*
types of armor	*armor*	*1*
what to do for poison ivy	*poison ivy*	*16*
if skunks can swim	*skunk*	*19*
how a telescope works	*telescope*	*20*
facts about horses	*horse*	*9*
where Cape Cod is located	*Cape Cod*	*3*
soccer rules	*soccer*	*19*
the life cycle of the butterfly	*butterfly*	*2*

Reading 3B: Skill Station Day, Lesson 96
Study skills: identifying key words and volume numbers to look up a topic in an encyclopedia

315

Road Runner Relatives

▶**Read and Color**

1. Read each entry.
2. Color the key word yellow.
3. Draw a red circle around the cross-references.

Yellow

Passenger pigeons flourished in North America in the 1500s. They were named passenger pigeons because they often flew to new locations to find food. Male passengers were characterized by their ruby-colored throats and long, pointed tails. These birds became extinct in the late 1800s.

See also Audubon, John J.

Yellow

Petrel is an ocean bird that can be found all over the world. It is either black, grey, or white and grows from 6 to 36 inches long. Most petrels feed by flying close to the water and snatching their prey from the waves.

See also Bird
Shearwater

Yellow

Pewee is a small bird in the "flycatcher" family. It grows from 6 to 8 inches long and is greenish gray in color. Usually there are two white stripes on each wing. The Pewee's name comes from its song that sounds like *pee-a-wee*. It feeds mainly on small insects.

See also Bird
Flycatcher

Yellow

Pintail ducks are the most common waterfowl. They get their name from their long, thin, black tail. The male is gray with a white chest and brown neck and head. It has strips of green feathers on its wings and a black line down the center of its blue-gray bill.

Cross-references provide additional key words.

▶Find the Answers

Use the encyclopedia entries on page 316 to answer the following questions.

1. Which entry does not have any cross-references?

   _____

   _____ *Pintail* _____

2. Why might you look up "flycatcher" to find more information about the Pewee?

   _____

   _____ *Answers will vary.* _____

3. Where did the pintail get its name?

   _____

   _____ *from its long, black, thin tail* _____

4. What cross-references might you look up to find more information about the petrel?

   _____

   _____ *Bird; Shearwater* _____

5. How are cross-references useful?

   _____

   _____ *Answers will vary.* _____

▶Bonus:

What is the name of the smallest hummingbird? Look in an encyclopedia.

   _____

   _____ *bee hummingbird* _____

Reading 3B: Skill Station Day, Lesson 96
Study skills: identifying key elements of an encyclopedia page;
recognizing cross-references as sources of additional information

317

What's Your Motive, Mates?

▶Think and Write

Listen to the story and choose a motive from the ship for each character.
Write his motive in the box with his name.

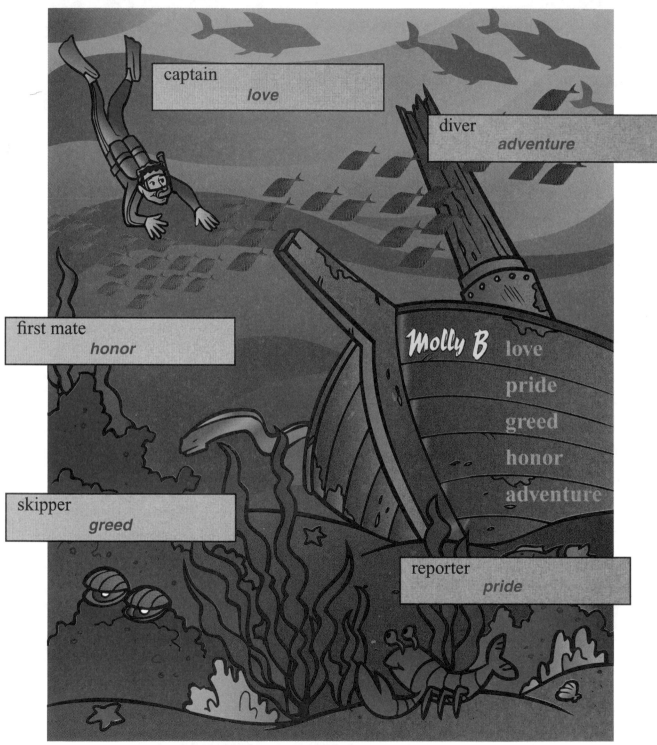

captain
love

diver
adventure

first mate
honor

Molly B love

pride

greed

honor

adventure

skipper
greed

reporter
pride

To understand a character's motives we
determine why he might have done things.

▶Finish the Story

Using what you know about each character, finish the story the way you think it happened.

"Will we be able to raise her?" the captain asked eagerly. Four pairs of eyes watched the skipper, waiting for his answer.

Answers will vary.

_____

_____

_____

_____

_____

_____

_____

_____

_____

_____

_____

_____

_____

_____

_____

_____

_____

_____

_____

_____

Reading 3B: Skill Station Day, Lesson 103
Comprehension: evaluating the motives of characters
Composition: writing a story ending

Operation Index

▶Study This Page

sheep ← **guide word**

sheep
  farming industry **F:73**
  wool industry **W-Z:135**

sheepdog ← **key word**
  canine pets **C:69**
  sheep farming **S:194**   } **topics**
  work animals **W-Z:294**

shelter
  disaster victims **D:175**
  homes **H:183**
  war victims **W-Z:54**

shepherd S:196
  sheep farming **S:194**

sherbet
  dairy products **D:51**
  ice cream **I-J:119**

sheriff
  government **G:220**
  law and order **L:30**
  protection **P-Q:341**

Shetland pony
  horses **H:216**
  show animals **S:210**
  work animals **W-Z:294**

shield
  armor **A:84** — **volume**
  battles **B:25** — **page number**

shilling S:199
  foreign money **F:264**

ship S:200
  famous voyages **V:52**
  ocean liners **O:46**
  shipbuilding **S:203**
  travel by boat **T:220**

ship repair
  shipbuilding **S:203**

shipping
  airmail **A:14**
  moving companies **M:213**
  postal service **P-Q:315**

ship's bell
  signals **S:219**

The encyclopedia index helps us find related topics.

▶Your Mission

Your mission is to answer these questions using the index page.
Write your answers in the blanks provided.

1. What topic would you look up to learn about a ship's bell?

   _____**signals**_____

2. How many topics are there relating to the key word *ship?*

   _____**four**_____

3. If you had to write a report on shields used by the military, where would you look?

   Volume ___**A**___ Page ___**84**___

4. If you wanted to find the sheriff's role in the protection of citizens, where would you look?

   Volume ___**P-Q**___ Page ___**341**___

5. What two key words have the related topic "sheep farming?"

   _____**sheepdog**_____

   _____**shepherd**_____

6. If you wanted to find information on shipping packages, where would you look?

   Volume ___**P-Q**___ Page ___**315**___

Reading 3B: Skill Station Day, Lesson 103
Study skills: using an encyclopedia index to locate additional information

321

Homes of All Kinds

▸What's the Big Idea?

Read the story. Find the main idea in each paragraph.

Log Cabins

Log cabins were popular homes that had many advantages for those who lived in them. Log cabins did not require nails or expensive materials to build. One man could build his own cabin even if he had no neighbors to help him. The log walls were thick and heavy. They protected the settlers from arrows and bullets.

With time, the settlers made many improvements to make the log cabins more comfortable. Stone chimneys replaced wooden ones, wooden roofs replaced straw roofs, and glass windows replaced greased paper. The log cabin became the sturdiest type of pioneer home.

▸Now for the Details

Read each paragraph again. Choose the details from the box that best describe each main idea. Write them in the outline.

Made without nails
Had stone chimneys
Made by one man
Protected from arrows
Had glass windows
Had wooden roofs

I. Advantages of Log Cabins

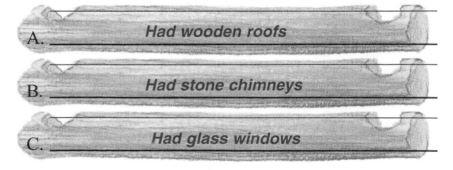

A. _Made without nails_

B. _Made by one man_

C. _Protected from arrows_

II. Improvements on Log Cabins

A. _Had wooden roofs_

B. _Had stone chimneys_

C. _Had glass windows_

A paragraph gives details that tell more about the main idea.

© 2000 BSU Press. Reproduction prohibited.

▶Read and Complete

Read the story. Use the words or phrases in the box to add the details to complete the outline.

First Homes in the New World

Many settlers in the New World copied the Indians' wigwams. Two rows of poles set into the ground were bent toward the center and tied together with vines. Each man covered his wigwam with mats of bark, skins, grass, or straw.

Other settlers built small, one-room houses called "mean" houses. The "mean" houses were built of woven branches and covered with mud.

Another type of house, called the "fair" house, was harder to build. The settler chopped down trees and shaped them into square beams. Then he raised the beams into place. The settler lined the floor, loft, and inside walls with planks. He covered the outside walls with rough boards.

Bent poles
Woven branches
Square beams
Mud
Mats
Rough boards

I. Building a wigwam

_____

A. _____ **Bent poles** _____

_____

B. _____ **Mats** _____

II. Building a "mean" house

_____

A. _____ **Woven branches** _____

_____

B. _____ **Mud** _____

III. Building a "fair" house

_____

A. _____ **Square beams** _____

_____

B. _____ **Rough boards** _____

What Do You Think?

▶Read and Think

This page is designed to be completed with teacher direction.

Read the table of contents below and imagine what the stories could be about.

▶Read and Predict

Answer the following questions, using the titles above.

1. If you were looking for a story about a war, which one

   would you read? **Friend or Foe**

2. If you wanted to read a fanciful story about a mushroom and
   some evil pickles, which story would you read?

   Mort and the Sour Scheme

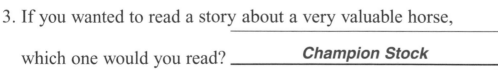

3. If you wanted to read a story about a very valuable horse,

   which one would you read? **Champion Stock**

4. If you wanted to read the story of a man's first flight over the
   ocean, which one would you read?

   Alone over the Atlantic

A title often gives clues to what the story is about.

▶Consider the Contents

Read each of the following story titles and imagine what the story could be about.

▶Match It

Draw a line between the story title and the sentence that tells what the story is most likely about.

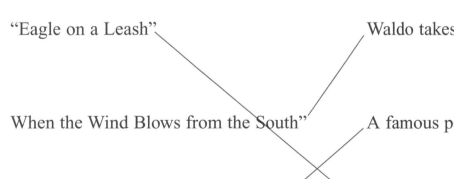

"The All-American Game"————————— Dr. Naismith invents basketball.

"Eagle on a Leash"   Waldo takes a vacation to Mexico.

When the Wind Blows from the South"   A famous person has an adventure.

"Story About George Washington"   Brent proves that his pet eagle does not kill lambs.

The Irrelevant Element

▸Choosing Together

Read the title and the items in each list. Draw a line
through the one item in each list that is irrelevant.

House Pets
fish
cat
~~horse~~
dog

Resource Books
dictionary
encyclopedia
almanac
~~book of fairy tales~~

Hymns
Amazing Grace
~~Old MacDonald~~
There Is a Fountain
The Old Rugged Cross

▸Finding Together

Read this paragraph to find the main idea and the details.
There are three irrelevant sentences in this paragraph.
Draw a line through each one.

Caleb got a horse for his birthday. It was reddish brown with a black mane. The horse stood higher than Caleb. Even though it was large, it was very gentle and obedient. ~~Mr. Cox's horse is strong and fast.~~ Caleb called his horse "Sox" because it looked like it had four white socks on its legs. ~~Caleb wore two pairs of socks in the wintertime to keep his feet warm.~~ Since Caleb owned Sox, he was in charge of taking care of him. He had to feed and water him every day and brush him several times each week. ~~The Kentucky Derby is a horse race.~~ Even though it was a lot of work, Caleb enjoyed taking care of Sox.

Irrelevant information is information
that is not related to the main idea.

▶Organize Your Information

1. Choose a person that you would like to write about.
2. On the lines below each category, write key words or phrases that describe your person.
3. Write a short paragraph about that person, using one of the categories. Be sure not to include any irrelevant information.

Appearance

1. _____

2. _____

3. _____

Character Traits

1. _____

2. _____

3. _____

Answers will vary.

_____
_____
_____
_____
_____
_____
_____
_____
_____
_____

Reading 3B: Skill Station Day, Lesson 123
Study skills: discriminating irrelevant information for the purpose of writing

327

A Formal Affair

▶Study It

Study the diagrams below.
How many things are we comparing in the first picture?
How many things are we comparing in the second picture?

bigger

biggest

▶Circle One

Circle the correct form of the word in each sentence.

1. Ryan thought he had the (greater, (greatest)) mother in the world.

2. First of all, she was the ((most,) more) beautiful lady he had ever seen.

3. Her cooking was even ((tastier,) tastiest) than Grandma's.

4. He knew that his mother was the (wiser, (wisest)) bargain hunter in the family.

5. Ryan thought his mom was a ((more,) most) talented soccer goalie than his friend James.

6. Guess who thought Ryan was the (more, (most)) special boy in the world.

Use *more* or *-er* when comparing two things;
use *most* or *-est* when comparing three or more things.

▶Look and Write

1. Read each word below.
2. Compare the items in each box.
3. Look at the item to which the arrow is pointing and write
   the form of the word used to compare that item.

colorful

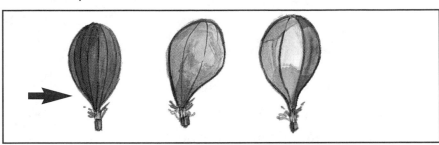

most colorful

long

longest

beautiful

more beautiful

deep

deeper

Setting the Stage

▶**Read and Discover**

Read the following paragraphs. List the words
or phrases that the author uses to tell us
where and **when** the story takes place.

God Provides

Heat pressed down on the dry land like a
blanket, smothering the thirsty ground. Elijah
pulled his cloak of camel's hair over his head
to protect himself from the burning sun. In the
distance he could see the walls of Zarephath.

"There will be water and food waiting for
me," Elijah thought as he shook the dust from
his sandals and garments. "God has said so."

As he came closer to the city, he saw a woman
gathering sticks. She was dressed in the clothes
of a widow. "Ah," thought Elijah. "She must be
the woman of whom God spoke."

in the desert	in Bible times
heat	Elijah
dry land	cloak of camel's hair
thirsty ground	Zarephath
burning sun	sandals and garments
dust from his sandals	woman of whom God spoke

The descriptions in a story help us
see the setting—where and when.

▶Pick the Place

Each of the following events took place in Bible times, but each happened in a different place. Complete the setting by finding the place. Write the letter of your answer beside the event.

A. the garden of a palace	D. a stable in a small village
B. a ship in the middle of a stormy sea	E. a dark cave
C. an island in the sea	

C 1. An apostle, traveling by boat to Rome, is shipwrecked. He and all the other people aboard the ship make it safely to shore. Many people on the shore are healed.

E 2. A king and his men stop to rest in the wilderness. They seek shelter among the rocks. They do not know that the men they are chasing are hiding in the shadows.

B 3. A man is disobeying God and traveling in the wrong direction. The sailors are about to throw him overboard.

A 4. A sick king asks for a sign from God that he will be healed. He asks that the shadow on the sundial go backward instead of forward.

D 5. A baby is born and is laid in a manger. Shepherds come to worship him.

▶Picture It

Read the following event from a familiar Bible story. Draw a picture that shows the setting.

Jesus is asleep and his disciples are afraid that they will die. At the moment they fear that all is lost, Jesus stands up and tells the wind and the waves to be still.

Concordance Creatures

A Bible concordance is a tool used to locate specific verses. To find a verse you must determine a key word.

▶Find the Keys

Look up each verse and find the missing key words. Write the words on the lines with the matching number.

1. _____ **Moses** _____

2. _____ **serpent** _____

3. _____ **Son** _____

4. _____ **sheep** _____

5. _____ **wolves** _____

6. _____ **serpents** _____

7. _____ **doves** _____

8. _____ **sheep** _____

9. _____ **praise** _____

John 3:14
"And as __1__ lifted up the __2__ in the wilderness, even so must the __3__ of man be lifted up."

Matthew 10:16
"Behold, I send you forth as __4__ in the midst of __5__: be ye therefore wise as __6__, and harmless as __7__."

Psalm 79:13
"So we thy people and __8__ of thy pasture will give thee thanks for ever: we will shew forth thy __9__ to all generations."

▶Find the Place

Write the references from the Bible verses above that mention the animals pictured below.

_____ **John 3:14** _____

_____ **Matt 10:16** _____

_____ **Matt 10:16** _____

_____ **Psalm 79:13** _____

▸Fill It In

Study these entries from a Bible concordance.
Answer the questions below.

scorpion
  Luke 10:19 tread on . . . scorpions
  Luke 11:12 offer him a scorpion?

serpent
  Prov. 30:19 way of a serpent
  Matt. 10:16 wise as serpents
  John 3:14 Moses lifted up the serpent
  II Cor. 11:3 the serpent beguiled Eve

sheep
  Psalm 79:13 sheep of thy pasture
  Luke 15:4 man . . . having an hundred sheep
  John 10:27 My sheep hear my voice

spider
  Prov. 30:28 spider taketh hold

swine
  Matt. 7:6 pearls before swine

1. How many Bible references are given for the key word *serpent*?   _____4_____

   List them. ____*Prov. 30:19; Matt. 10:16; John 3:14; II Cor. 11:3*____

2. Is Proverbs 30:28 a verse about scorpions or about spiders?   ___*spiders*___

3. If you wanted to find a verse about the serpent tempting

   Eve, where does this concordance tell you to look? ____*II Cor. 11:3*____

4. Write the rest of this verse: "My sheep hear my voice   _____

   _____*and I know them, and they follow me.*"_____

5. What verse tells about precious jewels and swine? ____*Matt. 7:6*____

Reading 3B: Skill Station Day, Lesson 130
Study skills: recognizing key words in a Bible verse; using a Bible concordance

333

Speech Can Show

▶Read and See

Read the following paragraphs and decide what each boy is like.

Jim followed Ben across the soccer field. "Ben, wait up. You're not mad, are you? I said I was sorry."

Ben crouched over his untied shoe.

"I know you don't believe this," Jim said. "But I didn't mean to trip you. You just kind of fell over my foot. And I wasn't laughing at you."

"Maybe not, but your friends were." Ben grabbed his bag off the bench. "Some way to make the new kid feel welcome."

"Ben, wait."

Ben did not stop. Jim ran to catch up.

"Listen, I'm sorry we got off to a bad start. I really would like to be your friend." Jim grabbed Ben's arm to stop him. "Maybe you could teach me some of your soccer moves."

"Maybe." Ben just stared at Jim. "Yeah, maybe."

 Jim

 Ben

▶Write It

Write each boy's name beside the qualities that best describe him.

angry _____**Ben**_____   kind _____**Jim**_____

concerned _____**Jim**_____   unfriendly _____**Ben**_____

unkind _____**Ben**_____   friendly _____**Jim**_____

▶Read and Choose

Read the story. Choose the best answer for each question.

"Friends," said the dog, "the squirrels' house has burned to the ground. We need to help them. Does anyone have any suggestions?"

"If we work and work," said the beaver, "we can build a new house and gather food for them before winter."

The wolf snarled. "While those tender little squirrels are out looking for food, I could catch some of them. They would make a tasty meal."

"Well, I don't know about you all," said the sloth, "but I'd rather just sleep."

"The squirrels have never done any harm," said the deer. "They have brought cheer to the forest. We ought to help them now."

___b___ 1. The dog is
      a. shy.
      b. thoughtful.
      c. lazy.

___c___ 2. The beaver is
      a. courageous.
      b. selfish.
      c. hard-working.

___c___ 3. The wolf is
      a. lazy.
      b. courageous.
      c. mean.

___b___ 4. The deer is
      a. mean.
      b. kind.
      c. selfish.

___a___ 5. The sloth is
      a. lazy.
      b. proud.
      c. kind.

What a character says shows what he is really like.

Reading 3B: Skill Station Day, Lesson 139
Literature: recognizing the author's use of the character's speech to reveal his traits

335

Discovering Treasure

▶Accent It
Read each word below, finding the accented syllable.
Place an accent mark above the last letter in each
accented syllable.

treas´ • ure

trin´ • ket

is´ • land

shov´ • el

lan´ • tern

ó • cean

pi´ • rate

pas´ • sage

In a two-syllable word,
the accent usually falls
on the first syllable.

men´ • tion

cre • á • tion

com • mó • tion

op´ • tion

at • ten´ • tion

In words that end in *tion*,
the accent usually falls on
the syllable before *tion*.

336

rep•tiles
dan•ger
jew•els

▶Fill In

Use words from the box above to complete sentences 1-3.
Use words from the box below to complete sentences 4-6.
Divide each word and mark the accents.

1. The storm caused everyone on the ship to be in great _____ dan ´ • ger _____ .

2. Large _____ rep ´ • tiles _____ lay sunning themselves on the bank.

3. The treasure box contained many fine _____ jew ´ • els _____ .

lo•ca•tion
in•ven•tion
mo•tion

4. It was difficult to determine the _____ lo • ca ´ • tion _____ of the hidden treasure.

5. They loosened the box from the dirt by using a rocking _____ mo ´ • tion _____ .

6. The men used a new _____ in • ven ´ • tion _____ to remove the box from the hole in the ground.

Reading 3B: Skill Station Day, Lesson 139
Structural analysis: applying accent generalizations: in a two-syllable word, the accent usually falls
on the first syllable; in words ending with *-tion,* the accent falls on the syllable before *-tion*

337

Trial by Fire

▶Read and Find

Read the following story carefully to find out which character has a great change of heart.

Mr. Sheffey approached the small shack slowly. "Hello, the house," he called. A small, dirty face peeked out from behind the door.

"Who are ya?" asked the young lady fearfully.

"I'm Mr. Sheffey. You wrote me a letter and asked if I would come."

To his surprise, the lady came rushing out the door toward him, crying as she came. "Oh, Brother Sheffey, I just knew you'd come! I do need yer help real bad!"

Mr. Sheffey looked down at the lady. She was badly bruised and had a cut under one eye. "It's your husband, isn't it?" he asked. "Does he drink the liquor?"

"Yes," she replied, "but he's a good man when he's sober—you must believe that."

"I'll help you if you promise to let me do what I must do. Lord willing, causing him a little pain tonight will save you both great pain in the future."

She agreed to the plan just as the man of the house stumbled through the door. He crashed into the bedroom and fell, unconscious, to the bed. Mr. Sheffey carried the large man up the hill behind the house and set him in a washtub full of whiskey. Then he built a wall of brush around the man and lit it on fire just as the man was waking from his drunken sleep. The man quickly became aware of the ring of fire and smoke surrounding him and of the liquor stinging his skin. Eyes wide with fear, he began screaming and crying, thinking he was actually in hell! He began repenting of his sin of drinking and hurting his family, but the fire continued to burn higher and hotter! Finally he could take no more. He ran right through the flames, down the hill, and into a tree.

Mr. Sheffey took the unconscious man back to the shack and cleaned up the remains of the fire. When he returned to the house, the man was sleeping peacefully. "When he wakes up, I promise you, he'll be a different man," said Mr. Sheffey.

"Oh, thank you, Preacher, thank you!" said the woman. "You brought my man a vision that will surely change his life. May the Lord bless you!"

What a character <u>does</u> shows what he is really like.

▶Match and Write

Find the action that matches the husband's character trait.
Look in the yellow sections on page 338. Use your own words
to write his action in the box.

cruel

_____

_____
bruised his wife

drunken

_____

_____
drank liquor or crashed through bedroom

peaceful

_____

_____

_____
slept peacefully

fearful

_____

_____
screamed and cried out in fear

▶What Do You Think?

Answer the following questions in your own words.

1. What do you suppose the husband thought had happened
   while he slept?

   _____

   _____*Answers will vary.*_____

   _____

   _____

2. Do you think the husband got saved? If so, how do you
   suppose the family will change?

   _____

   _____*Answers will vary.*_____

   _____

   _____

Reading 3B: Skill Station Day, Lesson 145
Literature: recognizing the author's use of character actions in characters' development

339

The Circuit Riders

▶**Read and Answer**

Read the story and the graph. Circle the answers to the questions.

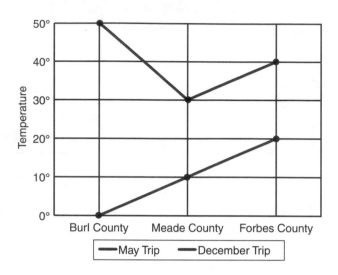

In pioneer days, frontier settlements often didn't have a church. That meant no preacher and no gospel preaching for Christians to hear. A minister from England found a solution to this problem: he became a "circuit-riding preacher." He rode horseback on a regular route or "circuit," trying to reach as many towns as possible, traveling in one big circle.

Soon other men became circuit-riding preachers. They rode from town to town, declaring the Word of God. Before long, townspeople in many backwoods frontier settlements looked forward to the days when the circuit-riding preacher would come riding into town. He would stay for several days, preach and counsel, and live in the homes of the townspeople. Most of these circuit riders depended on the people to care for their physical needs. The townspeople were usually glad to help because the circuit riders helped to care for their spiritual needs. It was a fair trade.

1. What would be a good title for this graph?
   A. Different Temperatures
   B. Three Counties
   C. Temperatures for Two Trips

2. What was the temperature in Meade County during the May visit?
   A. 10°
   B. 30°
   C. 40°

3. Which county was 50° in May and 0° in December?
   A. Burl County
   B. Meade County
   C. Forbes County

Line graphs compare two or more topics.

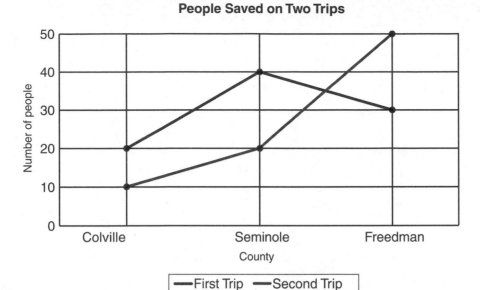

People Saved on Two Trips

—First Trip —Second Trip

▶Study and Answer

Study the graph above to find the answers to the following questions.

1. In which county were the most people saved during
   the second trip? _____*Freedman County*_____

2. How many people were saved in Seminole County during
   the circuit rider's second trip? _____*20 people*_____

3. How many people were saved altogether during the first trip?
   _____*90 people*_____

4. In which county were the fewest total people saved?
   _____*Colville County*_____

5. During which trip were more people saved? _____*the first trip*_____

Bonus: What is the purpose of a graph?
_____*to show a lot of information in a little space*_____

A Message to Parents

Ways You Can Help

Many parents ask the question "How can I help my child become a good reader?" Reading outside the instructional setting is an essential ingredient for his success. You can make a difference.

- *Read to your child.* Children of all ages benefit as they listen to an adult read. When a child hears material that is *above his own reading level,* his vocabulary is stretched and enriched, and he hears the more interesting syntax patterns that he will encounter in his own reading in the future. When a child hears material *at his present reading level,* he is given a model for the fluency that he needs to attain. When a child hears material that is *easy for him to read,* he is invited to take up that very book and read it for himself.

- *Visit the library with your child.* Help him to select easy, interesting books for his independent reading and more difficult, appealing books for read-aloud time.

- *Read the newspaper with your child.* Study the weather map and compare the map to the forecast given. Look at the sports page. If a sports article is particularly interesting to a child, he will read it eagerly. If any articles or editorials have content a child can reflect on, read them to him and discuss the facts and opinions given.

- *Ask your child to read to other family members.* Any homework that turns into family time has double benefits. A child's oral reading fluency will improve as he entertains younger children or elderly relatives by reading easy material to them.

- *Encourage meaningful writing.* Writing builds reading. Help your child to keep a journal of family trips. Enhanced with photographs or original art, it can become a record of his childhood that he will value all his life. Encourage him to write long letters to grandparents or aunts and uncles who live in other cities.

- *Show interest in your child's school papers.* Look with interest at the worktext pages that he has completed. Give value to his pages by commenting on their content rather than concentrating only on the incorrect answers. If he knows you are interested, he may become more diligent in his efforts.

- *Be enthusiastic about the stories in your child's reader.* After your child has completed the reading lessons for a story in his reader, he will benefit from some good follow-up.

  1. Encourage him to read all or part of the story again silently for himself.

  2. Select parts with ample dialogue and read just the conversation with him as a "play."

  3. Ask him to read the most exciting paragraphs aloud. Praise him specifically if he makes you hear the character's voice, if he communicates fear or other emotions, or if he changes the pace or pauses to show suspense.

Things to Avoid

Sometimes well-meaning parents cause problems unintentionally. Avoid practices that may become obstacles.

- *Allowing your child to read ahead in his reader is not a good teaching technique.* This will harm the book's effectiveness as a tool for teaching reading comprehension.

- *Avoid making your questions sound like a quiz.*

- *Don't allow your child to read his whole story aloud in a meaningless drone or in a hurried manner.* Good oral reading always communicates the message of the author.

- *Use caution as you correct misread words.* As your child begins to read fluently, he may say slightly different words. For example, the sentence *Jessie put her many toys away* might be read *Jessie put all her toys away.* This happens when his eyes begin moving across the text faster than his speaking voice can interpret it. In his mind the author's words and his own thoughts have become one. This is a sign of a good reader. It is the way you read. If you insist on asking him to go back to get each specific word, you are asking him to revert to being a word-by-word reader rather than a fluent phrase-by-phrase reader.

- *Your child needs a different kind of help when practicing words out of context, such as word family lists.* When he has difficulty with a given word, say, "What is the first sound? . . . Now look at the rest of the syllable." This will cause him to use phonics generalizations as well as letter/sound phonics knowledge. (This is important because in English each vowel letter represents several different sounds.)

Tools for the Job

READING *for Christian Schools* emphasizes comprehension and develops phonics systematically. These materials provide the tools not only to teach reading well but also to encourage growth in Christian character. A variety of selections—family stories, adventure stories, Christian realism, historical fiction, Bible accounts retold, biographies, information articles, folktales, poems, and plays—offer engaging reading that provides both pleasure and understanding.

We trust your child will enjoy the school year as he uses his third grade reading materials to become a confident, eager reader—one who will continue to read all his life.

Bob Jones University Press

A Summer Reading List

Rising fourth graders demonstrate a wide range of ability levels and represent an even wider range of interest levels. Not every book on the following list will appeal to your child. The annotations will help you to find books he may find interesting, but you need to exercise your evaluation of the difficulty level that fits your child. It is important that you keep your child reading during the summer months. His continued success in reading depends on it.

Atwater, Richard and Florence. *Mr. Popper's Penguins.* Illus. Robert Lawson. 1938. A paperhanger with a passion for the Antarctic receives as a gift a playful penguin named Captain Cook.

Benchley, Nathaniel. *Sam the Minuteman.* Illus. Arnold Lobel. 1969. Told from a young boy's viewpoint, this easy-to-read story provides helpful information about life during the days of the War for Independence.

Berry, Eileen. *Roses on Baker Street.* Illus. John Roberts. Journey Books, 1998. When Danae moves with her missionary family from France to America for a year of furlough, suddenly the familiar things of "home" are gone.

Bulla, Clyde Robert. *Dexter.* Illus. Glo Coalson. 1973. Although the townspeople are not very friendly to the strange new family and their pony named Dexter, Dave befriends them.

_____. *A Lion to Guard Us.* Illus. Michele Chessare. 1981. A search for their father brings three young English children to the colony of Virginia.

Caudill, Rebecca. *Did You Carry the Flag Today, Charley?* 1966. This book teaches the importance of learning and doing what is right at school. The pen-and-ink sketches enhance the simple story.

Dahl, Roald. *Charlie and the Chocolate Factory.* 1964. Five children win a contest that gives them a fun-filled visit to Willy Wonka's wonderful factory.

Dalgliesh, Alice. *The Thanksgiving Story.* Illus. Helen Sewell. 1954. This is the story of the Pilgrims sailing to America and their first year in the new country.

Daugherty, James. *Andy and the Lion.* 1938. Andy checks out a book about lions from the library and becomes so absorbed with his thoughts about lions that his imagination creates a fanciful adventure.

Davis, Tim. *Tales from Dust River Gulch.* Illus. Tim Davis. Journey Books, 1996. Sheriff J.D. Saddlesoap tolerates no trouble, and he is a fine-looking mustang besides. He faces down a passel of outlaws and solves a heap of problems to keep Dust River Gulch a dandy place for its citizens to live.

DeJong, Meindert. *Shadrich.* 1953. In this regional realism, set in the Netherlands, a black rabbit's problems help a little boy to grow.

Drury, Roger W. *Finches' Fabulous Furnace.* 1971. The Finches have moved, and the Fabulous Furnace is a volcano.

Dunckel, Mona. *Escape.* Journey Books, 1998. Charlie lives in Ethiopia with his missionary parents. The unusual bead he finds in the marketplace becomes his treasure as his family flees from rebel soldiers.

Edmonds, Walter D. *The Matchlock Gun.* Illus. Paul Lantz. 1941. Awarded a Newbery medal for literature, this historical story tells of a young hero who saves his family.

Gardiner, John Reynolds. *Stone Fox.* Illus. Marcia Sewall. 1980. Grandfather owes taxes that threaten the loss of the farm. Trying to help, Little Willy enters a sled race.

Henry, Marguerite. *Benjamin West and His Cat Grimalkin.* Illus. Wesley Dennis. 1947. Though Benjamin West is remembered today as the father of American painting, the child who reads this book will remember him as a painter who made his brushes from his cat's tail.

Hill, Elizabeth Starr. *Evan's Corner.* Illus. Nancy Grossman. 1967. Evan's mother allows him to choose a corner in the cramped two-room house and fix it up for himself.

Howard, Milly. *Captive Treasure.* Journey Books, 1988. Carrie Talbot's family sets out on a long trip west in spite of the danger of Indian attacks.

_____. *The Runaway Princess.* Journey Books, 1988. Princess Brenna tries to escape her ruthless uncle, Prince Zoran, who wants to rule her kingdom.

Lohr, Nancy. *Pelts and Promises.* Illus. Gabriela Dellosso. Journey Books, 1996. Jamie and his friends try out a great idea, end up in trouble, and think up a plan to set things right.

Longfellow, Henry Wadsworth. *Paul Revere's Ride.* Illus. Ted Rand. 1990. Beautiful, full-color illustrations portray Longfellow's famous narrative poem, re-creating Paul Revere's famous midnight ride in 1775.

McCloskey, Robert. *Lentil.* 1940. In this Caldecott Medal winner, a boy named Lentil loves to make music, so he saves up enough pennies to buy a harmonica.

_____. *Homer Price.* 1943. In this episodic tale the charming character Homer Price uses his intelligence and common sense to unravel mysteries.

Mowat, Farley. *Owls in the Family.* 1961. When Billy and his friends set out to have an owl as a pet, their adventures begin.

Pittman, Helena Clare. *A Grain of Rice.* 1986. Pong Lo, a humble farmer, requests the hand of the Emperor's beautiful daughter. The enraged Emperor grants Pong Lo's surprising request and learns how clever the young farmer is.

Seuss, Dr. *Yertle the Turtle and Other Stories.* 1958. Yertle the Turtle, Gertrude McFuzz, and several other Seuss creatures teach important lessons about pride.

Thurber, James. *Many Moons.* 1943. A young princess falls ill and thinks she will get well only if she can obtain the moon. This story is enhanced by the Caldecott award winning pictures.

Turkle, Brinton. *Thy Friend, Obadiah.* 1969. Obadiah, a little boy of colonial America, lives on Nantucket Island with his friend, a sea gull.

Voight, Virginia. *Nathan Hale.* Illus. Frank Aliose. 1965. An American volunteers to become a spy against the British and becomes known for his words "I only regret that I have but one life to lose for my country."

Waber, Bernard. *Ira Sleeps Over.* 1972. Ira's anticipated overnight stay with his friend becomes a special kind of struggle when his sister brings up the subject of his favorite sleep-time toy.

Watkins, Dawn. *Jenny Wren.* Journey Books, 1986. A shy young girl comes to her new foster home with misgivings.

White, E. B. *Charlotte's Web.* 1952. In this barnyard setting with Charlotte, the spider, and Wilbur, the pig, Charlotte is able to save the pig's life by spinning messages in her web.

Wilder, Laura Ingalls. *Little House on the Prairie.* 1953. In this second "Little House" book, Laura goes with her family into Indian country.

Yates, Elizabeth. *Sarah Whitcher's Story.* Illus. Nora S. Unwin. Journey Books, 1994. Sarah is lost in the woods during pioneer days. Search parties are unable to locate her. Sarah is protected by a bear in the woods and is eventually found by a man who has a dream about her.

Yolen, Jane. *Owl Moon.* 1987. This memorable account, winner of the Caldecott Medal in 1988, tells of a girl's first experience in owling.

Index